Emerson's Fall

B. L. Packer

EMERSON'S FALL

A New Interpretation of the Major Essays

CONTINUUM · NEW YORK

An earlier version of chapter 1, "The Lapses of Uriel: Emerson's Rhetoric," appeared in the *Georgia Review* (Summer 1977). Part of chapter 2, "The Riddle of the Sphinx: *Nature*," appeared in *Emerson's "Nature": Origin, Growth, Meaning*, 2nd edition, edited by Merton M. Sealts, Jr. and Alfred R. Ferguson.

Grateful acknowledgment is made to Alfred A. Knopf, Inc. for permission to reprint lines from "Tea at the Palaz of Hoon," copyright © 1923 and renewed 1951 by Wallace Stevens from *The Collected Poems of Wallace Stevens*, and lines from "The Greenest Continent," "A Duck for Dinner," and "Mr. Burnshaw and the Statue" from *Opus Posthumous* by Wallace Stevens, edited by Samuel French Morse, copyright © 1957 by Elfie Stevens and Holly Stevens.

1982

The Continuum Publishing Company
575 Lexington Avenue
New York, N.Y. 10022

Printed in the United States of America

Library of Congress Cataloging in Publication Data

Packer, B. L.
    Emerson's fall.

    1. Emerson, Ralph Waldo, 1803–1882—Criticism and
interpretation.   I. Title
PS1638.P28   814'.3   82-1439
ISBN 0-8264-0191-0   AACR2

To Nadine McCall Packer

Contents

Preface

"What is the front the world always shows to the young spirit?" Emerson asked in a lecture called "The Protest." "Strange to say, the Fall of Man."[1] His tone of mock wonderment would naturally have seemed more amusing to a New England audience still close to the ancestral religion than it does to most twentieth-century readers. But astonishment *is* the emotion uppermost in the typical youthful response to the fallenness of the world, since the testimony of consciousness is that indeed the world should be a better place than it is. Through such testimony we find that the world promised by the persistence of hope and the insatiability of desire is no illusion; that unfallen world is in fact our proper home to which we are (as Emerson says in a thoroughly American pun) entitled by our constitutions. And this is true even though the only evidence we have of the reality of this unfallen world is "a certain brief experience, which surprised me in the highway or in the market, in some place, at some time,—whether in the body or out of the body, God knoweth," which disappears almost as soon as it arrives. "Our faith comes in moments, our vice is habitual."

Two objections to accepting the reality of this unfallen world naturally suggest themselves, but Emerson dismisses both of them. The brevity of these flashes of illumination is no argument against their authority, for "there is a depth in those brief moments, which constrains us to ascribe more reality to them than to all other experiences." Nor is the historical failure of every attempt to realize this visionary kingdom in the world of the senses any argument against the possibility of ultimate satisfaction. "We give up the past to the objector, and yet we hope. He must explain this hope." If limitation were really the condition appropriate to us, we would be content with it. "We grant that human life is mean, but how did we find out that it was mean? What is the ground of this uneasiness of ours; of this old discontent? What is the universal sense of want and ignorance, but the fine innuendo by which the great soul makes its enormous claims?"

But if the soul is really unfallen, and if it is repeatedly granted glimpses of a world that might be adequate to its desires, what accounts for the mysterious persistence of evil, suffering, and death? We *feel* that the millennium ought to be imminent, yet every year leaves us reciting the verse from Jeremiah that Emerson had quoted in an early journal: "The harvest is passed, the summer is ended and we are not saved."[2]

Hence no sooner has Emerson freed himself from what he regarded as the inadequate biblical myth of origin sin than he found himself forced to fabricate his own fables in explanation of the fallenness of the world. Such fables are everywhere in Emerson: in the two chants of the Orphic poet in *Nature* and in the strange little visionary formula that separates them; in lectures like "The Protest"; in essays like "Circles" and "Experience." The laconic explanations altered as Emerson's thought developed, but they all exhibit certain family resemblances. They reject the notion that what we call the Fall of Man has anything to do with sin or disobedience; they interpret it instead as a consequence of "self-distrust," the self's ignorance or denial of its own divinity. And they treat the corresponding imperfections of the social and natural world not as adamantine limitations, but as parodic or entropic forms of the good. "Nonsense is only sense deranged, chaos is paradise dislocated, poverty is wealth decomposed; spite, apathy, bad blood, frivolity is only dispersed matter & light."

Emerson developed four chief fables or formulas for explaining the Fall in the years that begin with *Nature* and end with *Representative Men*. In *Nature*, faced with explaining man's curious position in the natural world—half related, half alienated—he invented the interlocking fables of *contraction* and *dislocation*. When, during his years of challenge, he turned his attention to the social world, seeking some underlying pattern that would explain the ceaseless warfare between the forces of conservatism and reform, he formulated his law of *ossification*, a principle that explains the Fall both in society at large and in the minds of the individuals who compose it. Finally, increasingly preoccupied with the vicissitudes of the inner life, he came to rest in an account of things that locates in *reflection* or self-consciousness the origin of suffering. Together these fables form a system of explanation as useful to Emerson as Genesis had been to his Puritan ancestors, a system which could organize the chaos of experience and the "Chaos of thought" into "a convenient mythus" equally applicable to the mind of the individual and to the social and natural world in which he lives. An understanding of these fables is essential to understanding the underlying forces at work in the years of Emerson's greatest power and productivity, the years that extend from *Nature* to *Representative Men* (1849).

My debts to earlier scholars are many. Like all students of Emerson, I owe the largest debt to the editors of *Emerson's Journals and Miscellaneous Notebooks, Early Lectures,* and *Collected Works.* Without their painstaking labors a book like mine would have been impossible. Two critical books—Stephen Whicher's *Freedom and Fate* and Northrop Frye's *Fearful Symmetry*—have influenced me in ways that the notes to this book are insufficient to express. And I repeatedly found that O. W. Firkins's brilliant, epigrammatic *Ralph Waldo Emerson* condensed as much critical wisdom into a single sentence or paragraph as could be found in the chapters of most books.

My personal debts to friends, colleagues, and students are a pleasure to acknowledge. I am grateful to Margaret Ferguson for her friendship and critical advice, and to Donald Weber, whose knowledge of American theology and church history greatly increased my own. I have benefited as well from conversations with the late W. K. Wimsatt, and with Ron Macdonald, Frances Ferguson, William Miller, Meredith Skura, Joyce Peterson, Gary Bjork, Carol and Richard Lanham, Robert Byrnes, Richard

Curtis, Elton Fukumoto, Joseph Kronick, Conrad Shumaker, and Eric Sigg. A Morse Fellowship from Yale University enabled me to begin the book, and a sabbatical leave from the University of California, Los Angeles, together with a grant from its Research Committee, enabled me to complete it.

The Lapses of Uriel: Emerson's Rhetoric

> Our highest insights must—and should—sound
> like follies and sometimes like crimes when they
> are heard without permission by those who are
> not prepared for and elected by them.
> Nietzsche, *Beyond Good and Evil*

Emerson once praised Landor for having "the merit of not explaining." Like most of Emerson's comments about rhetoric, this tribute celebrates the virtues of absence, the exhilarations of discontinuity. Late in life he remarked to a young admirer that the best writing is that which does not quite satisfy the reader. "A little guessing does him no harm, so I would assist him with no connections."[1] His own refusal to provide transitions was strategic, a sacrifice of judiciousness to power. But the strategy itself reflected a deep skepticism about the capacity of language to embody truth. "Thought," he once said, "is the manna which cannot be stored."

He had not always taken so suspicious a view of his medium of expression. In his youth he had been content simply to enjoy the pleasures of rhetoric without much concern for its truth value. In college he had been so intoxicated by the ravishing pulpit eloquence of Edward Everett that (as Emerson's biographer Ralph Rusk tells us) he not only memorized particularly affecting phrases, "he could say half the sermon from which he got them on the night after he had heard it."[2] And his college tastes were only an extension of his boyhood ones. William Henry Furness, a schoolfellow of Emerson's, thought that their boyhood days ought to be called "the era of rhetoric" because then even the youngest boy "went into ecstasies over a happy turn of expression or a brilliant figure of speech."[3] In declamation and debate boys found a form of self-display and combativeness that their parents, teachers, and ministers actively encouraged. In James Elliot Cabot's *Memoir* there is a touching story of Emerson's pride in bringing home a college prize for declamation in hopes that his winnings—thirty dollars—would buy his mother a new shawl; he was chagrined to learn that the money had to be spent to pay the baker's bill.[4] Even after graduation, when he had moved with his mother and brothers out into the country, his neighboring cousins could hear the Emerson boys making the woods resound with declamations and dialogues.[5] It was in such exercises as these that Emerson perfected that rich baritone that so moved and persuaded his hearers—a voice whose power and sweetness, issuing from his ascetic-looking New England body, was so surprising that it reminded one journalist of a huge magnolia blossom lodged in the bough of an aspen tree.[6]

Eloquence was the easiest road to success for a poor but gifted boy, whether he chose the pulpit or the political platform; it was also the surest way of reaching and influencing his fellow citizens. Foreign visitors were amazed at the apparently boundless appetite for sermons, lyceum lectures, and political debates that Americans displayed. We have lost this appetite so completely that it takes some effort of the imagination to recover it, but in Emerson's youth it was strong enough to hold out the promise of renown to any sufficiently talented speaker. Emerson himself was occasionally amused by the eagerness of his fellow citizens for oratorical entertainment. In a letter he wrote to his brother Charles he joked that he could announce a lecture on the Invisible Ox, to be *seen* at Faneuil Hall, and still be certain of an audience. As late as 1881 the American neurologist George Beard was led to adduce the well-known talent of his countrymen for oratory in support of his thesis that Americans were more highly strung than their European contemporaries (since "the masters in the oratorical art are always nervous"[7]).

With this sort of cultural background it is not surprising to find Emerson at the age of twenty-one confessing to his journal that he has inherited from his father "a passionate love for the strains of eloquence" and that he burns after that " 'aliquid immensum infinitumque' which Cicero desired." He had already determined to follow his father's profession, and though he realized that "entire success" in preaching was the lot of the few, he still "hoped to put on eloquence as a robe" and thereby "prevail over the false judgments, the rebel passions, and corrupt habits of men."

Nor is it surprising, given this notion of eloquence, that Emerson's early journals are virtually unreadable. The normal adolescent fondness for the saccharine and the overblown found little to restrain it in the prevailing literary taste of the surrounding society. Daniel Howe has remarked how far removed the "graceful sentimentality" of that taste had become from the "sparse utilitarianism" of the Puritan plain style, and adds: "In fact, could the Puritans have heard a nineteenth-century Unitarian sermon, they would probably have found its style similar to the flowery 'carnall eloquence' they detested in Anglican preachers."[8]

Emerson's embarrassment at his own youthful excesses and his dissatisfaction with the prevailing pulpit style grew at about the same rate during the years of his young manhood. Gradually in the journals and sermons one can witness the dawning of a livelier style as Emerson begins to abandon the "stock properties of college rhetoric" for the pungencies of the great seventeenth-century prose masters whose works he began to study and try to imitate. The *aliquid immensum infinitumque*, he decided, was something best left to each man's youthful and private meditations; he was growing to prefer instead the "homespun cloth-of-gold" of Donne, Jonson, Bacon, Browne.[9] True eloquence increasingly came to seem less a thing to be put on like a robe than a thing to be gotten at by stripping away the trite, the turgid, the flowery, the insincere. He longed to attain the state of simplicity described by Sampson Reed in his "Oration on Genius," delivered at Emerson's Harvard graduation exercises. Emerson was so taken with the address that he borrowed it and made a copy; he seems to have been particularly impressed by Reed's description of that blessed poetic state where "words make one with things, and language is lost in nature."[10] By 1831 Emerson was formulating his own maxim out of Reed's phrase: "In good writing words become one with things."

It is never entirely clear what this sort of assertion is actually supposed to mean, but what it usually suggests to native speakers of English is that good writing is writing in which words of Anglo-Saxon derivation are substituted for words derived from French and Latin, and simple nouns are preferred to poetic periphrases. That, at any rate, is what determination to achieve a "natural" or "thinglike" language has meant to every generation of linguistic reformers in English or American literary history from the Puritan opponents of "carnall eloquence" down to Pound and the Imagists.

And it was evident to Emerson's contemporaries that he saw himself as a reformer of this kind, that in his sermons and lectures he was attempting to reinvigorate language by returning it to its native roots, even if his efforts to do so obliged him to offend the reigning standards of good taste. Francis Bowen, who reviewed *Nature* for the *Christian Examiner*, thought the book marred by stylistic lapses; Emerson had gone a bit too far when he introduced aggressively "low" phrases like "pot and kettle," "huddled and lumped," and "dreams, beasts, sex" into serious philosophical discourse. But Bowen, while critical, could at least sympathize with the motives behind such offenses. He could see that the author of *Nature* was "in love with the Old Saxon idiom" and guessed that his sins against decorum stemmed not from ineptitude but from literary affectation. "He is sometimes coarse and blunt, that he may avoid the imputation of sickly refinement, and writes bathos with malice prepense, because he abhors forced dignity and unnatural elevation."[11]

Yet the very attempt to put Reed's advice into practice, though it eventually helped Emerson achieve the pungent, aphoristic style for which he is famous, revealed the flaws in the original project. Emerson could still invoke Reed when, in one of the first letters he ever wrote to Carlyle, he expressed his puzzlement and dismay at the "grotesque teutonic apocalyptic" style of the newly published *Sartor Resartus*. "I look for the hour with impatience when the vehicle will be worthy of the spirit when the word will be as simple & so as resistless as the thought, & in short when your words will be one with things." But a year later he is no longer so sure that such perfect blending is possible:

> The aim of the author is not to tell truth—that he cannot do, but to suggest it. He has only approximated it himself, & hence his cumbrous and embarrassed speech: he uses many words, hoping that one, if not another, will bring you as near to the fact as he is.
>
> For language itself is young & unformed. In heaven, it will be, as Sampson Reed said, "one with things." Now, there are many things that refuse to be recorded,—perhaps the larger half. The unsaid part is the best of every discourse.

Language is related to truth, it seems, as curve to asymptote, for "heaven" in Emerson is always defined as the candid child defined the concept of infinity in mathematics: "Infinity is where things happen that don't."

By the time of *Nature* (1836) metaphors of distance—the remoteness of language from truth—give way to metaphors of active hostility: Words "cannot cover the dimensions of what is in truth. They break, chop, and impoverish it." The man who seeks to refine a statement by careful qualifications, judiciously considered objections, gets no closer to truth. He only makes the inescapable poverty of language more abject, and ends in an "Iceland of negations." Hyperbole, or a certain "violence of direction" in rhetoric, is likely to prove more effective than restraint in counteracting the downward gravitational pull that language exerts on the writer who aims at truth. "We aim above the mark to hit the mark," Emerson observes. Hence his cheerful rule for rhetoric: "omit all the negative propositions."

A style that suggests rather than tells, that refuses to defend, that combines excess with reticence, carries its dangers, as Emerson realized. "Ah, so you shall be sure to be misunderstood." Refusal to modify or explain his more shocking assertions earned him a reputation for antinomianism; omission of negative propositions, for witless optimism. Such accusations clearly hurt him—he once confessed that his greatest weakness was an excessive desire for sympathy—yet he managed to survive caricature with his sense of humor intact. In the furor following publication of the Divinity School *Address* he writes in his journal:

> How soon the sunk spirits rise again, how quick the little
> wounds of fortune skin over & are forgotten. I am sensitive as a
> leaf to impressions from abroad. And under this night's beau-
> tiful heaven I have forgotten that ever I was *reviewed.*

In the end he came to suspect that a text's susceptibility to misinterpretation was itself a mark of greatness. He quotes with approval Aristotle's paradoxical remark that his works were "published and not published." The reader picks up a book to try the
author's merits; but the reader too is being tested. As Roland
Barthes puts it: "The text chooses me, by a whole disposition of
invisible screens, selective baffles: vocabulary, references, reada-
bility, etc.; and, lost in the midst of a text (not *behind* it, like a
deus ex machina), there is always the other, the author."[12] Ob-
scurities, enigmas, lacunae—like Biblical parables—are tests of
the reader's intelligence and generosity; they serve to divide the
elect from the nonelect. The reader can *hear* only those texts, or
portions of texts, for which he has ears. "Deep calls unto deep,"
Emerson notes, "& Shallow to Shallow."

A "deep" text is one that challenges the reader to intellectual
activity. And Emerson's best critics have always pointed out how
well his own works live up to his demand that a text must involve
the reader actively. W. C. Brownell, writing in 1909, pointed out
that the simple understanding of an essay by Emerson requires
virtues much more strenuous than passive receptivity. "Everything means something additional. To take it in you must go beyond it. The very appreciation of an essay automatically constructs a web of thought in the weaving of which the reader
shares."[13] The ambiguities, lacunae, paradoxes, and understate-
ments with which Emerson is so generous turn the sentences of
his essays into charged terminals that the reader must take the
risk of connecting; the latter's reward is a certain electric tingle.
"Search for eloquence in his books and you will perchance miss
it, but meanwhile you will find that it has kindled all your
thoughts,"[14] writes James Russell Lowell.

It must be admitted that Emerson did everything he could to
make the reader's task difficult. He deliberately rejected the carefully sloped introductions, the graceful transitions, the carefully
modulated crescendos and decrescendos of the popular essayistic

style. Emerson's beginnings are abrupt; his transitions, equally so. For the reader who fails to go beyond the sentences he is offered, and hence to take them in, the fragments of an Emerson essay can lie upon the page like steel filings when no magnet is present.

The connection between one sentence and another, one paragraph and another, or between anything within the essay and the world outside it, is something Emerson eliminates, something he offers the reader no assistance in forming. Self-reliance is to him first of all what it was to his Protestant ancestors: the liberty to interpret texts according to the Spirit. His scrupulous respect for the reader's liberty is what Laurence Stapleton has in mind when she entitles her chapter on Emerson in *The Elected Circle*, "Emerson and the Freedom of the Reader." There she observes that "in faithfully pursuing a writer's route to freedom, Emerson makes room for the reader. He does not wink or nod, coax or bully, scold or pontificate."[15] Stanley Cavell makes a similar point when he says that Emerson's prose leaves us "at liberty to discover whether he belongs to us or we to him." But it makes no effort to draw us in, to convert us. "It does not require us."[16]

Another feature of Emerson's style that makes his work difficult to interpret is its indeterminacy of tone. Emerson's sentences can usually be read in more than one way, and only the sophisticated reader will be able to supply an imagined tone or dramatic context that makes them interesting. "I was always in favor of the solid curse as one of the most beautiful of figures," Robert Frost remarked. "It depends for variety on the tones of saying it and the situations." And he goes on to apply this observation to Emerson:

> I had a talk with John Erskine, the first time I met him, on this subject of sentences that may look tiresomely alike, short and with short words, yet turn out as calling for all sorts of ways of being said aloud or in the mind's ear, Horatio. I took Emerson's prose and verse as my illustration. Writing is unboring to the extent that it is dramatic.[17]

That last sentence is surprising. I imagine most first-time readers of Emerson would claim that he is boring precisely because there

is so little drama in his work. To a reader who has never in his life
derived pleasure from a piece of oratory, nor even imagined that
oratory could be pleasurable, a volume of Emerson's essays will
at first seem to possess a lack of drama that can make *Walden*
seem by contrast almost a gothic romance. For Emerson's essays
belong to the oral, not the written, tradition. The printed text
bears about the same relation to the essays as they are meant to
be heard "in the mind's ear" as a score of the *Messiah* does to a
performance of it.

Emerson's contemporaries were much readier than we are to
respond to the text's call for dramatic renderings because they
had not left wholly behind the old oral-aural world in which eloquence flourished for the print-centered, visually oriented world
in which it languishes and dies. There were "voiceless" styles (or
at least the ancestors of such styles) in existence even then, of
course; Emerson could expect his readers to be familiar enough
with the deadpan impersonality of scientific prose to enjoy his
wonderful parody of it in the opening sentences of "Quotation
and Originality":

> Whoever looks at the insect world, at flies, aphides, gnats,
> and innumerable parasites, and even at the infant mammals,
> must have remarked the extreme content they take in suction,
> which constitutes the main business of their life. If we go into a
> library or a newsroom, we see the same function on a higher
> plane, performed with like ardor, with equal impatience of in-
> terruption, indicating the sweetness of the act.

But he could also count on his readers' familiarity with a whole
panoply of "voiced" styles—some, indeed, in which the sense
was scarcely more than an excuse for the sound. There were the
cadences of the King James Bible, the well-bred fluencies of the
periodical writers, the heavy sarcasm of religious and political
controversialists, and the pure "pleniloquence" of the popular
oratorical style. F. O. Matthiessen quotes the conclusion of
Everett's "very popular and many times repeated address for
Washington's birthday: '. . . the name and the memory of Washington on that gracious night will travel with the silver queen of
heaven through sixty degrees of longitude, nor part company

with her till she walks in her brightness through the golden gate of California, and passes serenely on to hold midnight court with her Australian stars.' "[18] Emerson himself recalled "what fools a few sounding sentences made of me & my mates at Cambridge," and gave as an example of the kind of thing he had in mind a sentence he still remembered from a classmate's oration: "And there was a band of heroes, & round their mountain was a wreath of light, & in the midst, on the mountain top, stood Liberty, feeding her eagle."

The eagle of Liberty was probably glad of such unaccustomed repose; according to Constance Rourke "orators kept the bird so continuously in flight from the peak of the Alleghanies to the top of Mt. Hood that its shadow was said to have worn a trail across the basin of the Mississippi."[19] But the existence of witticisms like this points out another important fact: the same audience that in one mood relished the pleniloquence also relished, in another, its parody in flights of pure "buncombe." (In the same way, the Augustan age in English poetry, with its worship of the ancients, was also the great age of mock-epic; and the Victorian striving after high seriousness is matched by the Victorian genius for nonsense verse.) The line between American bombast and American burlesque is very hard to draw; Rourke warns that it is "often impossible to tell one from the other without a wide context of knowledge as to the subject and the speakers. Popular declamation of the '30s and '40s has often been considered as bombast when it should be taken as comic mythology."[20]

Irony, like buncombe, is notoriously difficult to identify with any certainty. For, as Jonathan Culler has observed, "no sentence is ironic *per se*. Sarcasm may contain internal inconsistencies which make its purport quite obvious and prevent it from being read except in one way, but for a sentence to be properly ironic it must be possible to imagine some group of readers taking it quite literally. Otherwise there is no space between apparent and assumed meaning and no space for ironic play."[21] Culler's remarks suggest why irony provokes discomfort: it serves to divide the knowing from the innocent, the civilized from the boorish, the immature from the fully adult. In this it resembles parable, though it borrows its standards from earthly kingdoms rather than from heavenly ones. Those who can read it correctly belong to what we might call the world's elect.

The problem of recognizing irony is rendered acute when the text in question is ironic only at intervals. Emerson has many moods, but in general he adopts the stance of the Sage, a man who can give us guidance in the difficulties of living. Yet in certain crucial passages his texts seem to offer advice so radically at odds with normal standards of prudence and wisdom that they call into question the authority of the rest. If this advice is offered in all seriousness, then Emerson is either a "limb of the Devil" (as Yvor Winters calls him[22]) or a fool. If it is offered ironically, we still must decide what kind of complacency or dishonesty the irony is meant to expose.

For an ironist usually has some discernible target, some identifiable ethical purpose. His ironies are intended, as Martin Price puts it, "to shock men into recognition; not simply recognition of values they have deserted or duties they have neglected, but of the way in which the mind constructs a coherent system as a refuge from moral cognition and an asylum from its obligation." The mind does this by rhetorical evasion, by adopting "attractive labels for unsavory mixtures." An ironist like Swift exposes this evasion by carrying it to an extreme, where the "shock of ugly confrontation is doubled by the tone of disarming plausibility."[23] What makes Emerson baffling is that he seems to adopt Swift's technique while reversing its ethical intent. Emerson never sounds more like one of Swift's Modest Proposers than when he is urging upon us truths he professes to value most highly. This is certainly shocking, but it is harder to say what sort of recognition that shock is supposed to produce.

The problem of the misplaced Swiftian persona becomes especially acute in those rare passages in the *Essays* where Emerson pauses to answer objections to his position. Answering objections or defending assertions was something Emerson—in life or letters—usually refused to do, believing, with Blake, that "He who replies to words of Doubt/ Doth put the Light of Knowledge out."[24] The temptation to enter the arena of disputation was naturally strongest during the furor following the Divinity School

Address, but Emerson was able to surmount it—with a little help from the oracular wisdom of his wife:

> What said my brave Asia concerning the paragraph writers today? That "this whole practice of self justification & recrimination betwixt literary men seemed every whit as low as the quarrels of the Paddies." . . . But do you know, I asked, how many fine things I have thought of to say to these fighters? They are too good to be lost.—"Then" rejoined the queen, "there is some merit in being silent."

And he did preserve his public silence, though in the privacy of his journals he can sound as ferocious as Blake:

> And whilst I see this that you must have been shocked & must cry out at what I have said I see too that we cannot easily be reconciled for I have a great deal more to say that will shock you out of all patience.

By the time Emerson came to read selections from Blake in Gilchrist's *Life* he had long since abandoned the ambition to become the prophet of an imminent apocalypse. But he copied into his journal a proverb of Hell that appealed to him: "The tigers of wrath are wiser than the horses of instruction."

If Emerson never stoops to defend himself against external threats, still he sometimes allows a hypothetical adversary space to lodge objections in the body of an essay. And here something very curious happens. The Emerson who replies to these objections is not the vehement prophet of the journals but a mild and complaisant rationalist—who does not seem to notice that the bland evasiveness of his attempts at self-justification seem more damning than the outrageous statements they are intended to justify.

In the midst of one of his characteristic attacks on Emerson, Yvor Winters pauses to consider these oddly self-destructive excursions into self-defense. "Emerson," he says, "was not wholly unaware of the theoretical objections that could be made to his position, but unless we are to assume that he personally was a corrupt and vicious man, which I think we can scarcely do, we are forced to admit that he simply did not know what the objections meant."[25] Winters cites two passages from the *Essays* as examples of this failure of comprehension. The first, from "Self-Reliance," records an argument Emerson had with a "valued adviser who was wont to importune me with the dear old doctrines of the church."

> On my saying, what have I to do with the sacredness of traditions, if I live wholly from within? my friend suggested—"But these impulses may be from below, not from above." I replied, "They do not seem to me to be such; but if I am the Devil's child, I will live then from the Devil." No law can be sacred to me but that of my nature. Good and bad are but names very readily transferable to that or this; the only right is what is after my constitution, the only wrong what is against it.

Winters treats this as a perfectly serious attempt to refute a serious objection, and he disposes of it with the sneer: "Emerson appears to be ignorant of the traditional function of the Devil and of the viscera."[26]

But the language of the paragraph in which the little debate about impulses takes place is much shiftier than Winters seems to have noticed. It begins with one of Emerson's bold declarations, meant to rouse a cowardly and conforming nation as with a Spartan fife. "Whoso would be a man must be a nonconformist. He who would gather immortal palms must not be hindered by the name of goodness, but must explore if it be goodness." So far there is little to suggest that Emerson is doing anything more than his Protestant ancestors had always claimed the right to do: judge doctrines and practices according to the inner light in each redeemed soul.

But that traditional advice is suddenly shattered by the sentences that follow. We are told that nothing is at last sacred to us but the integrity of our own minds (not souls), and then encouraged to perform a remarkable sacrament: "Absolve you to yourself, and you shall have the suffrage of the world." It is only then that Emerson pauses to consider the "dear old doctrines" of his own church—as if they were a handful of cherished mementoes or treasured family anecdotes. But this, in Emerson's view, was what organized religion, or "historical Christianity," had come to represent: a collection of traditions that had no relationship to anything in the lives of its adherents. In the Divinity School *Address* he had pointed out that "the prayers and even the dogmas of our church, are like the zodiac of Denderah, and the astronomical monuments of the Hindoos, wholly insulated from anything now extant in the life and business of the people." If the religious sentiment is to survive, it must come from "this life within life, this literal Emanuel, *God within us.*" He was well aware that his new gospel courted dangers. In a journal entry written a few months before the Divinity School *Address* he cautions himself to "beware of Antinomianism," and candidly admits that his critics are right to worry that "the loss of the old checks will sometimes be a temptation which the unripeness of the new will not countervail." But clinging blindly to the old checks was a regimen that led to certain spiritual death; it created an "automaton man who is always needing directions & repairs."

Emerson's spiritual geography only makes sense if one understands that Emerson is trying to replace the old division of the world and the psyche—according to which good things were above and wicked things below—with a new division of his own—according to which good things come from within, wicked things from without. Not that *all* impulses from within are good: Emerson worries about the mind's "terrible freedom," and notes (in "Self-Reliance") that "the bold sensualist will use the name of philosophy to gild his crimes." But the law of consciousness abides. No imitation of something external to the self can produce true virtue; all it can produce is the sorry substitute ridiculed by Emerson. "Men do what is called a good action, as some piece of courage or charity, much as they would pay a fine in expiation of daily non-appearance on parade. Their works are done as an apology or extenuation of their living in the world,—as invalids and the insane pay a high board."

But the trusted adviser who asks questions about impulses can think only in terms of the older divisions offered by his culture: God and the Reason above, the Devil and the passions below. Emerson does not attempt to refute this position; he merely replies: "if I am the Devil's child, I will live then from the Devil."

The declaration of Byronic defiance is rendered comic chiefly by the circumstances: how could a decorous ex-minister in the town of Concord "live from the Devil" even if he wished to? At most he could do what Emerson had done: use the lecture platform to attack the derelictions of traditional Christianity, and be branded a heretic and an atheist as a result. "It is plain from all the noise that there is Atheism somewhere," he said after the Divinity School *Address.* "The only question is now, Which is the Atheist?" Your enemies will always call deviations from their own standards diabolic; the easiest thing to do is to accept the label and continue your authentic labor—the kind that is dictated from within, not from without.

It is easier to share Winters's bewilderment over the second passage he quotes, this time from "Circles." He does not give the full quotation, and since the sentences he omits are important ones, his reading is more than usually distorted. But the passage itself is difficult to explicate even in its unmutilated form. Emerson has been prophesying the inevitable obsolescence of all creations of the spirit. Every scientific discovery, every work of art, every religious system exists to be surpassed, he argues. All virtues are initial, none are final. No system will save us; nothing is secure but "life, transition, the energizing spirit." Emerson does not expect this doctrine to be welcomed by society. "The new statement is always hated by the old," he warns early in the essay, "and, to those dwelling in the old, comes like an abyss of skepticism." A voice of one of those dwellers suddenly rises up to question him:

> And thus, O circular philosopher, I hear some reader exclaim, you have arrived at a fine Pyrrhonism, at an equivalence and indifferency of all action, and would fain teach us that *if we are true,* forsooth, our crimes may be lively stones out of which we shall construct the temple of the true God!

There is something alien in the tone of this passage; its strangely hearty mockery reminds one of Carlyle. But if this glancing parody leads us to expect a grand, jesting refutation, we are immediately disappointed. Emerson's odd reply does not seem concerned to answer the objection at all, and it is couched in his characteristically elusive rhetoric of understatement. "I am not careful to justify myself," he begins; and though the remark looks at first like a mild non sequitur, it is in fact an expression of powerful contempt, Emerson's version of the Blakean declaration that what can be made explicit to the idiot is not worth his care. The reader of "Circles" who accuses Emerson of teaching an equivalence and indifferency of all actions is either careless or willfully stupid. "One man's justice is another's injustice; one man's beauty another's ugliness; one man's wisdom another's folly," Emerson says, but though these maxims may sound like mere variations on the proverb "one man's meat is another man's poison," they are not; since Emerson is careful to add an important qualification—"as one beholds the same objects from a higher point." If this is "thoroughgoing relativism,"[27] as Winters alleges, then so is the philosophy of St. Paul:

> For the preaching of the cross is to them that perish, foolishness; but unto us which are saved, it is the power of God.
> For it is written, I will destroy the wisdom of the wise, and will bring to nothing the understanding of the prudent.
> . . .
> For the wisdom of this world is foolishness with God.[28]

Emerson urges a new faith, not an old skepticism; mere Pyrrhonism he always equated with spiritual suicide. If his gospel looks to the orthodox Christian like an abyss of skepticism—well, Emerson might have replied, Christianity too was founded on a cornerstone that the builders had rejected: "unto the Jews a stumblingblock, and unto the Greeks foolishness."[29] But Emerson says nothing of the sort. Instead he suddenly performs a dizzying "sleight of mind," an elision so radical that it threatens to swallow up speaker and argument together, leaving only the reverberations of an oddly disembodied irony: the Tyger of Wrath as Cheshire Cat:

> I own I am gladdened by seeing the predominance of the saccharine principle throughout vegetable nature, and not less by beholding in morals that unrestrained inundation of the prin-

ciple of good into every chink and hole that selfishness has left
open, yea, into selfishness and sin itself; so that no evil is pure,
nor hell itself without its extreme satisfactions.

If we examine the rhetorical mode of this powerful and disturbing passage, we notice that parts of it are cast in the Swiftian
idiom remarked earlier. Emerson adopts the tone of the bloodless
empiricist, the Royal Society "projector" who is gladdened by
his observations of the saccharine principle, and who is cheered
at the thought that even the damned inhabit the best of all possible hells. No wonder Winters omits these sentences; to read them
straight would be to judge Emerson more than "corrupt and vicious." In "Circles" mere optimism, however foolish, has given
way to obvious lunacy—lunacy that combines the utilitarian
cheerfulness of Swift's "Digression on Madness" with the grisly
complacency of his *Modest Proposal.* Not even the sourest critic
is likely to take these opinions for Emerson's own.

But whose opinions are they? The journal entry upon which
this passage is based is, for once, unambiguously clear:

> And thus, o circular philosopher, you have arrived at a fine
> Pyrrhonism, at an equivalence & indifferency of all actions &
> would fain teach us that *if we are true,* forsooth, our crimes
> may be lively stones out of which we shall construct the tem-
> ple of the true God.
> The good Swedenborg was aware, I believe, of this won-
> derful predominance & excess of the saccharine principle in
> nature & noticed that the hells were not without their extreme
> satisfactions.

This is sarcasm rather than irony, but a sarcasm that is at least
susceptible of explanation. Swedenborg, who at the time of *The
American Scholar* had been one of Emerson's heroes, had by
1840 become one of his frequent targets of ridicule; in Emerson's
account of him in *Representative Men* the Swedish visionary
does in fact resemble one of Swift's creations: a cold, passionless
observer of Facts, whose humorless and pedantic manner never
deserts him, whether he is observing the ecstasies of heaven or
the torments of hell. Worse still, Swedenborg was essentially
Manichaean (as were all orthodox Christians, in Emerson's opin-

ion) for believing in devils and permanent damnation; and he was mean, vindictive, and morbid in his preoccupation with sin. "Except Rabelais and Dean Swift," Emerson complained, "nobody ever had such science of filth and corruption."

But if the visionary was a repellent figure, the visions themselves—taken as metaphors rather than dogmas—were sometimes surprisingly poetic and imaginative. (Blake thought so too; he said that Swedenborg's writings were "False philosophy according to the letter, but true according to the spirit."[30]) And Emerson was particularly attracted by the metaphoric truth of Swedenborg's vision of Hell: punishment there consisted in the *practice* of the same vices that had occasioned damnation in the first place. The deceitful continued to deceive, the covetous to rob, the lecherous to fornicate. These vices provide the same kind of pleasure they provide on earth, and ultimately occasion the same kind of misery.[31]

The notion that the evil in hell are punished by the consequences of their vices, if read as an allegory of life on earth, resembles Emerson's own beloved doctrine of compensation. But what is bold and imaginative as metaphor is, if accepted as literal truth, morally indistinguishable from the doctrine it replaces. "That pure malignity can exist," Emerson argues, "is the extreme proposition of unbelief. It is not to be entertained by a rational agent; it is atheism; it is the last profanation." And the alternative to a belief in pure malignity? Emerson commends the wild humor of Burns's "Address to the Deil":

> But fare you weel, auld Nickie-Ben!
> O wad ye tak' a thought & men'

Of this sentiment Emerson observes, "If it be comical, it yet belongs to the moral sublime." To say that evil can be converted into good is not quite the same thing as saying that there is no difference between good and evil, though the distinction is likely to be lost on the orthodox, of whom Swedenborg was ultimately one.

But Swedenborg's visions can be put to other uses than the ones he intended. Like Blake in *The Marriage of Heaven and*

Hell, Emerson discovers to his delight and amusement that evidence designed to support belief in eternal damnation can be cheerfully reversed to support a more generous eschatology. And this, after all, is what "Circles" is all about:

> There is not a piece of science but its flank may be turned tomorrow; there is not any literary reputation, not the so-called eternal names of fame, that may not be revised and condemned. The very hopes of man, the thoughts of his heart, the religion of nations, the manners and morals of mankind, are all at the mercy of a new generalization.

But of course the description I have just given of Emerson's irony fits only the 1840 journal entry, not the passage as it stands in "Circles." When Emerson rewrites the journal passage for inclusion in the essay, he expands it to include an explicit reference to the generosity of a vision that can joyfully await the conversion of evil to good (as Burns wishes the reclamation even of the Devil himself)—but he leaves out Swedenborg's name, and hopelessly blurs the distinction between Swedenborg's opinions and his own. He is *not* careful to justify himself: he mixes doctrines he finds offensive with beliefs he seriously supports, and he casts the whole passage into the kind of unconsciously self-destructive idiom that Augustan satire had reserved for its maddest or cruelest masks.

The passage gains in power what it loses in immediate intelligibility; indeed, its contempt for intelligibility is part of its power. Like some of the parables Jesus tells, it seems designed at once to invite misinterpretation and at the same time to radiate scorn for the misinterpreter. Emerson, like his own Uriel, simply withdraws behind a cloud, leaving it to his readers to decide whether his apparent "lapses" are the result of his incapacities or ours, whether he is unusually foolish or, on the contrary, "by knowledge grown too bright/ To hit the nerve of feebler sight."

Explaining how the strategy works is easier than guessing why it was chosen. In part, I think, Emerson had discovered that attempts to make fine distinctions were wasted effort when one's opponents were likely to condemn any revision of accepted ideas or practices with smug, undiscriminating zeal. There are only two ways of coping with resolute Philistinism—denunciation and insouciance. Emerson was sometimes tempted—particularly during the controversy following publication of the *Address*—to thunder and denounce, but he never appears as prophet outside the privacy of his own journal, for a number of reasons. One was a laudable awareness that the prose of prophet or martyr was—in nineteenth-century Boston, at any rate—a repellent affectation. Blake's opinions might have cost him his life. What did Emerson risk? After the Divinity School *Address* he could no longer speak at Harvard, but that hardly entitled him to a martyr's crown. A journal entry for September 1838 bears the contemptuous heading "The silken persecution":

> Martyrs with thumbscrews, martyrs sawn asunder, martyrs eaten by dogs, may claim with gory stumps a crown. But the martyrs in silk stockings & barouches, martyrs with venison & champagne, in ballrooms & picture galleries, make me sick.

The second reason is harder to define. Yet we can conjecture, from the tone and content of the remarks Emerson addresses to himself in the journals of the period, that he had formulated some version of Nietzsche's warning to philosophers: "Take care, philosophers and friends, of knowledge, and beware of martyrdom, of suffering 'for the truth's sake'! Even of defending yourself." In place of defense, Nietzsche advises a mocking retreat: "Rather, go away. Flee into concealment. And have your masks and subtlety, that you may be mistaken for what you are not, or feared a little."[32] *That you may be mistaken for what you are not*—that command (from Emerson to himself) seems to underlie those eerie and disturbing passages in which he invites the attack of hostile readers by appearing to offer them exactly the evidence they need to convict him. These passages, like the inkblots of a Rorschach, are less important for what they contain than for the response they evoke. They ask us above all to imagine a *voice*, and the voice we imagine determines whether we think the author an ironist, a Satanist, or a fool.

Yet Emerson's lapses are not the only things that ask us to imagine a presence behind the sentences on the page, nor are hostile readers the only ones to question his self-awareness. No one who reads much of the critical literature about Emerson can fail to be struck by the number of critics who assert that Emerson *was unconscious of* some significant implication contained in, or response likely to be provoked by, his own texts. Jonathan Bishop, for instance, praises Emerson's strategy of using "metaphors of eating and nourishment for the description of mental activity," but calls the strategy "sublimely unconscious."[33] John Lyndenberg points out that the "shudder, the feeling of awe" that characterizes what he calls the Dark Tradition in American literature appears with "startling clarity" in the essay "Experience," but then adds that "presumably Emerson did not intend to convey any such feeling, and possibly was not even aware that he had done so."[34] It seems to me that what Winters and Bishop and Lyndenberg are responding to is an effect of Emerson's style, which manages to sound offhand and fortuitous even when Emerson is treating of the most serious subjects. O. W. Firkins had something similar in mind when he remarked that although "Experience" seemed to him one of the boldest essays in literature, its boldness had a rather casual air, as if a man should blow up a cathedral by way of diversion to the monotony of an evening walk.[35]

This air of unselfconsciousness is one of the largest differences between Emerson's prose and Thoreau's. Thoreau has his paradoxes and enigmas too, but he never leaves the reader wondering who intended them, who stands behind them. Emerson's tendency from the first is to efface himself, to leave the reader no clues as to how his text is to be privately performed. If his reticence leaves room for the freedom of the reader, it also invites his distortions and mistakes. "Criticism has this defense, that, like poetry, it is the accommodation of things to the desires of the mind," he once dryly remarked, and he knew better than anyone that a strong desire of the mind was to be free of the text whose power one had been originally drawn to.

The mind does this by a curious evasive action, which gives it access to the power of a prior text without risking subjection to it. It grants the prior text its wisdom, but denies the author's intentionality. "It is remarkable . . . that we find it so hard to impute our own best sense to a dead author," Emerson observed. "The very highest praise we think of any writer, painter, sculptor, or builder is that he actually possessed the thought or feeling with which he inspired us. We hesitate at doing Spenser so great an honor as to think that he intended by his allegory the sense that we affix to it." The assertion that a text reveals a meaning its author did not consciously intend (whether of unwitting folly or oracular wisdom) is the constitutive gesture of interpretation. For it turns the text into a figure of which our explanation is the fulfillment, and hence is not the least powerful of the counterattacks we launch at the centuries who by their very existence are always conspiring "against the sanity and authority of the soul."

The Riddle of the Sphinx: *Nature*

> Is it any wonder that we should finally become
> suspicious, lose patience, and turn away impa-
> tiently? That we should finally learn from this
> Sphinx to ask questions, too? *Who* is it really
> that puts questions to us here? *What* in us really
> wants "truth"?
> Who of us is Oedipus here? Who the Sphinx?
> It is a rendezvous, it seems, of questions and
> question marks.
>
> Nietzsche, *Beyond Good and Evil*

The Sphinx, enigmatic propounder of a dangerous riddle—
the emblem was one of Emerson's favorites. He used it in
journals and essays; he chose it as the title for a notoriously inscrutable poem. Into an early journal he copies an
aphorism of Madame de Stael's: "The aenigma of ourselves swal-
lows up like the sphinx thousands of systems which pretend to
the glory of having guessed its meaning." Later on his brother
Charles had given the emblem a different referent. "I conversed
with him one day upon the agreement of so many thinkers in rep-
resenting Nature as the symbol of mind. He said, 'Yes, there sits
the Sphinx by the road-side, & every fine genius that goes by has
a crack with her.' "

Emerson recalled this conversation when he, too, found himself attempting to formulate a "theory of nature" that would explain all phenomena: the objective one of matter, the subjective
one of spirit, and all those curious borderline things in be-

tween—"language, sleep, madness, dreams, beasts, sex." On June 7, 1836, just a few weeks before he composed the little creation myth that later became the chant of the Orphic poet in *Nature*, he records his sense of amusement at his own brashness. "So you have undertaken to solve the problem of the world. God speed you, fair sir, in your modest attempt." *Nature* is Emerson's crack with the sphinx. Yet many of its readers have concluded that the answers it offers are more nearly a part of the problem than of the solution.

Emerson was well aware of his reputation for unintelligibility, and eventually learned to relish it. Late in life, when his memory had failed badly, he agreed to deliver an old lecture on education to a Concord audience, though he kept forgetting what the subject was even as he practiced reading his text. The piquancy of the situation amused him. "A funny occasion it will be," he remarked. "A lecturer who has no idea what he is lecturing about, and an audience who don't know what he *can* mean."[1] Still, one can detect a certain wistfulness in his discussion of the "innocent serenity" of the wise men of antiquity. "Well assured that their speech is intelligible and the most natural thing in the world they add thesis to thesis, without a moment's heed of the universal astonishment of the human race below, who do not comprehend their plainest argument." And if he adds that this innocence has a slightly comic look to us, he is probably imagining what would happen if the *Enneads* of Plotinus had been given to the *Christian Examiner* to review. What Emerson's contemporaries thought of him is perhaps most succinctly summed up in his report of a witticism that had circulated locally while he was abroad on a journey that had taken him up the waters of the Nile. "Mrs. Helen Bell, it seems, was asked, 'What do you think the Sphinx said to Mr. Emerson?' 'Why,' replied Mrs. Bell, 'the Sphinx probably said to him "You're another!"' "

Anyone who spends much time working with *Nature* develops, I think, a certain rueful admiration for Mrs. Bell's joke. Like de Stael's Sphinx, *Nature* has a way of swallowing up critics who pretend to the glory of having guessed its meaning; like Charles's Sphinx, it sits at the roadside, and no one seriously interested in

Emerson can avoid having a crack with it. Complex and difficult as it is, it is also his most exuberant and inventive work; in it he displays a speculative boldness he never afterward surpassed. To read *Nature* is to be alternately exhilarated, perplexed, amused, and charmed; to trace the history of its composition is to become intimately acquainted with the quality of its creator's mind—with its powers of assimilation and invention, with its skeptical restlessness and underlying intensity.

The difficulties in the text are real enough. And yet the greatest danger one faces in writing about it is not so much intellectual failure as failure of tact. The process of unriddling Emerson's attempt to unriddle the cosmos can become so absorbing a game that one ends by explaining everything about *Nature* except what made it memorable and influential in the first place: the quality of exhilaration, of buoyancy, that led Kenneth Burke to describe it as a Happiness Pill.[2]

Part of its charm comes from its considerable (if intermittent) beauty of language, a kind of fluency, as John Jay Chapman calls it, that gives *Nature* in places the quality of poetry. Such beauty is chiefly apparent in passages where Emerson recounts his "wild delight" in natural appearances, as in the lovely descriptions of sunrise and sunset from the chapter "Beauty":

> I have seen the spectacle of morning from the hill-top over against my house, from day-break to sun-rise, with emotions which an angel might share. The long slender bars of cloud float like fishes in the sea of crimson light. From the earth, as a shore, I look out into that silent sea. I seem to partake its rapid transformations: the active enchantment reaches my dust, and I dilate and conspire with the morning wind.

> Not less excellent, except for our less susceptibility in the afternoon, was the charm, last evening, of a January sunset. The western clouds divided and subdivided themselves into pink flakes modulated with tints of unspeakable softness; and the air had so much life and sweetness, that it was a pain to come within doors.... The leafless trees become spires of flame in the sunset, with the blue east for their background, and the stars of the dead calices of flowers, and every withered stem and stubble rimed with frost, contribute something to the mute music.

But the sense of exhilaration permeates the discursive parts of the book as well, where Emerson attempts to explain the origin and destination of the universe with a "theory" made of odds and ends borrowed from a bizarre assortment of poets, scientists, philosophers, and visionaries. *Nature* is a case study in the pleasures of eclecticism. Emerson takes a hint on dialectical method from Coleridge, hermeneutic techniques from a French Swedenborgian, a set of images from an English astronomer, and assembles from all this material a cosmogonic fable that might have been written by a laconic reincarnation of William Blake.

The resulting volume is a very strange work indeed, as hard to assess as it is to classify. On the whole, Whicher's description of the book as an "odd combination of provinciality and profundity, bookishness and originality, inhibition and power"[3] is accurate. Yet even if in the end its reach exceeded its grasp, *Nature* proved by the very extravagance of its ambition that a man at the tag end of time and on the outskirts of civilization could still build his own world from whatever driftwood washed up on his shores, and in so doing attain the state of grace promised by Emerson at the beginning of his book: an original relation to the universe.

What Helen Vendler said of another notable first book in American literature—that the whole of Wallace Stevens was in *Harmonium,* and not just in embryo—is also true of *Nature,* which includes condensed versions of every major Emersonian theme. The polemical aspect of the book—its overt protest against literary influence, its implicit protest against historical Christianity—looks forward to the trenchant orations of 1837–1838: *The American Scholar* and the Divinity School *Address.* The speculations on language and symbolism foreshadow the complexities of Emerson's later theories of poetry. And the curious little myths of Creation, Fall, and Redemption that end the book contain both an expression of his most extravagant millennial hopes and a subtle, skeptical analysis of the obstacles in the way of their fulfillment.

But if the study of *Nature* is rewarding, it can also be uniquely taxing, for certain qualities of the text make it more than usually "recalcitrant to the formulations of the discursive intelligence."[4]

There are at least three general areas of difficulty, two of which, in the canon of Emerson's works, are peculiar to *Nature* alone.

The first is stylistic. Emerson's rhetoric is nearly always unsettling, but the problem is particularly acute in *Nature*, where the succession of competing styles—rhapsodic, lapidary, lyrical, detached—is often so rapid as to leave the reader giddy. In part this confusion of tongues is the natural result of Emerson's habits of composition. Every one of his longer works is a kind of anthology of passages taken from the journals. And as anyone who has read the early journals knows, Emerson was a tireless imitator of prose styles he admired. His tastes were catholic; he liked the sonorities of Everett, the pungency of Jonson or Bacon, the lucid impersonality of the natural scientists whose works he encountered in the periodicals of the day, the marmoreal calm of Browne, the elephantine metaphysical humor of Carlyle. In the journals themselves this multiplicity of styles is rarely confusing, since each single paragraph (Emerson's natural unit of composition) is usually consistent in style, however much it may differ from the passages that surround it. We accept the blank space separating one journal passage from another.as a kind of signifier in its own right, rather like a glottal stop in phonemics: it stands for a presumed lapse of time in which a change of mood or attitude seems decorous. In the published works this hiatus is eliminated, and what in the journals is merely a change of mood acquires the formal status of a problematic transition.

Now of course Emerson was famous all through his career for the abruptness of his transitions. But the discontinuities of *Nature* are so radical as to seem almost different in kind from those of the later works, chiefly because Emerson was experimenting there with a variation on his usual mode of composition, one he had never used before, and never used again.

I have said that Emerson's works are anthologies, that Emerson-the-essayist works as an editor or compiler of material produced by Emerson-the-journalist. But in the lectures written before *Nature* and the lectures and essays written after it the compiler usually respects the structural integrity of the paragraphs composed by the journalist: words and phrases may be altered, but the order of the sentences is rarely disturbed.

In composing *Nature* Emerson's editorial techniques were more disruptive. Some paragraphs, it is true, are transferred intact from journal or lecture, but others are broken down, and sentences from them are distributed over several chapters. Since this process never entirely effaces the original style of the sentences, their juxtaposition with other similarly decontextualized sentences produces a perpetual series of small shocks or jolts.

This conflict of styles is not necessarily disagreeable even when it seems artless. Yet in certain places—like the Transparent Eye-ball passage—we are left to wonder just what it is we are confronting: adolescent high spirits (at one point in *Nature*, after all, Emerson advises us that we can experience a "low degree of the sublime" by looking at the landscape upside down through our legs!); deliberate metaphysical grotesquerie in the manner of Carlyle; or a simple blunder.

A second kind of difficulty arises from the presence in the text of several distinct "layers of purpose."[5] I borrow the phrase from a recent Biblical critic, who uses it to describe the complexities of certain Old Testament narratives in which legendary or historical material whose significance is no longer fully understood is at once preserved and reinterpreted by later compilers. Something of the same kind of sedimentation can be observed in *Nature;* in fact, I think that anyone who attempts to provide a diachronic account of the book's evolution ends up rather wishing that the evidence for single authorship were not so regrettably conclusive. It would be much easier to account for some of the peculiarities of *Nature* if one could simply adopt the analytic license of textual criticism and ascribe some parts of the book to *SR* (a pious "supernatural rationalist"[6] who assembles a collection of exempla designed to prove the wisdom of God from evidences of design in the creation), others to *A* (a furious antinomian who proposes an "infernal" or Blakean reading of these same exempla), and others still to *R* (the redactor—a shadowy figure, dispassionate and self-effacing, who attempts to reconcile the work of his predecessors by an exercise of hermeneutic ingenuity).

This tripartite division is not as fanciful as it sounds; it corresponds roughly to the sketchy external evidence we have about the book's mutations. We know that Emerson first planned a shorter essay, comprising at least Chapters I–VI of the book we now have, to be called "Nature." When he was nearly finished with this he planned to write a companion essay, to be called "Spirit"; he intended to publish the latter in the same volume with "Nature" but not under the same title. Sometime in the final month and a half of composition he decided to combine the two essays into one, but the work of unification caused him trouble; there was, he complained, a "crack" in the book "not easy to be soldered or welded."

The decision to unite the two essays in one is not in itself surprising. Emerson was drawn toward antithetical pairings. They seemed to him a mark of that dialectical agility that identifies a man as a "candidate for truth"—the willingness to "recognize all the opposite negations between which, as walls, his being is swung." Sometimes the opposite negations appear in a single title, like "Being and Seeming" or "Nominalist and Realist." Or else they will appear as the titles of two successive essays; "Prudence" is followed by "Heroism," "Politics" by "Private Life," "Fate" by "Power."

But why, when he had combined his two essays, did Emerson reduce the title of the second to a chapter heading and use the title of the first for the book as a whole, as if "spirit" were a subcategory of nature and not its antithesis? In *Aids to Reflection*, a book that was a kind of bible to Emerson in the early 1830s, Coleridge had defined "nature" and "spirit" as mutually exclusive terms: "the most general and *negative* definition of Nature is, Whatever is not Spirit; and *vice versa* of Spirit, That which is not comprehended in Nature."[7] If such a definition was at the back of Emerson's mind when he was planning his pair of essays in the summer of 1836, his final choice of a title for the volume is perversely misleading. It is as though Lévi-Strauss had decided to call *The Raw and the Cooked* simply *The Raw*. Certainly some of Emerson's contemporaries were mystified by a change of direction in the book that the title had not prepared them for. Readers who expected, not unreasonably, that a book entitled *Nature* would be about nature were baffled by the closing chapters. Francis Bowen, one of the first reviewers, found "beautiful writing and sound philosophy" in the earlier chapters, but complained that in the later ones Emerson "turns and aims a back blow at the universe, which he has been teaching us to admire and love. . . . Matter is nothing. Spirit is all. Man is alone in the vast inane with his God."[8]

The easiest way of explaining Emerson's decision about the title is to guess that something happened during the final weeks of composition that made him think a dual title unnecessary, *Nature* being neither more nor less misleading than *Nature and Spirit* would have been. But this in turn suggests that Emerson had realized that the insights contained in the final chapter of his book could not be accounted for by, and in fact were subversive of, the Cartesian or Coleridgean premises with which he had begun.

It is at this point that we encounter the third source of difficulty in the book, cracks or fissures that arise from antinomies in the subject itself. Is "nature" an aggregate of material particles or a system of signs? Is apocalypse a renovation accomplished in space or a revelation given discontinuously in time? Emerson's effort to mediate between these apparently irreconcilable alternatives generates the striking and peculiar figurations for which the final chapters of *Nature* is famous—the two chants of the Orphic poet and the strange, laconic formula that separates them: "The ruin or the blank, that we see when we look at nature, is in our own eye. The axis of vision is not coincident with the axis of things, and so they appear not transparent but opake."

The problem of arriving at a satisfactory reading of *Nature* lies in relating the second kind of difficulty to the third, without ignoring the local perplexities occasioned by the first—in other words, of finding a stylistically sensitive way of reconciling a diachronic account of the book's genesis and growth with a synchronic account of its structure. The accounts are neither wholly congruent nor wholly separable. *Nature* isn't merely an autobiography in disguise, but neither did it reach its present shape through the "self-development of a cold, pure, divinely unconcerned dialectic."[9] The terrible pressure of sudden catastrophe—the death of Emerson's brother Charles—precipitated the massive effort of reinterpretation that constitutes the second

half of the book, and in so doing revealed to Emerson the link between interpretation and desire. But the reinterpretation itself
only revealed the hidden presence of ideas at least implicitly
there in the book from the beginning—hence Emerson's conclusion that all revelation is really anamnesis: *quantum sumus,
scimus.* "I learn geology," he once observed, "the morning after
an earthquake."

It will be easier to chart this mazy, intricate story of discoveries, shocks, and sudden reappraisals if we divide it into four
roughly distinct periods. The first period, from 1831 to 1833,
covers the years of spiritual crisis that led Emerson to abandon
historical Christianity—and his own profession as a minister—in
search of a less compromised ground for faith. The second period
may be more precisely demarcated. It begins on July 13, 1833,
when Emerson had what his biographer rightly calls "one of the
memorable experiences of his life"[10]—a visit to the cabinet of natural history in the Jardin des Plantes at Paris that affected him
like a religious conversion and left him determined to become a
"naturalist." During his return voyage home from Europe he was
already toying with the idea of writing a book embodying his
new insights about nature and its relation to man. By June of
1835 he had defined his vague plans more precisely; he now
speaks of writing a book "chiefly upon Natural Ethics," a project
upon which he apparently began work the following winter. By
March of 1836 he was wholly absorbed in the process of composition. But work on the book was brought to a halt by the sudden
illness and death (May 9, 1836) of his brother Charles.

It may seem odd to regard the hiatus that follows this shock a
stage in the composition of *Nature*, and yet I think it can be argued that the final chapters of the book are largely shaped by
Emerson's complex response to Charles's death. For a while
Emerson abandoned work on his own manuscript in order to
search through Charles's papers in hopes of assembling a selection of posthumous writings. To Emerson's surprise and dismay,
the journals of his brother proved to contain nothing that resembled the brilliance of his conversation, and, what was worse, were
filled with "melancholy, penitential, self accusing" reflections.

The man whom Emerson had always admired for his sanity and effortless self-mastery proved to have been tormented by doubts far more crippling than Emerson's own.

What went on in Emerson's mind during this painful period can only be guessed at, reconstructed with the help of laconic comments in the letters and journals of the time. Yet by June of 1836 there are indications that a considerable revolution of thought had taken place, a revolution that was to alter the direction of *Nature* radically.

The first sign of this change appears in a journal entry for June 7, 1836. The brief entry (which I have already quoted) is an amused note from Emerson to himself, and it indicates that his little book about nature has become something very different from the book of natural ethics he started out to produce. "So you have undertaken to solve the problem of the world. God speed you, fair sir, in your modest attempt." He makes clear, too, that he is aware of the relationship between his new boldness and the personal loss he has just suffered. "It were a wise secret inquiry for the bosom," he notes, "to compare point by point especially at eras or remarkable events our own biography with the rise, progress, & practice of Ideas in us."

What those ideas were becomes apparent in a sudden rush of journal passages composed during the closing days of June. From "helpless mourning" Emerson is suddenly catapulted into a vision of greatness in which all forms of suffering or alienation— even the otherness of nature itself—are revealed as temporary delusions in the mind of a godlike human creator. (Why Charles's death should have had this effect is, of course, the question most in need of resolution.) This burst of creative activity seems to have given him the energy he needed to complete his old project—he writes to his brother William on June 28 that his little book on nature is nearly finished. But the new journal passages (which will become part of "Spirit" and "Prospects") suggest an expansion of his original plan: a new essay, to be called "Spirit," that will incorporate his new insights and will indicate their relation to his previous views.

The evidence for what went on during the final weeks of composition—July and August of 1836—is again rather sketchy, and comes mostly from the letters. But Emerson was clearly troubled by the difficulty of working out the relationship between his new material and the now-completed earlier book. Should he print the new material in a separate essay, and if so, should he publish it together with *Nature* or separately? Or was there perhaps a way of subsuming both old and new material under some larger rubric? He considered each of these possibilities in turn before settling on the last. The work of splicing caused him some trouble; in early August he is still complaining about his inability to solder the two halves of his book together. But by August 27 he reports that the proofs for the finished book have returned from the printer, and the book itself was offered for sale on September 9.

The agility of Emerson's mind—its endless willingness to revise its previous interpretation under the pressure of new facts, new thoughts, new experiences—is what makes it perennially interesting; and in tracing the history of *Nature*'s growth we can observe the process of reinterpretation with particular clarity. It is true that in later essays Emerson manages to get more of his dialectic into his text. The structure of *Nature* as we have it is designed rather to camouflage than to exhibit the upheavals that produced it. But if the cracks and fissures in the text make its surface rough, they also have the merit of providing a rare glimpse of the deeper strata of Emerson's imagination.

1831–1833: "Correspondence" and the Moral Law

What led Emerson to choose his topic in the first place? His youthful literary ambitions had never included anything so bold as an attempt to discover the secret of the universe. When he was twenty-one he confided to his journal that he hoped to write "one of those books which collect & embody the wisdom of their times & so mark the stages of human improvement," and had listed, as instances of the kind of thing he had in mind, the essays of Montaigne and Bacon and the Proverbs of Solomon. As a forecast of the genre of his later writings (if not quite of their content) this shows considerable prescience; both before and after *Nature* Emerson's characteristic form was the lecture or occasional essay, and his prose style in them tends to be strongly aphoristic. But *Nature* itself is something of an anomaly.

Emerson's early journals and theme books show relatively little interest in nature or natural science. His interest in the general topic seems to have begun during the months in which he was struggling with his decision to leave the ministry, and for this reason it is worthwhile reviewing briefly some aspects of that spiritual crisis.

Religious doubt was nothing new to Emerson. Throughout the 1820s he struggled with various demons of skepticism, and when he finally was ordained, it was into the most liberal denomination of organized Christianity then available. But even this mild faith proved to be at once too constricting and too unsatisfying: constricting because it still imposed a weight of traditional forms upon the observer, unsatisfying because it placed all direct contact with the divine in the distant past. As he was later to complain in the Divinity School *Address*, "men have come to speak of the revelation as somewhat long ago given and done, as if God were dead."

He had given concise expression to the problem that plagued him as early as 1823, in a letter to his Harvard classmate John Boynton Hill:

> An exemplary Christian of today, and even a minister, is content to be just such a man as was a good Roman in the days of Cicero or of the imperial Antonines. Contentment with the moderate standard of pagan virtue, implies that there was no very urgent necessity for Heaven's last revelation; for, the laws of morality were written distinctly enough before, and philosophy had pretty lively views of the immortality of the soul.

In this mood of disgruntlement he could look back with envy at one aspect of ancestral religion. "Presbyterianism & Calvinism," he admitted, "at least make Christianity a more real & tangible system and give it some novelties which were worth unfolding to the ignorance of men." But the breezy dismissal that follows— "this, I think, is the most which can be said of orthodoxy"— shows that Emerson assumes no enlightened mind can take seriously orthodoxy's claims to historical accuracy or exclusive possession of truth.

The doctrines of orthodoxy, then, were incredible; those of liberal Christianity, unnecessary. But a third alternative—atheism or agnosticism—was never really available to him. Once, after a combative skeptic had challenged him, he remarked that men seemed to be constitutionally either believers or unbelievers. And he knew that his own opinions, affections, even whimsies, placed him firmly in the party of belief.

But merely possessing a constitutional tendency to believe did not solve the problem of locating something to believe in. Throughout the 1820s and early 1830s Emerson searched for a faith that would satisfy both his intellect and his emotions. Meanwhile he clung to the one belief inherited from his immediate intellectual tradition that still seemed unquestionable—a belief in the existence of a "moral sentiment" or "moral sense."

Much excellent scholarly work has been done to trace the intellectual ancestry of this concept, which postulated a special faculty in the soul capable of intuitively apprehending ethical truths. What the concept meant to Emerson, according to Stephen Whicher, "was that conscience was not to be explained naturalistically. It was, as religion taught, the voice of God in the soul, teaching us an unquestionable law of conduct, testifying to the reality of a divine authority, and assuring us of the moral administration of the universe."[11]

Undoubtedly Whicher is right to say that one value of this belief for Emerson was that it provided "an early answer to the problem of scepticism."[12] But the emotional intensity in Emerson's tone whenever he speaks of the moral sentiment suggests that the belief had a far greater importance for him than that. And it is just this intensity that seems so peculiar to a modern reader, and so unpalatable. It is easier to sympathize with ordinary religious enthusiasm than to understand Emerson's worship of an abstract principle of righteousness within his soul, or share in the exhilaration he evidently feels when he thinks he can trace evidences of its existence in the workings of external nature. When he argues, in *Nature*, that "all things are moral" and that the outward beauty of nature exists only to the end of illustrating the Ten Commandments, his propositions are likely to sound to us not only incredible but (what is more damning) preachy and smug.

It is often dangerous, though, to take an alien terminology at face value. One thinks of Nietzsche's remarks about post-Kantian Idealism: "One can do no greater wrong to the whole of this exuberant and enthusiastic movement, which was really youthfulness, however boldly it disguised itself in hoary and senile concepts, than to take it seriously, or worse, to treat it with moral indignation."[13] Before we succumb to the temptation to treat the moral sentiment with moral indignation, we should examine more carefully what it actually meant to Emerson.

The first thing one notices is that Emerson's relationship to this sentiment is anything but reassuring. He may conceive of it as located within his soul, but its presence there makes the rest of him feel like "feebleness & dust." If it was in one sense a beacon of hope, something that "cannot be defeated by my defeats," in another sense its counsels were difficult to tell from despair. "It has separated me from men. It has watered my pillow; it has driven sleep from my bed. It has tortured me for my guilt."

Why should Emerson have wanted so demanding an inner guest? For one thing, it satisfied a strong emotional need for at least one point of certitude in a world of radical evanescence. An early meditation on the seventh verse of Psalm 112—"He shall not be afraid of evil tidings; his heart is fixed, trusting in the Lord"—turns into an evocation of flux that might have been written by Walter Pater:

> We are the changing inhabitants of a changing world. The night & the day, the ebbing & flowing of the tide, the round of the seasons, the waxing & waning moon, the flux & reflux of the arts & of the civilization of nations & the swift & sad succession of generations, these are the monitors among which we live. . . . This general report coming from the creation around us of swift decay in which we are also partakers,—this is one species of the evil tidings that are current in the world.

The search for a fixed idea to serve as a stay against this confusion receives ever increasing emphasis as his dissatisfaction with traditional certitudes fades. He chose an abbreviated version of Archimedes' famous assertion—"Give me a place to stand on and I will move the world"—as the epigraph to an early journal; and it is pretty clear that for a long time the Moral Sentiment *was* for Emerson this Archimedean point that gave him leverage on the slippery world of experience. Its freedom from mutability was what distinguished it from mere "affections of the heart" or "faculties of the mind":

> The affections are undiscriminating and capricious. The Moral Sense is not. The powers of the intellect are sometimes wakeful and sometimes dull, alive with interest to one subject, and dead to the charm of another. There are no ebbs and flows, no change, no contradictions in *this*. Its approbation never loses its pleasure; its aversion never loses its sting.

But its immunity to fluctuation was the least of its attractions. Its chief merit for Emerson was that it represented a force operating *in the present and within the self*—though it is doubtless misleading to state the matter as if it were a question of choice, as if Emerson merely preferred truths acquired intuitively to truths mediated by tradition. Emerson himself argued that intuition was in fact the only possible ratifier of truth. Even those doctrines inherited from tradition must receive the assent of intuitive affirmation in order to be accepted by the subject. Arguments from tradition alone are "a very operose way of making people good"—operose, because any truth so received will have to be confirmed later by the soul anyway.

> You must be humble because Christ says, "Be humble." "But why must I obey Christ?" "Because God sent him." But how do I know God sent him? "Because your own heart teaches the same thing he taught." Why then shall I not go to my own heart at first?

Emerson was aware, of course, that official Christianity had a different answer to the third of the questions he proposed: we know Christ was sent by God because he performed miracles impossible without divine aid. Yet the sermon Emerson preached on miracles in 1831 exhibits the same reversal of emphasis evident in his little dialogue on humility. The record of Jesus' miracles, instead of being the triumphant confirmation of his status, becomes merely another thing needing confirmation from the certainty of the intuitive consciousness: "since I perceive the divine truth of the doctrine, I know the miracle must have been wrought which they say was wrought."

As Whicher points out, it was only a short step from increasing reliance on the promptings of the moral sense to a full belief "that the soul of man does not merely, as had long been taught, contain a spark or drop or breath or voice of God, it *is* God."[14] As Emerson put it, "Blessed is the day when the youth discovers that Within and Above are synonyms." The religion appropriate to this revelation might very well dispense with public rituals, for which Emerson always had a great deal of distaste. "Is not Solomon's temple built because Solomon is not a temple, but a brothel & a change-house? Is not the meeting-house dedicated because men are not?"

But if Emerson could cheerfully contemplate the withering away of public worship, he was less confident about dispensing with another "external" aid to devotion: Scripture. He knew that many would worry about the radical subjectivity of this new gospel. To a certain extent he shared their anxiety. He often notes in his journal the disturbing fact that a great licentiousness seems to tread on the heels of a reformation; cautions himself to beware of antinomianism; and worries that an exclusive reliance on the inner life of faith can sometimes impoverish the very ardor it was intended to exalt.

But if the maxims of ethics were *written* somewhere else? In a form potentially available to everyone? Then Emerson could convince himself, and others, that this new gospel—which looked to the orthodox like an abyss of skepticism—was a faith that could subsume the old without abrogating it. It is not surprising to discover, then, that Emerson began to look to nature as a possible alternative to Scripture at precisely the point when his dissatisfaction with organized religion reached a head. The editors of Emerson's early lectures note that "a correlation of the journals in the early crisis months of 1832 when Emerson was making up his mind to leave the ministry with Kenneth W. Cameron's lists of his withdrawals of books from the Boston Athenaeum and the Harvard libraries suggests an upsurge of interest in natural science at that time."

An aphorism of de Stael's that had caught his fancy in 1831—"Almost all the axioms of physics correspond to the maxims of morals"—expresses the hope that directed this eclectic reading in natural science. He quotes or alludes to this remark often in his journals, and eventually toyed with the idea of basing a literary project on it—doubtless the same book of "Natural Ethics" he referred to in a letter to a friend. "It occurs that a selection of natural laws might easily be made from botany, hydraulic, natural philosophy, & c., which should at once express an ethical sense." Most of the time he was content to amuse himself wth the unexpectedly appropriate "ethical sense" of laws like the ones he quotes in the "Language" chapter *Nature:* "reaction is equal to action" (the law of compensation?) or "the smallest weight may be made to lift the greatest, the difference of weight being compensated by time" (the principle of self-reliance?). But occasionally he pursues the principle beyond a playful noting of resemblances into something uncannily close to divination, as when he vows "to learn the law of the diffraction of a ray" in hopes that when he understands it "it will illustrate, perhaps suggest, a new truth in ethics." (This resolution was in fact carried out, and it had, as we shall see later on, profoundly important consequences for the final chapter of *Nature.*)

The same impulse led him to a lively interest in the Swedenborgian doctrine of "correspondence." Swedenborg offered independent confirmation of the truth Emerson had found in de Stael, and his testimony was particularly valuable because of his prestige as a natural scientist. (Before the revelation that had turned him into an interpreter of Scripture and founder of a new religion Swedenborg had conducted original research in astronomy, anatomy, and metallurgy.) According to Swedenborg, "if we choose to express any natural truth in physical and definite vocal terms, and to convert these terms only into the corresponding and spiritual terms, we shall by this means elicit a spiritual truth, or theological dogma, in place of the physical truth or precept."[15] And he carried the theory even further. Not only natural laws, but individual natural objects corresponded to spiritual truths.

This seminal notion found in Emerson's mind a receptive soil, for the common appearances of nature had often teased him with an uncanny sense of lurking significance. "Every object suggests to me in certain moods a dim anticipation of profound meaning, as if, by & by, it would appear to me why the apple-tree, why the meadow, why the stumps stand there & what they signify." But the doctrine of correspondence did more than confirm a hunch; it satisfied a spiritual appetite.

This point is worth emphasizing. We will find it difficult to understand the eagerness with which Emerson—and many of his contemporaries—embraced the doctrine of correspondence unless we remind ourselves how strong the hunger for raw significance had become after the starvation diet of the Lockean-Unitarian tradition in which they had been raised. Not that the world presented by Lockean empiricism and Unitarian theology was, strictly speaking, meaningless. It simply did not mean *enough.* What impresses us about the methodologies of all these separate disciplines—scientific, philosophical, exegetic—is their extreme reductiveness, their insistence upon eliminating every hint of polysemy from nature, psyche, or sacred text. The natural world is an aggregate of indestructible particles operated on by uniform and continuous laws; experience is a series of sense impressions inscribed on a mind originally empty; the Bible is a historical record of God's successive revelations to mankind of the ethical laws he wishes them to obey.

This cheerless trinity of beliefs removed all sense of the numinous from nature and restricted man's hermeneutic freedom; it turned poetry into an exercise in triviality and bad faith. In his journal Emerson sketches his own little conjectural account of this dissociation of sensibility:

> The ancients probably saw the moral significance of nature in the objects without afterthought or effort to separate the object & the expression. They felt no wrong in esteeming the mountain a purple picture whereon Oreads might appear as rightly

> as moss; . . . because they . . . believed the gods built it & were not far off, & so every tree & flower & chip of stone had a religious lustre, & might mean anything.
>
> But when science had gained and given the impression of the permanence, even eternity of nature & of every substance . . . the mountain became a pile of stones acted on by bare blind laws of chemistry, & the poetic sense of things was driven to the vulgar and an effort was made to recal [sic] the sense, by the educated & so it was faintly uttered by the poet & heard with a smile.

It is easy to mistake the real nostalgia here, which is not for those vanished Oreads—Romantic Hellenism bored Emerson—but for the infinite richness of a world in which sensuous particulars might mean anything. What he calls religious luster, the poetic sense of things, *is* this susceptibility to multiple interpretation, and Emerson is as consistent as Blake in denouncing the single vision that reduces the world to an Ulro, a "pile of stones acted on by bare blind laws." The deepest pleasure in life, Emerson thought, came from "the occult belief that an unknown meaning & consequence lurk in the common every day facts." And the "highest minds" are those that "have never ceased to explore the double meaning, or, shall I say, the quadruple or the centuple or much more manifold meaning" of these facts.

The fascination Swedenborg exercised over the young Boston intellectuals is, in a way, prompted by the same delight in the revelation of unexpected significance in trivial facts that is in our day so large a part of Freud's appeal. Of course there are obvious differences. Swedenborg's category of interpretable things is much larger than Freud's, including as it does not only the human but also the material world; and Emerson is as sure that the truth revealed by an interpretation will always be ethically admirable as we are sure of the reverse. But the differences are perhaps less important than they seem. "That something signifies, delights,"[16] as Nietzsche remarked. *What* something signifies matters less than the fact of significance itself. In the end, what the doctrine of correspondence does for Emerson is to transform nature into a text, mysteriously encoded but potentially decipherable, like a dream or a symptom to a Freudian analyst.

Nature is a language & every new fact that we learn is a new word; but rightly seen, taken all together it is not merely a language but the language put together into a most significant and universal book. I wish to learn the language not that I may know a new set of nouns & verbs but that I may read the great book which is written in that tongue.

July 13, 1833–May 9, 1836: The Jardin des Plantes to the Death of Charles

But why should the text of nature be inscrutable in the first place? What catastrophe—or long, slow process of historical decline—first made the text of nature opaque to our understanding? In Emerson's early, delighted playing with the notion of correspondence this question seems hardly to have occurred to him; he treats it as a tool, not as a symptom. But the visit he paid to the Jardin des Plantes during his European tour of 1833 placed the entire question of "correspondence" in a new light. Standing before the specimens in a cabinet of natural history he experienced a moment of illumination that made him feel (the simile is surprising) "as calm & genial as a bridegroom."

> The Universe is a more amazing puzzle than ever, as you look along this bewildering series of animated forms,—the hazy butterflies, the carved shells, the birds, beasts, fishes, insects, snakes,—& the upheaving principle of life everywhere incipient in the very rock aping organized forms. Not a form so grotesque, so savage, nor so beautiful but is an expression of some property inherent in man the observer,—an occult relation between the very scorpions and man. I feel the centipede in me—cayman, carp, eagle, & fox. I am moved by strange sympathies, I say continually, "I will be a naturalist."

In one way, the occult relation Emerson here apprehends resembles the earlier doctrine of correspondence, in that it suggests a relationship between the forms of nature and those of truth: Emerson speaks of worms and scorpions as "expressions."

But the differences are noteworthy too. In place of the static correspondential universe Emerson sees one everywhere stirred by "the upheaving principle of life." And there is nothing particularly ethical about this universe, either. The forms of animate life Emerson singles out for mention as stirring the strange sympathies of a suddenly acknowledged kinship are notable for their wildness or even venom—a kind of confession we associate more readily with Whitman than with Emerson:

> I too knitted the old knot of contrariety,
> Blabb'd, blush'd, resented, lied, stole, grudg'd,
> Had guile, anger, lust, hot wishes I dared not speak,
> Was wayward, vain, greedy, shallow, sly,
>   cowardly, malignant,
> The wolf, the snake, the hog, not wanting in me. . . .[17]

But the most significant change in Emerson's conception of correspondence is the hint, here barely touched upon, that the text of nature is not something given to us but something emanating from us. "Not a form so grotesque, so savage, nor so beautiful but is an expression of some property inherent *in man the observer*" (emphasis added).

The radical implications of this notion were not fully explored until "Prospects," the final chapter of *Nature*. But there is evidence that the experience itself provided a new focus for Emerson's powerful but vague literary ambitions, and gave new cogency to his desultory speculations on the relationship between man and nature. On the voyage home from Europe he was evidently meditating a book on the subject, and—like many another hopeful author—speaking of it as though it were a *fait accompli*. "I like my book about nature," he writes, and though the book he was planning did not take final shape for another three years, there is a new note of urgency in the lectures and journal entries he wrote following his return. (His private faith in a beneficent Providence, built, as he said once, on happy coincidences, must have received an infusion of strength when he disembarked to find waiting for him an invitation to lecture before the Boston Natural History Society. According to Charles Emerson, natural history had become a craze in Boston: everybody was "making catalogues of birds, reading memoirs of Cuvier, hearing lectures about Crustacea, Volcanoes, entomology, & the like.")[18]

It has occurred to Emerson that the various topics he has been pursuing—the moral law, the identity of the soul with God, the doctrine of correspondence—are not so much reassuring answers to questions as hints of a much greater question he had not yet thought of asking. "Insist on seeing Nature as a problem to be solved," he now writes. "It is a question addressed to you." What chiefly needs explaining is the paradox of man's relationship to nature, its curious blend of kinship and estrangement. If nature were wholly other, how could we account for the "occult relation" we perceive between "visible things and human thoughts"? On the other hand, if nature is somehow related to us, what accounts for our painfully evident alienation from it? "The fox and the deer run from us; the bear and tiger rend us." We need a theory of origins that can explain both how nature came to resemble us and why it presently holds itself aloof from us—is permeated with human meaning, yet not subject to human will.

There are religious and mythological explanations of this problem, of course, but Emerson finds them so unsatisfying that he is sometimes surprised that the human race has seemed content with them. "How few cosmogonies have we," he muses in his journal. "A few have got a kind of classical character & we let them stand, for a world-builder is a rare man. And yet what ghosts & hollow formless dream-gear these theories are; how crass & inapplicable! how little they explain; what a poor handful of facts in this plentiful universe they touch. . . ." Contemporary science, on the other hand, has no lack of facts; the problem here is rather in knowing what to do with them.

The immense chasm separating the wild imaginings of cosmogonic poets from the lifeless systems of classification proposed by empirical scientists may seem too wide to bridge, yet Emerson remains hopeful. "The Idea according to which the Universe is made is wholly wanting to us; is it not? Yet it may or will be found to be constructed on as harmonious & perfect a thought, self explaining, as a problem in geometry." For Emerson, like Blake, refuses to believe in the existence of impenetrable mystery. In the "Introduction" to *Nature* he asserts, with Johnsonian firmness: "We must trust the perfection of the creation so far, as to believe that whatever curiosity the order of things has awakened in our minds, the order of things can satisfy." (Even as late as *The Conduct of Life* we find him arguing that Fate "is only a name for facts not yet passed under the fire of thought, for causes which are unpenetrated.")

Poetry can provide hints and guesses. But if thought is to penetrate the mystery of nature, it must do so systematically: constructing a *theory* that will classify thoughts *methodically* until it reduces the multiplicity and confusion of the sensible world to the shining simplicity of underlying *law*. Emerson took these terms from Coleridge, whose "Essays on the Principles of Method" in *The Friend* he began studying assiduously after his return from Europe. In those essays Coleridge was concerned to distinguish between true and false science, between systems that contained within them an ordering, self-explanatory principle of development, and ones that presented a mere dead arrangement of facts. Nineteenth-century science liked to think of itself as purely inductive, and took as its motto Newton's famous *hypotheses non fingo*. But Coleridge—who here anticipates contemporary theorists like Thomas Kuhn and Karl Popper—pointed out the logical flaws in such a model. Facts themselves can never suggest their own arrangement, since "what shall determine the mind to abstract and generalize one common point rather than another?"[19] The ordering principle *must* come from the mind first; "*the solution of Phaenomena can never be derived from Phaenomena.*"[20]

Coleridge distinguishes two kinds of ordering principle. The first is *law* or *idea*, which fully and exhaustively accounts for the behavior of phenomena. In its perfection, a knowledge of law is "conceivable only of the Supreme Being,"[21] yet Coleridge accepts the term's extension to describe any science (like mathematics or geometry) in which the relation of the parts to one another and to the whole is predetermined by a truth originating in the *mind,* and not abstracted or generalized from observation of the parts. The second and lesser kind of principle is *theory,* in which "the existing forms and qualities of objects, discovered by observation and experiment, suggest a given arrangement of many under one point of view."[22] Theories occupy a sort of intermediate position between random observations and true laws;

without theory true method in science is impossible, but the final goal of theory is to wither away into the mathematical purity of law. How does this happen? Coleridge instances the various theories of electricity, from which true philosophers, "rejecting the imagination of any material substrate,"[23] were able to "contemplate in the phenomena of electricity the operation of a law which reigns throughout all nature, the law of Polarity."[24] What made the reduction to law of competing theories of electricity possible was their common possession of a single *idea* "which required little more than the dismission of the imagery to become constitutive like the ideas of the geometrician."[25]

Emerson seized upon Coleridge's terminology as eagerly as he had seized upon the crucial distinction between the Reason and the Understanding (and, as in the earlier borrowing, used the terms in ways Coleridge could not possibly have sanctioned). The "fact" Emerson wants to explain is the occult relation between man and nature he had sensed in the Jardin des Plantes, and since that relation includes everything in the cosmos, he is merely being accurate when he cheerfully proposes that the sole experimental test of a "true theory of nature" is that "it will explain all phenomena."

What Emerson is looking for in the various "theories of nature" he gathers in his eclectic reading, then, is the glimmering of a single *idea* or pattern common to them all, an idea that might be expressed as compactly as a mathematical formula. And what would happen if he succeeded in discovering one? He himself is not always clear on this matter. At times he writes as if he expected a solution to the Sphinx's riddle to do no more than satisfy our curiosity or stimulate our pious admiration of God's elegant design. But mixed in with these unexceptionable sentiments we can discern others less orthodox: apocalyptic and even frankly gnostic. At the end of that first lyceum lecture to the Boston Natural History Society, after having urged us to study natural laws, "for herein is writ by the Creator his own history," he advances a more daring surmise: "it may be, all this outward universe shall one day disappear, when its whole sense hath been comprehended and engraved forever in the eternal thoughts of the human mind." The goal of natural science, in this view of things, is to make nature publish *and* perish. Like the wildest of gnostic visionaries, Emerson looks forward to the day when the "outward universe" will no longer be external to the mind at all; its enigmas will no longer be able to frustrate our desires for omniscience, nor its cruel otherness, our desires for joy.

This apocalyptic hope had always been latent in Emerson. The meditations of his college notebooks have a way of sliding— whatever their original subject—into orotund evocations of the Day of Judgment, as in the 1820 journal (*Wide World* 1), where a long passage on the subject of eloquence ends in a consideration of its "noblest theme," the Apocalypse. And *Wide World* 2 contains the engaging memorandum: "Also Mr. Waldo if you would like to find the sublimest attainable sayings of the destruction of Nations—Vide 4rth book of the Sybilline collections." Nor were his speculations confined to traditional Christian apocalyptic. When Emerson was only twenty he wrote in his journal a declaration of imaginative independence as emphatic as Blake's "To Tirzah": "Who is he that shall controul me? Why may I not act & speak & write & think with entire freedom? ... I say to the Universe, Mighty One! Thou art not my mother; Return to chaos, if thou wilt, I shall still exist." His rejection of the natural world is usually phrased more gently, but the apocalyptic emphasis remains unmistakable. In 1820 he copied into his journal a letter from his Aunt Mary arguing that "we love Nature,—to individuate ourselves in her wildest moods, and to partake of her extension and glow with her colors and fly on her winds; but we better love to cast her off and rely on that alone which is imperishable."

What is surprising about the outline Emerson drew up for *Nature* in March of 1836, though, is how little these bolder wishes—the quest for a key to all of nature's riddles, the apocalyptic desire that nature herself might vanish—seem to enter into the scheme:

> ... through Nature there is a striving upward. Commodity points to a greater good. Beauty is nought until the spiritual element. Language refers to that which is to be said.
> Finally; Nature is a discipline, & points to the pupil & exists

for the pupil. Her being is subordinate, his is superior. Man
underlies ideas. Nature receives them as her god.

I take it that this plan, if it had been carried to completion as it
stands, would have given us a *Nature* consisting of Chapters I
through VI of the present work ("Nature" through "Idealism").[26] In these chapters Emerson's raising of the ontological
question receives the perfectly reverent, perfectly ministerial answer that everything in nature exists in its present shape because
God has designed it that way for man's use and education. Nature ministers to our animal needs, satisfies our hunger for
beauty, provides us with language. Even its bruteness and immobility—the resistance it opposes to our desires—are intended to
exercise and toughen our spirits, to wean us from a childish attachment to things of this world. If one way of explaining the
reason for God's decision to create nature in the first place is to
say that Spirit needs to evolve an opposite, as the sole means and
condition of its manifestation (a notion Emerson took over from
Coleridge, who had it from Schelling), then nature returns the
dialectical favor by conspiring with Spirit to "emancipate us"—
not just from *attachment* to the material world, but even from
belief in its substantial existence, until we can finally see the
whole outward creation as a mere spectacle designed for our edification: "one vast picture, which God paints on the instant eternity, for the contemplation of the soul."
A stalwart empiricist like Francis Bowen might object to the
dangerous consequences of that final leap into Idealism (he ends
his review by advising the young Transcendentalists to close
their Platos and open their Franklins), but even Bowen would
have been obliged to commend the *piety* of the sentiment Emerson recorded in his journal on April 2, 1836: "In these Uses of
Nature which I explore, the common sense of Man requires that,
at last, Nature be referred to the Deity, be viewed in God."
What, we may ask, has become of the apocalyptic hope expressed at the end of that first lyceum lecture, the wish that outward nature might be transformed or even vanish? Idealism is a
doctrine congenial to apocalyptic thinkers, but in itself is not nec-

essarily apocalyptic. It affirms that what we call "matter" is a phenomenon rather than a substance, but it does not necessarily hold out any hope that the phenomenon can be altered, much less disappear. As Emerson was later to complain, the Ideal theory contains nothing "progressive."

Even more importantly, what has become of that central belief upon which Emerson's life was based—that the soul in its essence was not to be distinguished from the Divine essence, that the soul *was* God? It is all very well to explain the existence of nature by saying that God designed it for man's use and edification if you accept the conventional belief that the soul is one of God's creatures. But once you have abolished the distinction between God and man you place that relatively simple explanation forever out of reach. It does not on the face of the matter make much sense to say that We designed nature for the benevolent purpose of teaching Ourselves to transcend it.

Whether the logic of composition alone would finally have driven Emerson to recognize the contradictions in his original scheme I cannot say. That he did attain such a recognition is demonstrable; in listing the deficiencies of the "Ideal Theory" I am only paraphrasing Emerson's critique of it in "Spirit," Chapter VII of the final version of *Nature*. But the journal passages upon which that chapter is based were written after a great catastrophe, and the final shape of Emerson's answer is largely determined by the new and brutal way the Sphinx had suddenly found to pose the question.

May–June 1836: "The eye is closed that was to see nature for me . . ."

Emerson was no stranger to catastrophe. There were the early childhood losses: deaths, illnesses, and grinding poverty. A brief period of adult happiness had come to an end with the death of his beautiful young wife, Ellen, in 1831, followed by that of his brilliant younger brother, Edward, in 1834. But the death of Charles Emerson, on May 9, 1836, was the greatest shock Emerson had yet suffered. Ellen and Edward had both been ill for many years before their deaths; Charles had in recent years seemed vigorous and healthy. Less than five weeks elapsed between the appearance of Charles's illness and his sudden death; and the illness itself was diagnosed by the doctors as nothing worse than a bad cold until the final week of Charles's life. Emerson had only a few days to adjust to the notion that his brother was in fact terminally ill with tuberculosis before arriving in New York (where Charles had gone to recuperate) to find him already dead.

The loss would have been devastating at any time, but it was particularly brutal because it came at a moment when Emerson could at last reasonably expect the dawning of a happier life. He was a successful lecturer and an aspiring author; he could derive confidence in both enterprises from his growing personal security as a kind of *paterfamilias.* He had married again, and his new wife, Lidian, was expecting a child. His purchase of a house in Concord made it possible to offer his mother the first settled home she had had since his father died. He was adding rooms to the house to accommodate Charles and his intended bride after their marriage. After so many years of gypsy existence, shifting between one set of rented rooms and another, Emerson at last had a home, a community, and the promise of intimacy with the people he loved most. In a letter to his friend Henry Hedge dated March 14 he wrote: "I think at times I shall never be unhappy again."

The prospect of having Charles at last under the same roof with him must in some ways have seemed the most glorious good fortune of all. In Charles, Emerson had enjoyed the "inestimable advantage" of having "a brother and a friend in one." Charles was at once his sounding board and his sparring partner, his most enthusiastic audience and his severest critic. He and Charles were tied together by an "occult hereditary sympathy" that gave the widest possible latitude to free censure and honest praise— and this, to a man whose desperate shyness frustrated most chances for human companionship, made Charles's presence a "society" that indemnified Emerson "for almost total exclusion from all other."

And Charles had been valuable not only for what he gave, but for what he had seemed to represent: an effortless self-mastery, a responsiveness to the natural world ("his senses were those of a Greek"), in short, a kind of health that Emerson himself admired without hope of attaining. In Charles, Emerson's dream of a "spheral" man—philosopher, poet, hero, Christian—had achieved actual incarnation. Now the world seemed suddenly empty, and for a time Emerson's despair was absolute. "When one has never had but little society—and *all that society* is taken away—what is there worth living for?"[27]

Grief was complicated by the guilt of discovering that Charles had not, in fact, been as free from internal division as Emerson had confidently assumed, that his gaiety and courage had concealed much that was melancholy, even self-tormenting. Reading through his journals made Emerson aware of how much of Charles's life had remained hidden even from him; aware, too, of how much Charles's perfection had been a creation of his own need to find in Charles qualities he himself lacked. "Every ship is a romantic object, except that we sail in," as he was later to put it.

Yet the curious thing about Emerson's response to all this devastation is that he does *not* announce a chastening of imagination, as Wordsworth did after a similar loss:

> I have submitted to a new control:
> A power is gone, which nothing can restore;
> A deep distress hath humanised my Soul.[28]

Confronting the brutal otherness of nature, the mystery of disease and death, the shattering of human hopes, Emerson proclaims not the loss of power but its sudden exhilarating influx. "Power is one great lesson Nature teaches Man," he now writes. "The secret that he can not only reduce under his will, that is, conform to his character, particular events but classes of events & so harmonize all the outward occurrences with the states of mind, that he must learn." *All* occurrences? Even death itself, even Charles's death? That is indeed what Emerson means; he struggles to attempt such a reduction in a journal passage scarred with many cancellations and revisions, which later became the closing paragraph of the chapter "Discipline" (I quote the version that appears there):

When much intercourse with a friend has supplied us with a standard of excellence, and has increased our respect for the resources of God who thus sends us a real person to outgo our ideal; when he has, moreover, become an object of thought, and, whilst his character retains all its unconscious effect, is converted in the mind into solid and sweet wisdom,—it is a sign to us that his office is closing, and he is commonly withdrawn from our sight in a short time.

One can see how this deeply disturbing passage arose. The hardest thing to *know*, Emerson pointed out, is the death of someone else (one's own death is much easier to contemplate with equanimity, and Emerson never at any time in his life showed the slightest concern about the matter). Either you accept the death as meaningless, part of the brutality of a world in which the coherence demanded by consciousness is the exception rather than the rule; or else you do what Wordsworth did—accept it as a chastening and find your solace in the traditional forms of consolation. If neither of these alternatives is emotionally acceptable to you, then you are driven to the curious position Emerson adopted. You insist that the event has a meaning that, like the meaning of everything else, bears a necessary relation to the perceiving self—even if such logic drives you to the cruelty of "Discipline" or to broodings that at times border on the psychotic, as when Emerson supposes that "the roots of my relation to every individual are in my own constitution & not less the causes of his disappearance from me." When earth has become a paradise, Wallace Stevens wryly observed, it will be a paradise full of assassins. What Marvell expressed as a wish—"Two paradises 'twere in one/ To be in paradise alone"—was for Emerson an inescapable fact. We are alone in paradise whether we like it or not, for the reason he made frighteningly explicit in the essay "Friendship": "I cannot deny it, O Friend, that the vast shadow of the Phenomenal includes thee also in its pied and painted immensity,—thee also, compared with whom all else is shadow." Hence his eerie version of the Golden Rule, a kind of Golden Rule for solipsists, in "Experience": "Let us treat the men and women well; treat them as if they were real; perhaps they are." The grim humor of these later passages is absent from the journal meditations in 1836, which exhibit instead a spooky, manic exhilaration. To read the journal entries written during the crucial months of May and June is to come to the inescapable conclusion that Charles's death liberated forces in Emerson that had always been present but had previously lain dormant; he suddenly becomes aware that, like the oblivious travelers in *Nature*, he has been using the cinders of a volcano to roast his eggs.

Kenneth Burke remarked that the paragraph from "Discipline" is the equivalent in dialectic of the sacrifice of the ritual victim in tragedy,[29] a judgment expressed even more frankly by James M. Cox, who does not scruple to say that "there is a sense in which Emerson literally feeds off the death around him." He points out the connection between Ellen's death and the influx of imaginative energy that follows, between the death of Charles and the "strong assertion" of *Nature*. He knows that some people will find this vision of the relationship between Emerson's life and work appalling, but points out—rightly, I think—that much of the covert resentment directed at Emerson by scholars "discloses attitudes which could well be considered expressions of precisely this vision held *unconsciously*."[30] Emerson ought to have been crippled by his losses, they seem to feel, and they resent him for springing back with renewed force, Antaeus-like, at each contact with disaster.

Is it really so appalling, after all? Defensive measures adopted by the ego can become—to use Reich's vivid term—*Characterpanzerung*, the armor-plating of character, and if Emerson had not developed such defenses very early on in life, it is hard to see how he could have survived as a man, let alone a writer. Two defense mechanisms, in particular, seem characteristic of Emerson's response to loss: incorporation and denial. Charles, with whom Emerson had felt so strong a kinship that he could speak of the two of them as forming "one man," is not lost when he dies; he is simply incorporated into Emerson's own character—"converted in the mind into solid and sweet wisdom" (the oral metaphors are significant). At the same time, the helplessness of mourning is suddenly transformed into its polar opposite, a vision of power so absolute that even the bruteness and immobility of matter itself must yield to its "instantaneous in-streaming causing" force.

This peculiar pattern of conversion is evident in a network of imagery and allusion in Emerson's writings that links Charles and Emerson himself with Milton, vision with blindness. Burke, with his uncanny instinct for the revelatory detail, was the first to notice the faint Miltonic echo in the final chant of the Orphic poet in "Prospects," where the end of the sentence prophesying the glorious revolution attendant upon the influx of the spirit—"So fast will disagreeable appearances . . . vanish; they are temporary and shall be no more seen"—comes close to the phrasing of a line from "Lycidas":

> But O the heavy change, now thou art gone
> Now thou art gone, and never must return!
> · · ·
> The willows and the hazel-copses green
> Shall now no more be seen
> Fanning their joyous leaves to thy soft lays.[31]

Now the curious thing about the line from "Lycidas" is that we would expect to see it quoted in a lamentation, not a prophecy of apocalypse. And as a matter of fact, in its first appearance in Emerson's journals it does occur in the midst of a lamentation. Immediately after Charles's death Emerson lists the things he now regards as irrevocably lost: "the soul that loved St. John St. Paul . . . the hilarity of thought which awakened good humor wherever it came, and laughter without shame; and the endless endeavor after a life of ideal beauty;—these are all gone from my actual world & will here be no more seen."

The verbal echo here may seem slight. But "Lycidas" was a poem Emerson knew by heart, and there are obvious reasons why it should have been in his mind at this moment. And Charles had stronger ties to Milton in Emerson's mind than the mere fact of his resemblance to the subject of Milton's elegy. Emerson once said that Charles reminded him more strongly of Milton himself than anyone he knew, and in listing Charles's virtues after his death Emerson simply applied to Charles some of the phrases he had used to describe Milton in a lecture he had delivered the preceding year. Emerson's idea of Milton's character is largely derived from William Ellery Channing's influential essay of 1826, where Milton is praised for his magnanimity, courage, and above all, power of mind—that "gift or exercise of genius, which has power to impress itself on whatever it touches,"[32] and which is capable of fusing nature and imagination into a new unity higher than either. This power was what had seemed most luminous about Charles (though apparent only in his conversation, not his written work, as Emerson discovered to his sorrow). "The fine humor of his conversation seemed to make the world he saw. His power of illustration & the facility of his association embroidered his sentences with all his reading & all his seeing," Emerson recalled. "I used to say that I had no leave to see things till he pointed them out, & afterwards I never ceased to see them." *Had no leave* is an odd phrase—as if Emerson had needed his younger brother's permission to look at the world—and it recurs in the striking synecdoche into which Emerson condensed his feeling of irreparable loss: "The eye is closed that was to see Nature for me, & give me leave to see. . . ." With the loss of Charles—his only society, his eye—Emerson himself becomes a kind of Milton, not the lordly figure of Channing's essay, but the blind and lonely poet of the Invocation to Book III:

> . . . from the cheerful ways of men
> Cut off, and for the Book of Knowledge fair
> Presented with a Universal Blanc
> Of Nature's works to me expung'd and ras'd,
> And wisdom at one entrance quite shut out.[33]

In linking Charles, via Milton, to themes of blindness and isolation, Emerson was giving voice to some of his deepest anxieties, for the fear of blindness—both literal and spiritual—is one of the dominant obsessions in Emerson's life, as the extraordinary proliferation of visual imagery in his works testifies.

He had already had one frightening brush with actual blindness. When he was beginning his studies at the Divinity School in 1825, he found his eyes refusing to read. He was obliged to give up reading and writing, though he still attended lectures and, in vacations, kept school. Aunt Mary, according to Rusk, "seems to have imagined at one time that he might turn out to be a laureate of religion and a sort of second Milton, with poetry a sufficient compensation for blindness,"[34] but it is doubtful that Emerson shared her opinion of the adequacy of that compensation. In the confident declaration of recuperative powers that introduces the Transparent Eye-ball passage in *Nature*, he is careful to insert one significant qualification: "In the woods, we return to reason and faith. There I feel that nothing can befall me in life,—no disgrace, no calamity (leaving me my eyes), which nature cannot repair."

Nor was the fear merely a memory in 1836. Although Emerson had regained most of his sight by early 1826, he continued to be troubled by weak and painful eyes. And some fascinating remarks he makes in the journals in 1835 and 1836 seem to give sanction to the psychoanalytical explanation we itch to give of the Divinity School episode. Emerson was struck by the fact that his vision seemed intimately connected with his will. "If you sit down to write with weak eyes & awaken your imagination to the topic you will find your eyes strong. ⟨& all pain vanished.⟩" This kind of experience was still in his mind when he came to assemble a list (later revised for inclusion in "Prospects") of those rare "examples of the action of man upon nature with his entire force," actions effected by the Reason alone without the mediation of the Understanding:

> Animal Magnetism, the Miracles of enthusiasts as Hohenlohe & the Shakers & the Swedenborgian, prayer, eloquence, *self healing as weak eyes*, the achievements of a principle as in Revolution & the abolition of the Slave Trade—& the wisdom (often observed) of children. . . . (emphasis added)

Yet the most vehement denial of reality's power to threaten vision is, of course, the Transparent Eye-ball passage itself. There Emerson does not fear losing sight because he has become, as it were, all eye; and he does not fear isolation because society itself is dismissed as irrelevant:

> I become a transparent eye-ball. I am nothing. I see all. The currents of the Universal Being circulate through me; I am part

> or particle of God. The name of the nearest friend sounds then
> foreign and accidental. To be brothers, to be acquaintances,—
> master or servant, is then a trifle and a disturbance.

Mastering anxiety through denial and reversal in fantasy is,
according to Anna Freud, a normal defense mechanism employed by the developing ego (it informs those fairy tales in
which children tame wild animals and humble powerful kings,
for instance), but she warns that its recurrence in adult life indicates an advanced stage of mental disease. The ego always remains capable of denying reality, but this "capacity for denying
reality is wholly inconsistent with another function, greatly
prized by it—its capacity to recognize and critically test the reality of objects,"[35] and the mature ego's need for synthesis makes it
impossible for these opposite tendencies to coexist. Against this
practical wisdom one can only remark that poets keep the joy of
infantile omnipotence alive in their embers longer than other
people, that Keats *defined* negative capability as the powers of
forgoing premature synthesis, and that in any case Emerson
(who, as John Jay Chapman said, is mad only when the wind is
nor'-nor'-west) neatly solved the problem of accommodating the
ego's need both to deny and to test reality by splitting the ego itself into two mutually exclusive parts—Reason and Understanding—that simply divide the tasks between them, like Jack Sprat
and his wife.

Emerson would not have put the matter that way, of course,
because he would not have agreed that the world accessible to
empirical observation—the world of "experience" (a technical
term for him as it was for Blake)—deserved to be dignified by the
term "reality." The *real* world is the world as it appears to the
Reason, and its defiant slogan is the "sublime remark" Emerson
attributes to the Swiss geometrician Euler, concerning his Law of
Arches: "This will be found contrary to all experience, yet it is
true." "Sublimity" is in fact Emerson's term for the sudden up-
welling of pleasure and awe that occurs when we suddenly perceive the insubstantiality of the world of experience, and hence
realize that the common use of the terms "real" and "unreal" exactly inverts the truth.

Wordsworth draws his great declaration of faith in the Reason from a trivial, even a foolish circumstance: the disappointment of a pair of youthful travelers at discovering that the Alps are more easily crossed in fact than in imagination. We know what Dr. Johnson, that personification of common sense, would have made of the incident. "The use of travelling," he says, "is to regulate imagination by reality, and instead of thinking how things may be, to see them as they are."[36] But for Wordsworth the traveler's chagrin testifies not to the vanity of human wishes but to their preternatural plenitude; the soul is

> Strong in herself and in her beatitude
> That hides her, like the mighty flood of Nile
> Poured from his fount of Abyssinian clouds
> To fertilise the whole Egyptian plain.[37]

A new conviction of the soul's centrality is apparent in the aggressive tone Emerson now takes in the journals. No longer content merely to list the "uses" of nature, he begins to see nature's very existence as the problem to be solved. "What is a child? What is a woman? What is a year or a season? What do they signify & say to ME?" The Idealist's answer is no longer satisfactory. "The Idealist says, God paints the world around your soul. The spiritualist saith, yea, but lo! God is within you. The self of self creates the world through you, & organizations like you." Idealism itself, once the goal of speculation, is now seen as a temporary landing-place in a larger dialectic. It now occurs to Emerson to wonder "whether the Ideal Theory is not merely introductory to spiritual views. It diminishes and degrades matter in order to receive a new view of it, namely this, that the world is the new fruit of Spirit evermore."

June–August 1836: The Apocalypse of the Mind

What, exactly, does it mean to say that the world is the fruit of Spirit? It is intelligible enough to say that "spirit does not act on us from without, that is, in space and time, but spiritually, or through ourselves" if you are explaining phenomena like con-

science or intuitive wisdom. But nature? To say that "the Supreme Being does not build up nature around us, but puts it forth
through us, as the life of the tree puts forth new branches and
leaves through the pores of the old" seems to suggest that natural
phenomena are somehow being extruded through us like tooth-
paste—or, as Burke prefers to put it, like offal. He points out the
"strong hints of a fecal motive"[38] in Emerson's quotation from a
French Swedenborgian in "Language": "Material objects . . . are
necessarily kinds of *scoriae* of the substantial thoughts of the
Creator" (*scoriae* means slag or dross and is ultimately derived
from the Greek word for dung). The same motive is apparent in
the single phrase Emerson remembered from the conversation of
Amos Bronson Alcott, who paid him a visit toward the end of
June. "He made here some majestic utterances but so inspired me
that even I forgot the words often. The grass, the earth seemed to
him 'the refuse of the spirit.' "

Alcott's visit has long been recognized as having had a catalytic
effect upon Emerson, so much so that Alcott used to be identified
as the Orphic poet of "Prospects." It is certainly true that the
journal passages that later became the fable of the Orphic poet
were composed, evidently in a state of great intellectual excite-
ment, in the week following Alcott's departure. But I doubt that
the Orphic chants owe much of their *content* to Alcott; his works
were chiefly valuable as a stimulus to rival productions. In the
words of one of Emerson's favorite Arabian proverbs, "a fig tree
looking on a fig tree becometh fruitful." (After a later visit from
Alcott Emerson wrote: "When I see a man of genius he always
inspires me with a feeling of boundless confidence in my own
powers.")

For Alcott was engaged in the same kind of enterprise as
Emerson's: to comprehend the origin of things. "Mr. Alcott has
been here with his Olympian dreams," Emerson wrote on June
22. "He is a world-builder. Ever more he toils to solve the problem, Whence is the world?" And some of Alcott's home-grown
Neoplatonic theories bore a striking resemblance both to Swedenborgian theories of correspondence and to Emerson's own
éclaircissement in the Jardin des Plantes. But though Alcott's visionary schemes bore the names *Genesis* and *Lapse* they were

remarkable for their freedom from the ruinous error that vitiated most mythical attempts to account for the existence of nature: their persistent habit of accounting for the disparity between the perfect world we can imagine and the ruined world we perceive by postulating a Fall caused by sin or disobedience.

As early as 1824 Emerson was proposing to write an essay on the Evils of Imagination, which would treat of "the most signal instances of this captivity in which the Imagination has held the Reason of Man." Chief among these, Emerson thought, was "the most picturesque dogma of a *ruined world*" that has had "a most pernicious fascination over nations of believers. It was an error locked with life." In 1837 he was still elaborating irritably upon the theme:

> What means all the monitory tone of the world of life, of literature, of tradition? Man is fallen Man is banished; an exile; he is in earth whilst there is a heaven. What do these apologues mean? These seem to him traditions of memory. But they are the whispers of hope and Hope is the voice of the Supreme Being to the Individual.
> We say Paradise was; Adam fell; the Golden Age; & the like. We mean man is not as he ought to be, but our way of painting this is on Time, and we say *Was.*

But Alcott showed that it was possible to combine a poetic account of creation with an unswerving belief in the divinity and innocence of man. In fact, the point at which he began his account was "the Mystery of the Birth of a child," which Alcott conceived of, more or less in the manner of the "Intimations" ode, as a descent into the finite of an infinite and perfect spirit. His example must have been profoundly reassuring; it removed whatever scruples Emerson still had about giving his solution to the riddle of nature a narrative form.

For fable, in general, had much to recommend it. It was a time-honored way for mediating between the contradictory demands of the Reason and the Understanding, between the truths of Eternity and the hard facts of Time.

> Why must always the philosopher mince his words and fatigue us with explanation? He speaks from the Reason & being of

course contradicted word for word by the Understanding, he stops like a cogwheel at every notch to explain. . . . Empedocles said bravely "I am God; I am immortal; I contemn human affairs"; & all men hated him. Yet every one of the same men had his religious hour when he said the same thing.

Fable avoids the difficulty, is at once exoteric & esoteric, & is clapped by both sides. Plato & Jesus used it.

The coupling of Jesus and Plato is at first surprising, but in fact is rather acute. What parable and Platonic fable have in common is the representation through narrative of a truth that lies outside of time altogether. The kingdom of God is *like* a sower who went out to sow his seed; the soul is *like* a charioteer who attempts to drive an ill-matched team.

Fable is not truth, only the image of truth. Yet in our present fallen condition, when our faculties and even our virtues are at war with one another, it is as close as we can come to that theory of nature, that "idea of creation" a true science would afford. The "facts" this fable must account for are the dark hints and inferences now seen to be buried beneath the pious surface of the Ur-*Nature* like so many land mines waiting to be detonated by the Self's new insistence on its divinity. In the first chapter of the book we are introduced to the central mystery a true theory of nature must account for:

> The greatest delight the fields and woods minister is the suggestion of an occult relation between man and the vegetable. I am not alone and unacknowledged. . . . The waving of the boughs is new to me and yet old. It takes me by surprise, and yet is not unknown.

This curious sense of *déjà vu* gives rise to a question: Was our knowledge of external objects once more complete than it is now? If so, what accounts for our present ignorance?

The delight we feel in nature teases us with a sense of nature's concealed significance. "What was it nature would say? Was there no meaning in the live repose of the valley behind the mill, and which Homer or Shakespeare could not re-form in words for me?" The chapter entitled "Language" answers that question affirmatively, and offers the doctrine of "correspondence" (here for the first time explicitly named) as a key to the meanings concealed in the external world. Words are emblematic because things are; natural facts are the symbol of spiritual facts; there is a "radical correspondence" between visible things and human thoughts.

Separate instances of correspondence are all parts of one great Correspondence. "The world is emblematic. Parts of speech are metaphors, because the whole of nature is a metaphor of the human mind." Toward the close of the chapter Emerson first attempts to provide a genetic explanation for the phenomenon: "A Fact is the end or last issue of spirit. The visible creation is the terminus or circumference of the invisible world." If the whole of nature is a metaphor of the human mind, and if external objects are the "last issue" or circumference of spirit, then perhaps we can venture the formula "the visible creation is the circumference of the human mind." This hybrid proposition would explain the mystery of correspondence. Nature resembles man because nature is man: "man imprisoned, man crystallized, man vegetative."

But if natural forms are imprisoned men, how did they get that way? "Discipline" suggests an answer. There Emerson remarks that all natural objects "appear to be degradations" of the human form. But the human form as we know it is also degraded; everyone we meet "bears the marks as of some injury; is marred and superficially defective." But if the world presents us only with images of greater and lesser degradations, where do we get our standard of perfection, our concept of the unfallen human form whose lineaments are the universe? "We grant that human life is mean," Emerson says, "but how did we find out that it was mean?"

Every nation possesses myths and legends that trace man's descent from a higher and nobler race of godlike beings with powers far surpassing our own:

> There are always two histories of man in literature contending for our faith. One is the scientific or skeptical, & derives his origin from the gradual composition, subsidence, & refining. . . . The other is the believer's, the poet's, the faithful history, always testified by the mystic & the devout, the history of the Fall, of a descent from a superior & pure race, attested in

actual history by the grand remains of elder ages, of a science
in the east unintelligible to the existing population. . . . The
faithful dogma assumes that the other is an optical show, but
that the Universe was long already complete through law, and
that the tiger & midge are only penal forms, the Auburn and
Sing Sing of nature; men, men, all & everywhere.

If the believer insists upon the doctrine of the Fall it is not because he takes delight in calling attention to man's weakness and
depravity, but because he knows that man possesses powers infinitely greater than any he currently exercises; and the easiest way
to reconcile belief in man's powers with evidence of his impotence is to assume that man reached his present condition by
falling into it. The believer's history has another advantage: it
regards the tiger and midge not as abortive men but as imprisoned men. And imprisoned men may be set free. In "The Uses of
Great Men" Emerson says, speaking of natural objects, "it would
seem as if each waited, like the enchanted princess in fairy tales,
for a destined human deliverer. Each must be disenchanted and
walk forth to the day in human shape."

"Discipline" brings us to the threshold of vision. But before
Emerson can draw together the scattered fragments of wisdom
into a coherent fable, he must relax the despotism of the senses
by introducing the "noble doubt" of "Idealism"—the hint that
what we call outward nature exists only "in the apocalypse of the
mind." The phrase is beautifully suggestive; it combines both the
etymological and conventional meanings of the word "apocalypse" in that vibrant tension Emerson thought characteristic of
the best poetry. The mind *is* an uncovering, a revelation of significance; it also may be the consuming fire in whose flames the
dross of nature will be burnt up. Perhaps its most significant
contribution to the argument of *Nature* is its implicit assertion
that the mind is not a place but a process; not an isolated inner
space passively receiving sense impressions, but an active power
incessantly striving to reveal the meaning of creation.

For the world as it appears now is only intermittently intelligible, and only partially subject to human control. It may be true
that the Supreme Being puts forth nature through us, as Emerson
asserts in "Spirit," but if so, the process is hardly so serene as the

illustrative metaphor of the tree with new leaves would seem to suggest. At the end of the chapter he admits as much: "The world proceeds from the same spirit as the body of man. It is a remoter and inferior incarnation of God, a projection of God in the unconscious. But it differs from the body in one important respect. It is not, like that, now subject to the human will." If nature is the unconscious part of the universal Mind, then we need some sort of hypothesis—like primal repression in Freud—to explain the trauma that split it off from consciousness.

In "Prospects" Emerson will at last attempt to give his account of this trauma or Fall—two accounts, really. Since I intend to devote a fair amount of space to these accounts, I should say why I think they are important. It seems to me that it is in "Prospects" that Emerson first really becomes "Emerson"—the figure we think of when his name is mentioned; in this final chapter of his first work he demonstrates not only an impressive originality but also a degree of artistic control that has not, I think, been sufficiently appreciated. In "Prospects" the interplay of different voices—the genial reasonableness of the essayist, the rhapsodic intensity of the Orphic poet, and the chilly impersonality of the strange visionary who speaks the book's most important sentence ("the axis of vision is not coincident with the axis of things, and so they appear not transparent but opake")—is for the first time made part of a larger design. In "Prospects" Emerson becomes aware of the representational possibilities of stylistic differences, and if his rhetorical modulations seem crude in comparison to the far more fluent oscillations of "Circles" or "Experience," they at least point out the direction his mature work was to take.

Contraction and Dislocation: Two Fables of the Fall

"Prospects" begins quietly enough, with a restatement of the themes expressed in the "Introduction." The split between empirical science and the intuitions of Reason places a "true theory" of nature at present out of reach, and hence postpones to a future time the satisfaction of that desire for a redemption from suffering that is really the source of our inquisitiveness. "Not whilst

the wise are one class & the good another, not whilst the physiol-
ogist & the psychologist are twain, can a Man exist, & Messiah
come." But in the meantime we have the testimony of poets and
philosophers that there is a deeper relation between man and nature than experimental science has yet succeeded in establishing.
The quotation from Herbert's poem "Man" summarizes the central mystery—the correspondence between macrocosm and microcosm—that the Orphic chants will account for, though Herbert's joyous tone of celebration is as far as possible from the
Orphic poet's defiant insistence on treating correspondence as a
symptom of man's fall into division. The relation between Herbert's poem and the Orphic chants is like the relationship between Wordsworth's famous lines from *The Recluse*, proclaiming:

> How exquisitely the individual Mind
> (And the progressive powers perhaps no less
> Of the whole species) to the external world
> Is fitted:—and how exquisitely, too—
> Theme this but little heard of among men—
> The external world is fitted to the Mind[39]

and Blake's equally famous marginal comment on these lines:
"You shall not bring me down to believe such fitting & fitted."[40]
For the way things are is not the way we want them to be, and if
nature "fits" man, it fits him very badly, like a shoe that pinches
the foot. At the beginning of "Prospects" Emerson tells us that
"a dream may let us deeper into the secret of nature than a thousand concerted experiments," but what dreams reveal is the "dislocation" between man and nature that makes our existence here
one of suffering. "The very landscape and scenery in a dream
seem not to fit us, but like a coat or cloak of some other person to
overlap and encumber the wearer; so is the ground, the road,
the house, in dreams, too long or too short, and if it served no
other purpose would show us how accurately Nature fits man
awake."

Explaining how this dislocation occurred is now Emerson's
task, and to introduce it he defers to "some traditions" sung by a

"certain poet," which, "as they have always been in the world, and perhaps reappear to every bard, may be both history and prophecy." The model for this diffident gesture is probably the Platonic dialogue, where Socrates too is fond of introducing poetic "traditions" about the origins of things, offered in a spirit that combines an ironic attitude toward their form with a genuine reverence for their content. Attributing his own daring speculations to an anonymous Orphic bard whose hyperbolic style is in deliberate and startling contrast to everything else in the chapter is a maneuver that neatly surrounds the forces of faith with the defenses of skepticism; it allows Emerson at once to offer and partially to disavow the radical suggestions the chants contain.

The first chant comprises four loosely related paragraphs: three covering different aspects of man's fallen condition, the fourth providing the cosmogony proper—a vision of the unfallen state, and an account (if not quite an explanation) of man's lapse from it.

The chant begins:

> The foundations of man are not in matter, but in spirit. But the element of spirit is eternity. To it, therefore, the longest series of events, the oldest chronologies are young and recent. In the cycle of the universal man, from whom the known individuals proceed, centuries are points and all history is but the epoch of one degradation.

The opening sentence is unfortunate, since it reintroduces that troubling dualism "Idealism" had been at such pains to dispel. True, the foundations of man are *not* in matter—but then, neither are the foundations of matter: both are emanations from a common soul. That revelation can wait, though. Emerson is here concerned to show that all historical evidence that can be marshalled against a theory proclaiming the divinity of man is simply irrelevant. In "The Over-Soul" he declares that "the argument, which is always forthcoming to silence those who conceive extraordinary hopes of man, namely, the appeal to experience, is for ever invalid and vain. We give up the past to the objector, and yet we hope. He must explain this hope." And in his journal he writes:

> I acknowledge that as far back as I can see the procession of
> humanity the marchers are lame & blind & deaf; but, to the
> soul, that whole past is but the finite series in its infinite scope.

Historical evidence is invalid because all history is, by definition,
fallen history. Time and Space are relations of matter, and matter
is the unhappy product of man's self-alienation. Hence the irrele-
vance of history, with its gloomy and inevitable moral—which
Emerson, at nineteen, had somberly drawn:

> This fact that the seeds of corruption are buried in the causes
> of improvement strikes us everywhere in the political, moral, &
> natural history of the world. It seems to indicate the intention
> of Providence to limit human perfectibility & to bind together
> good & evil, like life & death by indissoluble connection.

Nature's Orphic poet is able to dismiss the whole dismal spectacle of historical rise-and-fall in one sentence: in the cycle of universal man "all history is but the epoch of one degradation."

If the first paragraph of the chant gives us the glimpse of a figure like Blake's Albion, a "universal man" whose proper element
is eternity and whose fall generates history, the second paragraph
presents a vision of his contrary: fallen man, natural man, wholly
degraded—"like Nebuchadnezzar, dethroned, bereft of reason,
and eating grass like an ox." (The choice of Nebuchadnezzar as
an emblem of fallen man is another striking resemblance to Blake,
who drew the image of Nebuchadnezzar on the last plate of *The
Marriage of Heaven and Hell*.) From this nadir of vision the
chant rises with the hopeful rhetorical question that closes the
second paragraph: "But who can set limits to the remedial force
of spirit?"

For man is a god, though presently a god in ruins. Human life
as we know it runs relentlessly downhill, and if we could not
witness around us examples of radiant narcissism in the as-yet-
unconquered eye of Infancy, we might forget that redemption is
possible. Infancy is the Messiah; as Wordsworth said, the "Eye
among the blind."

The magnificent fourth paragraph, beginning with the sentence "Man is the dwarf of himself," is the climax of the chant,

the long awaited cosmogony. Originally, the Orphic poet tells us, man was not only a god but a cosmos: what we now call nature was his perpetual emanation. All "Time" was human time; the laws of man's mind externalized themselves into days, years, seasons. But something stopped this continual outward flow of world-creating spirit; man began to ebb, to shrink, leaving the body of nature surrounding him like a vast shell. That shell still bears his impress, but instead of "fitting" him like a garment it now merely "corresponds" to him, and he worships it with timid adoration, forgetting that it is his own creation.

The general shape of Emerson's cosmogony is very close to Blake's, even down to details of phrasing. The description of man as "shrunk to a drop" recalls the savage parody of Genesis in Blake's *Book of Urizen:*

> Six days they. Shrunk up from existence
> And on the seventh day they rested
> And they bless'd the seventh day, in sick hope:
> And forgot their eternal life.[41]

There is nothing in the Orphic chant to explain the reasons for this catastrophic shrinkage, but then attempts to provide reasons for the origin of evil are always somewhat less than convincing, always open to the sensible question the Indian asked John Eliot: "Why God did not kill the devil?" (As Emerson says when he relates this anecdote, one would like to know what Eliot replied.) Even Blake, whose machinery for detailing the intermediate stages of the collapse is so much more elaborate than Emerson's, is silent on the subject of First Causes. As Thomas Frosch notes, "Blake never tells us why it is that the dismemberment of Albion and his massive externalizations, or repressions, begins in Luvah, nor why it is that Urizen has fallen asleep."[42] Both Emerson and Blake are less concerned with the etiology than the phenomenology of the Fall: how the fallen world presents itself to the senses, how a redeemed one might appear. Since Emerson in the Orphic chant is considering the fallen world in its guise as a resistance to the *will* of man, his imagery is strongly tactile. Fallen nature is fixed, redeemed nature is fluid. (In the axis-of-vision passage, where the emphasis is rather on nature's resistance to man's *intellect*, he employs visual imagery instead: fallen nature is opaque, redeemed nature is transparent.)

Matter is only another form of energy, or rather is the detritus left behind by a failure of energy's dissolving power. Its recalcitrance is an illusion, though as immediately convincing and hard to dispel as the pain of a hysterical symptom is to the hysteric. In both cases what manifests itself as resistance to desire is in reality the disguise the subject uses to deny its existence.

Acknowledging the presence of desire frankly—as Emerson does when he suggests that the only faculty we have left capable of reminding us of our divinity is *Instinct*—will liberate that portion of it now projected into the "unconscious" as matter. If Emerson does not go quite so far as Blake, who links renovation to "an improvement of sensual enjoyment,"[43] still a careful reader of the Orphic chants could detect in them premonitory hints of the explicit antinomianism of "Circles" and "Self-Reliance." As R. A. Yoder has argued, if Blake had read *Nature*, he "might have pronounced the divine energy in the chapter on 'Spirit' as of the body and Satanic. Indeed, Emerson's Orphic poet edges toward Orc or Prometheus, the classical Lucifer."[44]

If matter is the product of a failure of energy, then a new influx of that same energy will dissolve it again. "Nature is not fixed but fluid. Spirit alters, molds, makes it. The immobility or bruteness of nature is the absence of spirit; to pure spirit, it is fluid, it is volatile, it is obedient." From these sublime heights of speculation the Orphic poet of the second chant can dismiss all the miseries of existence in a remarkable litotes: "So fast will disagreeable appearances, swine, spiders, snakes, pests, madhouses, prisons, enemies, vanish; they are temporary and shall be no more seen."

It is easy to see why Christopher Cranch thought this passage, like the Transparent Eye-ball passage, worthy of comic illustration. But here we feel more secure in judging the comedy fully intentional. The Orphic poet's sentence seems moved by an attitude that can only be described as a curious mixture of bravado, high spirits, and tenderness. Emerson wants disagreeable appearances to vanish, but he does not hate them, and of all apocalyptic thinkers he is surely the most nonviolent. He manages to combine, with little apparent strain, precisely those traits of Blake and Wordsworth that one would have thought least susceptible of combination: a tenderness for natural appearances and a fierce refusal to accept natural limitations. A pair of sentences from *Essays: Second Series* neatly sums up this precariously balanced attitude, and seems to me a better epigraph for *Nature* than either of the ones Emerson affixed to it: "Nature is loved by what is best in us. It is loved as the city of God, although, or rather because there is no citizen."

It is harder to know what to make of the swelling peroration that closes the book:

> As when the summer comes from the south, the snow-banks melt, and the face of the earth becomes green before it, so shall the advancing spirit create its ornaments along its path, and carry with it the beauty it visits, and the song which enchants it; it shall draw beautiful faces, and warm hearts, and wise discourse, and heroic acts, around its way, until evil is no more seen. The kingdom of man over nature, which cometh not with observation,—a dominion such as now is beyond his dream of God,—he shall enter without more wonder than the blind man feels who is gradually restored to perfect sight.

Of this passage Kenneth Burke observed: "One can't do anything with that, other than to note that it disposes of many troublesome things in a great hurry."[45] But the language of the passage is more ambiguous than it looks at first. What *kind* of renovation is the Orphic poet envisioning, and how does he expect it to take place? He borrows much of his imagery, as many people have noticed, from the "Prospectus" to Wordsworth's *Excursion:*

> —Beauty—a living Presence of the earth,
> Surpassing the most fair ideal forms
> Which craft of delicate Spirits hath composed
> From earth's materials—waits upon my steps;
> Pitches her tents before me as I move
> An hourly neighbor. Paradise, and groves
> Elysian, Fortunate Fields—like those of old
> Sought in the Atlantic Main—why should they be
> A history only of departed things,

> Or a mere fiction of what never was?
> For the discerning intellect of Man,
> When wedded to this goodly universe
> In love and holy passion, shall find these
> A simple produce of the common day.[46]

But Emerson characteristically warps Wordsworth's language in the direction of solipsism. One cannot really say that Emerson expects renovation to come through a *wedding* of mind and nature, for mind and nature are less like bridegroom and bride than like Narcissus and his reflection. "Not in nature but in man is all the beauty and worth he sees. The world is very empty and is indebted to the gilding and exalting soul for all its pride," he writes; then makes the revision of Wordsworth explicit: " 'Earth fills her lap with splendors' *not* her own." The "advancing spirit" of Emerson's second Orphic chant is the ancestor of Stevens' Hoon; the beauty it visits is not a neighbor but a creation of the self:

> Out of my mind the golden ointment rained,
> And my ears made the blowing hymns they heard.
> I was myself the compass of that sea:
>
> I was the world in which I walked, and what I saw
> Or heard or felt came not but from myself.[47]

Then is the apocalypse to come only an "apocalypse of imagination" that will renovate man by renovating his perceptual organs? The Orphic poet does not say so explicitly, but hints as much through his Berkleian language—phenomenon, appearances, no more seen—as well as through his final metaphor—the blind man restored to perfect sight. On the other hand, there is also an equally strong insistence in the second Orphic chant upon the stickiness, the solidity, of material objects that keep intruding themselves into the discussion like Dr. Johnson's rock: not only pests and madhouses, but "sordor and filths." Can we really get rid of these by ceasing to perceive them? It is hard to see how a private apocalypse can effect a revolution in *things*.

A related contradiction occurs in Emerson's curious use of a Biblical allusion in the book's final sentence. The phrase "cometh not with observation" is taken from the seventeenth chapter of Luke, where Jesus is rejecting the Pharisees' demand that he fix a date for the coming of the kingdom. He replies: "The kingdom of God cometh not with observation: Neither shall they say 'Lo here!' or 'Lo there!' for, behold, the kingdom of God is within you."[48] The kingdom of God is not something that will come, in time and space, but an inner paradise accessible *now.*

It is easy to understand why this text should have been one of Emerson's favorites, but hard to understand why he should have introduced it here, since it seems to explode the chant that contains it. As Joel Porte points out, Emerson is on the one hand promising an even greater dominion in time and space than the Pharisees had asked for—a kingdom of man *over nature*—yet on the other hand "he now surprises us by associating the gradual nature of this redemption with Christ's insistence that the kingdom does not come 'with observation': the visionary perfection we seek has stolen upon us unawares and lies waiting within."[49] But how can dominion over nature steal upon us unawares? To return us from the contemplation of disagreeable appearances to the inner kingdom of perfection does not *solve* the problem a fable of the Fall is supposed to explain; it *is* the problem. What kind of influence can the inner kingdom have on the outer?

Swedenborg's solution to this problem was inventive, and Emerson—who was reading Swedenborgian works like Reed's *Growth of the Mind* and Oegger's *True Messiah* with great interest during the period that spans the composition of *Nature*—seems to have adapted it to his own purposes. Swedenborg, who was as convinced as any primitive visionary that the precise date of the apocalypse could be fixed, sidestepped the danger that always attends such prophets—having the appointed day pass without producing the expected conflagration—by a maneuver both elegant and original. We must not, he says, take the threats of destruction in Revelations literally: this earth will exist eternally, and the renovation that will change it into an earthly paradise will be a gradual process, manifesting itself by a growing rejection of empty formalism in religion and of tyranny in politics.

There *is* a Last Judgment in Swedenborg's system (the earthly benefits just described flow from it) but it takes place only in the spiritual, not the natural, world. In fact, it already *has* taken place—in 1757, to be precise.[50]

I am not suggesting that Emerson took this notion to be literally true; he adapted it, as he adapted everything from the Swedenborgians, to suit his own heretical purposes. But its double structure—instantaneous revolution in the spiritual world followed by gradual renovation in the material one—was the only form in which Emerson, however briefly, could entertain the millennial hopes that were intoxicating the youth of the 1830s. (For a description of the comic excesses these hopes could give rise to, one need only consult the opening pages of James Russell Lowell's essay on Thoreau.) But of course the "spiritual world" Emerson sought was not above this world but within the self, and any redemption imaginable must begin there. Like Blake again, who weaves into his basic myth—the fall of Albion, the Universal Man, into division—passages describing the disastrous malformations of the different organs of perception, Emerson interposes between his two Orphic chants an account of the Fall as it is reenacted within each individual perceiver:

> The problem of restoring to the world original and eternal beauty is solved by the redemption of the soul. The ruin or the blank, that we see when we look at nature, is in our own eye. The axis of vision is not coincident with the axis of things, and so they appear not transparent but opake. The reason why the world lacks unity, and lies broken and in heaps, is, because man is disunited with himself.

The passage is difficult to understand for a number of reasons—unlike Emerson's first account of the Fall, it makes few concessions to the Understanding. We cannot even begin to construe it unless we notice that he is both drawing upon and revising his earlier account. This new formula depends upon an implicit assumption that the mind is a center from which nature radiates, yet it differs from the Orphic chant in assigning the cause of the mind's alienation to an error in vision rather than a failure of energy.

The first and last sentences of the passage, taken alone, could pass for a mere précis of the preceding Orphic chant—as though Emerson at last felt confident of asserting in bare formula what his Orphic poet has advanced as fable. But the middle sentences introduce a new idea. To say, as the Orphic poet does, that nature is a shell from which we have shrunk is very different from arguing that the "ruin or blank" of nature is in our own eye. The former places the Fall in some mythical past; the latter, in the present. Moreover, the axis-of-vision formula hints that this Fall is really nothing more than a mis-seeing, an optical illusion. The problem is not so much in nature as in the way we see nature. "The axis of vision is not coincident with the axis of things, and so they appear not transparent but opake."

But what *is* an "axis of vision"? The book from which Emerson seems to have derived the metaphor is a *Life* of Newton written by the English astronomer David Brewster and published in 1831.[51] Brewster's book is largely concerned with presenting summaries of Newton's scientific and mathematical discoveries in a form intelligible to the layman. Chapters 3 through 10 contain accounts of the various experiments on light and color that Newton describes in his *Opticks*. But Brewster does not merely paraphrase the *Opticks*: he also attempts to furnish hypotheses for phenomena Newton left unexplained, and he details changes in optical theory that had taken place since Newton's time. Chapter 6 of Brewster's work, which deals with Newton's experiments on the colors of thin plates, contains the passage that probably suggested Emerson's axis-of-vision formula; Chapter 7, which deals with the colors of natural bodies, may have suggested the related images of transparence and opacity.

In the second book of his *Opticks* Newton discusses a number of puzzling optical phenomena. What causes the interference rings produced when a beam of light is shined through a very thin, curved, transparent medium? Or the rings of colors on soap bubbles? Why do the surfaces of all thick transparent bodies reflect part of the light incident upon them and transmit the rest? The chief thing these rather disparate phenomena have in common is that they cannot be accounted for by the purely corpuscular theory of light that Newton attempted to establish in the first book of the *Opticks*. If light really is composed of small material particles identical in size and shape and propagated in straight lines, why should some of the particles bounce off the surface of a transparent medium while others bend through it?

In order to account for this phenomenon Newton is forced to introduce an undulatory principle somewhere in his theory. At first he tries to restrict the undulatory motion to the medium alone. The undulatory motion excited in the medium by impinging light particles (or "rays"), like waves in a pond when a stone is pitched into it, puts the particles into "Fits of Easy Transmission and Reflexion":

> ...when any Ray is in that part of the vibration which conspires with its motion, it easily breaks through a refracting Surface, but when it is in the contrary part of the vibration which impedes its Motion, it is easily reflected; and, by consequence, ... every Ray is successively disposed to be easily reflected, or easily transmitted, by every vibration which overtakes it.[52]

This hypothesis, which accounts for the behavior of the particles by attributing undulatory movement to the medium, not the particle, explains the interference rings produced by thin transparent bodies. But even thick transparent bodies reflect some light and refract the rest; hence Newton is finally forced to conclude that "Light is in Fits of easy Reflexion and easy Transmission, before its Incidence on transparent Bodies. And probably it is put into such fits at its first emission from luminous Bodies, and continues in them during all its progress."[53] Newton does not even begin to offer a hypothesis for this "property," since it is pure supposition, but Brewster feels called upon to attempt one:

> We may form a very intelligible idea of it by supposing, that the particles of light have two attractive and two repulsive poles at the extremities of two axes at right angles to each other, and that the particles revolve round their axes, and at equidistant intervals bring one or the other of the axes into the line of the direction in which the particle is moving. If the attractive axis is in the line of the direction in which the particle moves when it reaches the refracting surface, the particle will yield to the attractive force of the medium, and be refracted

and transmitted; but if the repulsive axis is in the direction of the particle's motion when it reaches the surface, it will yield to the repulsive force of the medium, and will be reflected from it.[54]

In the following chapter he gives Newton's explanation of the phenomena of transparence and opacity—recording Newton's belief that "the least particles of all almost all natural bodies are in some measure transparent."[55]

Details of this theory may seem rather recondite for Emerson to have bothered mastering, but his own eye troubles may have given him a more than casual interest in the science of optics. His visual metaphors are always quite precise. Then, too, there was that resolve recorded in his journal—"to learn the law of the diffraction of a ray, because when I understand it it will illustrate, perhaps suggest, a new truth in ethics." He even makes up a term of his own—"Theoptics"—to cover this new visionary science, and uses it to index material in his journals.

Apparently Emerson stuck by his resolve, for Brewster's terms blended in his mind with material he had assimilated from Coleridge and the Swedenborgians to form the basis of a complex symbolic system that he retained to the end of his life. "Axis," for instance, comes from Brewster's book, but "coincidence" does not, despite its vaguely scientific ring (cf. "the angle of incidence is equal to the angle of reflection"). Emerson probably adopted the term from Coleridge or from Sampson Reed, who both employ it in discussion of epistemology. In *Observations on the Growth of the Mind*, Reed argues that a man who aspires to true philosophy must "bring his mind into coincidence with things as they exist, or in other words, with the truth."[56] And in the *Biographia Literaria* Coleridge asserts: "all knowledge rests on the coincidence of an object with a subject."[57]

Whatever Emerson took from other sources, though, Brewster's book seems to have been the primary stimulus behind his development of a coherent symbolic system. References to transparence and opacity, coincidence and dislocation (in the peculiar sense they bear in the axis-of-vision passage), do not occur in the journals before 1831, the year Brewster's book was published, but they are frequent after then.

The world becomes transparent to wisdom. Every thing reveals its reason within itself.

Whenever a man comes, there comes revolution. . . . When a man comes, all books are legible, all things transparent, all religions forms.

If *I see*, the world is visible enough, clothed in brightness & prismatic hues. If again I see from a deeper energy,—I pierce the gay surface on all sides, & every mountain & rock & man & operation grows transparent before me.

Every body, I think, has sublime thoughts sometimes. At times they lie parallel with the world or the axes coincide so that you can see through them the great laws.

Do something, it matters little or not at all whether it be in the way of what you call your profession or not, so it be coincident with the axis of your character.

There is a certain fatal dislocation in our relation to nature, distorting all our modes of living and making every law our enemy. . . . Poetry and prudence should be coincident.

We can only guess why these images appealed so strongly to Emerson. He himself could not have explained it, but he was content to accept their significance in the belief that "the soul's emphasis is always right." In "Spiritual Laws" he argues that a man is "a selecting principle, gathering his like to him wherever he goes." From the multitude of images offered to him by life or by books a man selects only what belongs to his "genius." "Those facts, words, persons which dwell in his memory without his being able to say why, remain, because they have a relation to him not less real for being unapprehended. They are symbols of value to him, as they can interpret parts of his consciousness which he would vainly seek words for in the conventional images of books and other minds." With uncharacteristic patience Emerson declares his willingness to wait upon his genius' revelation of its own nature, secure in the faith that salient images held in the mind's solution will someday precipitate out into intelligible form.

If, then, "coincidence" and "dislocation," "transparence" and "opacity," were symbols of value to Emerson, what traits of consciousness did they interpret? The periodicity that Newton had discovered in the behavior of light matched Emerson's own discovery of the periodicity of vision. At times he could invoke Newton in a relatively trivial context, as when he notes that "there is . . . in moon gazing something analagous to Newton's fits of easy transmission & reflection. You catch the charm one moment, then it is gone, then it returns to go again." But Newton's law also appears in an important passage from the 1833 journals, where it is used as the scientific counterpart to Wordsworth's lines from *The Excursion* on the impermanence of vision, lines that haunted Emerson all his life:

> As the law of light is fits of easy transmission & reflexion such also is the soul's law. She is only superior at intervals to pain, to fear, to temptation, only in raptures unites herself to God and Wordsworth truly said
>
> > *Tis the most difficult of tasks to keep*
> > *Heights which the soul is competent to gain.*

This imagery helped express a puzzling yet centrally important feature of the inner life—polarity. "Every body perceives the greatest contrasts in his own spirits and powers," he writes. "Today he is not worth a brown cent—tomorrow he is better than a million." "I write laboriously after a law, which I see, and then lose, and then see again." And finally: "I am God in nature; I am a weed by the wall."

It was predictable, then, that Emerson would try to assimilate his system of contraries to his favorite philosophical distinction. (Coleridge himself may have suggested the blending: in *The Friend* he speaks of "that eternal Reason whose fulness hath no opacity, whose transparency hath no vacuum."[58]) Reason, transparence, and coincidence versus Understanding, opacity, and dislocation: the six terms became a kind of private shorthand for recording the discontinuous splendors of the inner life.

Each pair of terms in this triad of contraries expresses a slightly different aspect of the central fact of discontinuity. The distinction between the Reason and the Understanding accounts for a dualism within consciousness itself, and so represents an advance upon more conventional dualisms, like the Christian or Cartesian. The distinction between transparence and opacity transfers the characteristics of that primary dualism from consciousness to the phenomenal world that is its shadow. Finally, the distinction between coincidence and dislocation indicates with great precision the statistical rarity of visionary moments: there is an infinite number of possible dislocations, but only one possible position of coincidence for the diameters of two concentric circles. There is a good deal more Understanding than Reason in the operation of our minds; a good deal more opacity than transparence in the world we perceive around us. "Our faith comes in moments," he notes, "our vice is habitual."

But if visionary moments are rare, they are also surprisingly effortless. Vision always takes us by surprise. When we least expect it, the axis of vision suddenly snaps into place, and the universe dissolves in light. "But suddenly, in any place, in the street, in the chamber, will the heaven open, and the regions of wisdom be uncovered, as if to show how thin the veil, how null the circumstances." Emerson uses the language of traditional apocalyptic in describing the moment of vision—the uncovering of heaven, the rending of the veil—yet insists upon the remarkable nature of its surroundings.

If one can begin to understand why the terms from Newton and Coleridge became primary symbols of value to Emerson, one does not find it hard to understand why he decided to employ them in constructing a new account of the Fall. They were the most resonant words in his private vocabulary. With formulaic terseness Emerson offers the theory that explains all phenomena: "The ruin or the blank, that we see when we look at nature, is in our own eye. The axis of vision is not coincident with the axis of things, and so they appear not transparent but opake."

Perhaps the easiest way to characterize this theory, which attempts to blend scientific objectivity and religious enthusiasm, is to say that Emerson conceived the startling idea of treating the "inner light" of the radical Protestant tradition as though it behaved according to Newton's laws. In this project he may have been encouraged by some sentences in Guillaume Oegger's *Le Vrai Messie* (Paris, 1829), a manuscript translation of which he read during the summer of 1835. (Oegger is the "French philosopher" quoted in the "Language" chapter of *Nature*.) Natural or "dead" light, according to Oegger, always corresponds to "some variety of truth":

> All the phenomena of reflected light, all the colors, preserve some distant relation with the moral world; from white, which represents complex truth, to black, which recalls the darkness of absolute ignorance.... And this amazing comparison of dead with spiritual light, may be carried into the mysteries of refraction and transmission.[59]

One might wish to object that even Emerson could hardly have hoped to explain the structure of the universe in two sentences. But in "Idealism" he implies that a certain laconism is a sign of the highest reasoning. In physics, once the mind "has penetrated the vast masses of nature with an informing soul, and recognized itself in their harmony, that is, seized their law," then "the memory disburthens itself of its cumbrous catalogues of particulars, and carries centuries of observation in a single formula." By the time Emerson ventures the axis-of-vision formula his memory has disburdened itself not only of cumbrous particulars but also of any subsidiary propositions upon which that formula was based. But they may be roughly conjectured:

1. Emerson uses the term "inner light" as a synonym for soul or Reason; he also identifies the soul with vision. "In the highest moments we are a vision." It follows, then, that the soul may be spoken of—by metonymy—as an Eye. (Oegger calls man's eye "the emblem of his soul," and Coleridge calls it "the Micranthropos in the marvellous microcosm.")[60]

2. This Eye resembles a Newtonian particle in having "poles" or "axes." In his journal Emerson records a bizarre anecdote told him by a friend about a "boy that was cross eyed when ever he lied, but the axes of the eyes parallel when he spoke the truth." Of Swedenborg's attempt to formulate a science of correspondences Emerson wrote: "It required such rightness of position that the poles of the eye should coincide with the axis of the world."

3. This Eye is the center of the visible world. "The eye is the first circle; the horizon which it forms is the second; and

throughout nature this primary emblem is repeated without end." And he hints at the Eye's possible transcendence by associating this "emblem" with a mighty paradox he habitually attributed to the father of spiritual autobiography: "St. Augustine describes the nature of God as a circle whose center was everywhere, and its circumference nowhere."

4. All natural objects are opaque, but they may become, or be made, transparent. (That "transparence" and "opacity" denote spiritual rather than physical states is apparent from a charming sentence in "The Poet": "I shall mount above these clouds and opaque airs in which I live,—opaque, though they seem transparent. . . .") Opacity is the condition Blake called Mystery: the threatening and unknowable otherness of the material world. Transparence is Revelation or Apocalypse, the state in which the mute characters of nature become wholly intelligible, like hieroglyphics translated by Champollion.[61]

Coleridge, significantly, resorts to a similar metaphor in his influential "Essays on the Principles of Method" in *The Friend*. A man who studies nature without method is like the "rude yet musing Indian" who has come into possession of an illuminated manuscript of the Bible. If he studies it diligently, he may begin to notice that the symbols on the page fall into recurrent patterns; but he can get no further until the helpful missionary arrives to translate the book for him. "Henceforward, the book is unsealed for him; the depth is opened out; he communes with the spirit of the volume as a living oracle. The words become transparent, and he sees them as though he saw them not."[62]

When Emerson calls the world transparent, then, he is referring not to its appearance but to its intelligibility. Behind his assertion that "the ruin or the blank, that we see when we look at nature, is in our own eye" lies Milton's moving complaint that in his blindness the "Book of knowledge fair" is now a "Universal Blanc/ Of Nature's works to me expung'd and ras'd."[63] In Milton's lines the blankness of the book of knowledge is a metonymy of effect for cause. But in Emerson the question of figuration is not so easily resolved. On one level the axis-of-vision formula functions perfectly well as a striking though rather peculiar figure of speech. To say that we see a ruin or blank when we look at nature is, on the face of it, a hyperbolic protest against the gloom of the Christian or the emptiness of the Cartesian vision of nature; to say that the ruin or blank is in our own eye identifies perception with projection.

But in another sense the formula is not figurative at all. If the Orphic poet is right, then projection is the cause of nature. "Perhaps these subject-lenses have a creative power; perhaps there are no objects," Emerson muses in "Experience." But if there are no objects, then what is "the great apparition, that shines so peacefully around us"? Only a hieroglyphic text that we wrote, then lost the key to; only a kind of giant parapraxis, a slip or dislocation of the mind. "Nonsense is only sense deranged, chaos is paradise dislocated."

From these principles, or something like them, Emerson derives his prescription for apocalypse. When the poles of the eye, the first circle, coincide with the poles of the second, the horizon that it makes, the particulars of the natural world dissolve into the transparency of pure significance. One cannot really call the formula a program for uniting subject and object, since it denies, at least implicitly, that what we call "objects" really exist, just as it denies the existence of any essential difference between the inner light and the light of higher laws, the god within and the god without. "The simplest man who in his integrity worships God becomes God, at least no optics of the human mind can detect the line where man the effect ceases, and God the cause begins."

We are now in a position to understand, too, why Emerson cast his formula in negative terms. I have been attempting to describe the state of Coincidence; Emerson would have denied that any such description was possible. Discursive language is the language of the Understanding; it can hint at the truths of Reason only through fable, paradox, or negation.[64] The Orphic chants are fables; the Transparent Eye-ball passage is a web of paradoxes ("I am nothing. I see all."). Here Emerson approaches the subject through negation. He cannot say that the problem of restoring original and eternal beauty to the world would be solved if the axis of vision *were* coincident with the axis of things, because in the state of Coincidence there are no separate things. The object-world is the product of dislocation, and will vanish when that dislocation is remedied.

The question then arises: If there is no "axis of things" in the state of perfect Coincidence, what is it that the "axis of vision" deviates *from?* I think we have to say (with some violence both to language and to sense, as Dr. Johnson might remark) that it deviates from itself. Geoffrey Hartman notes Blake's belief that "all myths are creation myths and tell of man's self-alienation."[65] Emerson's creation myths, too, are myths of self-alienation; and the "dislocation" of the formula, like the "contraction" of the first Orphic chant, is a way of describing man's lapse from his own divinity. But the formula does something the chants cannot: it evades temporality.

Most myths of the Fall express differences between states as differences between times, and hence obscure or pervert (in Emerson's opinion) the meanings they were supposed to convey. In his journal he tries to explain the causes of this persistent misrendering:

> Reason, seeing in objects their remote effects, affirms the effect as the permanent character. The Understanding listening to Reason, on one side, which saith *It is,* & to the senses, on the other side, which say, *It is not,* takes middle ground and declares *It will be.* Heaven is the projection of the ideas of Reason on the plane of the Understanding.

In the Orphic chants that surround the axis-of-vision formula, Emerson is willing to make concessions to the time-bound Understanding. But in the axis-of-vision formula itself he speaks uncompromisingly from his Reason to ours. The image of "dislocation" neatly avoids locating perfection either in a remote past or a distant future. It is a spatial rather than a temporal image, a formula rather than a plot. If the kingdom of man over nature does not seem to be in any hurry to establish itself, "it is only the feebleness and dust of the observer that makes it future, the whole *is* now potentially in the bottom of his heart."

* * *

Nature certainly ends on a note of hope and rejoicing, a "rapt vision of redemption."[66] Yet one is tempted to ask, as Northrop Frye did of the apocalyptic vision that ends *The Four Zoas*, how far the finale "is a real climax of the vision, and how far it has been added as an effort of will, perhaps almost of conscience."[67] James Cox complains that the second Orphic chant is "weak vision and weak language."[68] I think that it is more complicated and more interesting than that, but there is certainly a sense of strain about the passage that leads us to wonder whether the will isn't trying to do the work of the imagination.

For the collective redemption envisaged at the end of the book depends upon the possibility of renovating the vision of the individual perceiver, and the axis-of-vision formula, which is concerned with that renovation, leaves one giant question unanswered. Are the ruined, blank eyes of man capable of "self-healing" by an effort of will *or* imagination? Or are they passively subject to the endless alternations, the "fits of easy transmission & reflexion," that give to our organs of perception a nature first opaque, then transparent, then opaque, then transparent, and so on to eternity? That may sound at first like the description Blake gives of the "Characters of the great Apocalypse" as they appear to the renovated body's perceptual powers:

> every Word & Every Character
> Was Human according to the Expansion or Contraction, the
>   Translucence or
> Opakeness of Nervous fibres such was the variation of Time &
>   Space
> Which vary according as the Organs of Perception vary . . .[69]

But the important thing about *this* kind of fluctuation, as Thomas Frosch points out, is that in Blake's Eden "the relative translucency or opacity of substance is under the perceiver's control."[70]

Are the "transparence" and "opacity" of the world in Emerson's final vision under our control? Or is their alternation not rather the chief sign that we are fallen? At certain times "I can . . . with a mountainous aspiring say, *I am God,*" Emerson knows. "Yet why not always so? How came the Individual thus armed &

impassioned to parricide thus murderously inclined ever to traverse & kill the divine life?" Before that final riddle Emerson—like another riddle-solving parricide before him—is silent. "Into that dim problem I cannot enter. A believer in Unity, a seer of Unity, I yet behold two."

I do not wish to distort *Nature* by overemphasizing its unresolved contradictions, its cracks not to be soldered or welded. Surely what every reader remembers about the book is its "idealistic upsurge,"[71] the faith and hope it expresses that the transparent universe we perceive in those moments of "perfect exhilaration" will someday be our permanent home, that the whole that is potentially in the bottom of our hearts will organize itself as well around our organs of perception. Yet in the end it is difficult to say whether the hope we are offered in "Prospects" belongs among the visions from Patmos or the views from Pisgah; whether we are being shown the Jerusalem in which we will someday live, or the Promised Land we will never be permitted to enter.

III

Portable Property

> For where your treasure is,
> there will your heart be also.
> Matt. 6:21

The Empty American Parnassus

By 1837, the year in which Emerson delivered his address to the Phi Beta Kappa Society, the chair of Mental Philosophy at Harvard had been vacant for over eight years, a circumstance one foreign visitor found distressingly symbolic. The national mind of a self-governing people, Harriet Martineau observed, may be judged in two ways: as it manifests itself in legislation, and in literature. For the wisdom of our laws she had the highest praise. But our literature was another matter. "If the American nation be judged of by its literature," she said, "it may be pronounced to have no mind at all."[1] Tocqueville was more polite in his phrasing, but his judgment of the American literary scene was scarcely less devastating. Americans themselves were so convinced of the imitativeness of their own literature that they left the task of evaluating it to the English—"just as a painter may be held to judge the merit of a copy of his own work."[2]

The sorry state of American letters was particularly galling in view of the high hopes various eighteenth-century thinkers had expressed that the achievement of political independence, coupled with the economic prosperity for which the country was already celebrated, would produce a cultural flowering to rival the Golden Ages of the past. The arts, they observed, moved northward and westward in the course of history, flourishing among prosperous and free peoples and declining among despotisms. Armed with such conventional wisdom, George Berkeley had not hesitated to predict the most glorious future for the American *polis:*

> There shall be sung another golden age,
> The rise of empire and of arts,
> The good and great inspiring epic rage,
> The wisest heads and noblest hearts.
>
> Not such as Europe breeds in her decay;
> Such as she bred when fresh and young,
> When heavenly flame did animate her clay,
> By future poets shall be sung.
>
> Westward the course of empire takes its sway;
> The first four acts already past,
> A fifth shall close the drama with the day;
> Time's noblest offspring is the last.[3]

Berkeley's lines express a hope that the products of American civilization will not merely rival the art of the refined and sophisticated nations, but will somehow return to the primitive vigor of the earliest beginnings of European civilization, producing heroes as bold as Achilles, as wise as Nestor, and bards as "naïve" (in Schiller's sense) as Homer to enshrine their deeds in verse.

And Berkeley was not alone in his hopes; by the time of the Revolution prophecies of American cultural greatness had become a favorite theme for liberal poets and essayists on both sides of the Atlantic. As Emerson reminded his audience when he delivered the address entitled "Literary Ethics": "This country has not fulfilled what seemed the reasonable expectation of mankind. Men looked, when all feudal straps and bandages were snapped asunder, that nature, too long the mother of dwarfs, should reimburse itself by a brood of Titans, who should laugh and leap in the continent, and run up the mountains of the West with the errand of genius and of love."

But by 1837 the snapping asunder of the feudal bands was six decades in the past, and what had America produced in the way of Titans, or epic rage? There was Joel Barlow's *Columbiad,* and (after the War of 1812) Emmons's *Fredoniad*—but only the most undiscriminating patriot would be likely to exhibit these pitiful leavings of the Muses as evidence of a new Periclean Age. The failure of the eagerly awaited and confidently predicted cultural flowering to manifest itself had in fact become both a national scandal and an embarrassment to liberal thinkers everywhere. Political freedom was supposed to make men fearless, but in no country on earth was there *less* freedom of opinion than in America, where, as Tocqueville noted, the "tyranny of the majority" produced a degree of intellectual conformity that the most brutal and repressive of despotisms had never achieved. Prosperity was supposed to nourish art, but the quest for wealth had simply become an end in itself, with results that everyone acknowledged and deplored. Emerson's wry comment on the advantages of his own place in cultural history shows how very far he thought American literature was from its promised Golden Age. "We early men at least have a vast advantage," he admitted. "We are up at 4 o'clock and have the whole market: We Enniuses & venerable Bedes of the empty American Parnassus."

If the problem really had been only a literary one, it might have deserved the good-natured dismissal it gets in James Russell Lowell's essay, "Nationality in Literature". Lowell is equally amused by the European critics who kept demanding that America produce a literature of its own "as if it were a school composition to be handed in by a certain day" and by the Americans who allowed themselves to be buffaloed by the demand. "Other nations kept their poets, and so must we. We were to set up a literature as people set up a carriage, in order to be as good as our neighbors. It was even seriously proposed to have a new language. Why not, since we could afford it?"[4]

But the literary problem was only one symptom of a more serious malaise, and if there was something comical in American attempts to produce an epic that would satisfy a jaded European public hungry for primitive poetic vigor, there was nothing at all amusing about the malaise. Conservatives and royalists around the world, who had perhaps been disappointed in their hopes that the infant republic would collapse shortly after its founding, could at least take comfort from the fact that nearly all the virtues

associated with aristocratic societies—courage, nobility, self-sac-
rifice—and all of their cultural achievements as well, were evidently impossible in a democracy. Here John Jay Chapman's
vivid portrait of the world Emerson confronted as a young man,
familiar as it is, deserves quoting:

> The South was a plantation. The North crooked the hinges of
> knee where thrift might follow fawning. It was the era of Mar-
> tin Chuzzlewit, a malicious caricature,—founded on fact. This
> time of humiliation, when there was no free speech, no litera-
> ture, little manliness, no reality, no simplicity, no accomplish-
> ment, was the era of American brag. We flattered the foreigner
> and we boasted of ourselves. We were oversensitive, insolent, and
> cringing. As late as 1845, G. P. Putnam, a most sensible and
> modest man, published a book to show what the country had
> done in the field of culture. The book is a monument of the
> age. With all its good sense and good humor, it justifies foreign
> contempt because it is explanatory.[5]

That Emerson was not only aware of foreign contempt but acknowledged its justice is evident from the unusually strong language he employed in the peroration of *The American Scholar:*

> The spirit of the American freeman is already suspected to be
> timid, imitative, tame. Public and private avarice make the air
> we breathe thick and fat. The scholar is decent, indolent, com-
> plaisant. See already the tragic consequence. The mind of this
> country, taught to aim at low objects, eats upon itself. There is
> no work for any but the decorous and complaisant. Young men
> of the fairest promise, who begin life upon our shores, inflated
> by the mountain winds, shined on by all the stars of God, find
> the earth below not in unison with these,—but are hindered
> from action by the disgust which the principles on which busi-
> ness is managed inspire, and turn drudges, or die of disgust,—
> some of them suicides.

In the final sentences of the paragraph Emerson is alluding to the
great financial crash that had occurred in the spring of the year;
doubtless there were many in his audience who shared his disgust at the greed and speculation that had helped produce the disaster. Still, the frank confession of spiritual deformity Emerson's
words contain strikes me as a remarkable one to make at a college

commencement festivity, and must have seemed even more so in 1837, when what Americans ordinarily got from their ceremonial oratory was outrageous flattery. "The public orators," Martineau noted, "flatter the people; the people flatter the orators. Clergymen praise their flocks; and the flocks stand amazed at the excellence of their clergymen. Sunday-School teachers admire their pupils; and the scholars magnify their teachers."[6] She did not think that the practice stemmed from any real corruption of spirit, only from a genuine kindliness unfortunately mixed with a false idea of honor. And she noted with approval that many of the citizens were as disgusted by it as she was. After attending a Forefather's Day speech that "consisted wholly of an elaboration of the transcendent virtues of the people of New England," she heard it criticized by her hostess's daughter in these words: "I am heart-sick of this boasting. When I think of our forefathers, I want to cry, 'God be merciful to us sinners!' "[7] One can begin to see why Emerson's address seemed so revolutionary when it was delivered. It was a frank confession of what many people had been thinking, but no one had had the courage to admit.

There had, of course, been attempts to explain the nonappearance of American literature before Emerson's. Educated Americans were often only too eager to agree with visiting European aristocrats that America could never have a literature of its own until it had an established leisure class. Martineau was repeatedly surprised to discover American intellectuals expressing a contempt for the "masses" with "as much assurance as if they lived in Russia or England," and not in a country "whose profession is social equality, and whose rule of association is universal self-government."[8]

On the other hand, there was a noisily nationalistic party—mostly in the popular press—who kept loudly insisting that all foreign and "feudal" ideas be rejected as demeaning to the spirit of the American freeman. But Emerson was the first to say that the debate, as it was usually conducted, missed the real point. Our sympathetic *liberal* critics were the ones who ought to be listened to. The real problem with the American "freeman" was neither that he was insufficiently aristocratic nor insufficiently American, but that he was insufficiently free. He was inhibited in every area of intellectual and moral life by that peculiar form of tyranny Tocqueville judged more dangerous to the spirit than all the machinery of despotism:

> Princes made violence a physical thing, but our contemporary democratic republics have turned it into something as intellectual as the human will it is intended to constrain. Under the absolute government of a single man, despotism, to reach the soul, clumsily struck at the body, and the soul, escaping from such blows, rose gloriously above it; but in democratic republics that is not at all how tyranny behaves; it leaves the body alone and goes straight for the soul.[9]

He wrote this eloquent paragraph in an attempt to explain something to himself that, as Chapman notes, was exceedingly puzzling to all intelligent foreigners who inspected the American scene. Why were Americans—hedged round as they were with every constitutional defense of their civil liberties—the most timid, canting, anxious nation of intellectual and social conformists on earth? Martineau was astonished to find that a kind of self-protective caution intruded itself into even the most intimate of conversations. Such "want of social confidence" seemed to her "little short of disgusting" in its selfishness and implied mistrust, and at times manifested itself in a dread of responsibility that she did not hesitate to label "insane." Americans themselves were so accustomed to this habit of caution that they were "unaware of its extent and singularity," but a wider acquaintance with the world would make them realize how odd they really were:

> They may travel over the world, and find no society but their own which will submit to the restraint of perpetual caution, and reference to the opinion of others. They may travel over the whole world, and find no country but their own where . . . the youth of society determine in silence what opinions they shall bring forward, and what avow only in the family circle; where women write miserable letters, almost universally, because it is a settled matter that it is unsafe to commit oneself on paper; and where elderly people seem to lack almost universally that faith in principles which inspires a free expression of them at any time and under all circumstances.[10]

This perpetual caution, this "want of moral independence," was doubly puzzling because it seemed anomalous. Americans were not *generally* timid or fearful, and they did not bring up their children to repress their opinions or defer unquestioningly to the authority of others. Foreign visitors were often astonished by the freedom American parents permitted their children. They treated their children with friendliness and respect, encouraged them to speak their minds freely, and seemed delighted by the candid and amusing responses they got.

But the happiness and fearlessness of American children only made the moral timidity of American adults more incomprehensible. It is evident that Emerson shared Martineau's perception of the discrepancy between youthful and adult behavior in America; he makes it the theme of a key paragraph in "Self-Reliance."

> The nonchalance of boys who are sure of a dinner, and would disdain as much as a lord to do or say aught to conciliate one, is the healthy attitude of human nature. A boy is in the parlor what the pit is in the playhouse; independent, irresponsible. . . . You must court him; he does not court you. But a man is, as it were, clapped into jail by his consciousness. As soon as he has once acted or spoken with eclat, he is a committed person, watched by the sympathy or the hatred of hundreds whose affections must now enter into his account. There is no Lethe for this.

It is easy enough to be as sincere as a child when one is alone, but the "voices which we hear in solitude grow faint and inaudible as we enter the world. Society everywhere is in conspiracy against the manhood of every one of its members."

Emerson's condemnation of society ought doubtless to be qualified by the phrase "in America." His European tour of 1833 had given him only the most superficial glimpse of other cultures, and it was not until his visit to England in 1848 that he had an opportunity to observe the workings of a different kind of social system. But the charges he levels at American society in *The American Scholar* and "Self-Reliance" echo the criticisms of

Tocqueville and Martineau: America seemed geared to produce a race not of Titans but of cowards.

The difficulty that the whole antebellum North presents to our intellect, according to Chapman, is accounting for this cowardice. "It is incredible that the earth should ever have nurtured such a race of cowards as the dominant classes in our Northern States seem to have been. And yet we know that they were no worse, nor very different, from other persons recorded in history; they furnish merely an acute, recent example of how self-interest can corrupt character, of how tyranny can delude intellect."[11] Emerson himself makes this point with particular distinctness in "Self-Reliance," when, after urging each person to take up the frightening task of becoming a law unto himself, he explains the need for such extremities of moral isolation. "If any man consider the present aspects of what is called by distinction *society*"—by distinction to the self, that is—"he will see the need of these ethics. The sinew and heart of man seem to be drawn out, and we are become timorous desponding whimperers. We are afraid of truth, afraid of fortune, afraid of death, and afraid of each other."

The contempt implied in that qualifying phrase "by distinction" shows why Emerson dismissed out of hand all attempts to oppose the legitimate needs of society to the extreme claims he makes for the "supreme authority" of the moment of vision. He simply refuses to agree that the atomized collection of frightened individuals he sees around him deserves to be dignified by the term "society." What people commonly call by that name appears to him nothing more than a "joint-stock company, in which the members agree for the better securing of his bread to each shareholder, to surrender the liberty and culture of the eater."

This point is worth emphasizing. The severest attacks on Emerson's character and sanity in this century have come from men who accuse him of harboring and fostering in others an infantile disregard for the realities of associated life. The untrammeled spiritual freedom he urges his hearers to cultivate, the reliance only on inner promptings, would result in anarchy and murder if actually applied to the world of natural and social reality. And even if it is argued that Emerson was himself fully conscious of this fact (the journals supply ample material on this subject) and that he always insists on respecting the absolute distinction between the world of the senses and the world of the soul, the very fact that he sees the world in this way and encourages other people to do the same is a strategy that trivializes the inner world and drains the outer one of significance and even life itself. The self may be "imperial," but it is impotent; the world may be conquerable, but then it is worthless.[12]

What complicates this subject is Emerson's own ambivalence about whether this split between soul and senses, Reason and Understanding, is to be regarded as humanity's greatest sickness or its greatest defense. No simple answer to this question is possible. As long as Emerson is thinking of Man as he appears to the eye of eternity, his state of alienation from nature, other men and his own body naturally appears as the greatest curse of existence. Attempting to formulate a "theory" that would account for such a disaster is the subject of Emerson's first book, *Nature*, as recording its human costs is made the subject of his greatest essay, "Experience." Yet if Emerson turns his attention from the eternal Man to his poor, frightened American avatar, Man as he is in the Boston of 1837, the soul's immense capacity for alienation can come to seem a positive virtue. In a society wholly dominated by a debasing fear of Opinion, whose literature is a pitiful attempt to appease European criticism by aping its approved literary forms, isolationism is increasingly difficult to distinguish from integrity itself. It was doubtless pleasing to an admirer of the law of compensation to discover that the malady he had spent his first major work trying to understand and so dispose of turns out to be, by the time of his second, the remedy for a different disease.

Bruno Bettelheim makes a similar point when, in *The Informed Heart*, he describes the changes in psychoanalytic theory that his own experience in the German concentration camps forced him to make. "According to psychoanalytic convictions then current, the test of the well functioning, well integrated personality, the goal of psychoanalysis, was the ability to form freely intimate relations, 'to love,' to be in ready contact with the forces of the unconscious, and to sublimate in 'work.' Aloofness from other persons and emotional distance from the world were viewed as weakness of character." Yet Bettelheim was surprised to discover that many apparently well integrated persons disintegrated almost immediately under the extreme conditions of camp life, while two groups of aloof and rigid people—members of the high nobility, and Jehovah's Witnesses—were able to survive the camp experience virtually unchanged, the former because their conviction of inner superiority gave them a detachment from the debasing conditions of camp life that let nothing touch them, the latter because their faith in a transcendent order gave them courage to endure sufferings that destroyed other men. He also mentioned another noncamp group that resembled them: people raised in communal children's houses in the socialist kibbutzim of Palestine. They too seemed aloof and unrelated, and most would have been diagnosed as neurotic by conventional psychoanalysts. Yet many of them became heroic leaders during the war of liberation, and all endured extreme hardship with no signs of personality disintegration. Bettelheim's point is not that rigidity or aloofness is a desirable human characteristic; merely that no theory of personality can say what constitutes "integration" or health unless it takes into account the "human and social environment" with which the "total man" has to deal. What is normal in one environment may be suicidal in another.[13]

Now the human and social environment Emerson found himself confronting in his prophetic period was dominated by a single emotion: fear, or, as Chapman calls it, "moral cowardice." No one can possibly understand the essays and addresses written between 1837 and 1841 who fails to recognize that in all of them Emerson's adversary is fear, and that his therapeutic goal is the development in his hearers of an ego strong enough to resist its crippling influence. A failure to recognize this central fact can lead a reader as intelligent as Quentin Anderson to interpret as a retreat from society what was actually a virulent attack upon it; it even leads him to make the astonishing statement that "in [Emerson] alone was the social voice stilled in his great years."[14]

But fear of what? Not, really, of physical persecution, though Garrison was mobbed and Elijah Lovejoy murdered. Most of

Emerson's hearers risked no such persecution; and even that degree, by historical standards, was rather mild. As he reminds them in the lecture "The Transcendentalist," "All that is clearly due to-day is not to lie. In other places, other men have encountered sharp trials, and have behaved themselves well. The martyrs were sawn asunder, or hung alive on meat-hooks. Cannot we screw our courage to patience and to truth, and without complaint, or even with good-humor, await our turn of action in the Infinite Counsels?" What was causing men to lie to one another and to themselves, so that Emerson's voice came to seem, to a whole generation, an agent of liberation? Was there some underlying fault that would explain those puzzling splits in the surfaces of the American character that left the sympathetic foreigners so perplexed—the good temper and the mob violence, the mutual kindliness and the terror of opinion, the candor of children and the hypocrisy of adults?

The Morning After the Earthquake: Emerson and the Depression of 1837

In *The American Scholar* Emerson explains the despair of the younger generation attempting to move into the adult world by saying that they are hindered by disgust at the principles upon which business is managed. Recent events in the world had given him an unusually clear glimpse of what those principles were, and how they were related to the desires and aspirations of the people he hoped to reach. Although Emerson had joked to Carlyle about the importance of money to the American psyche—he called it the "innate idea of the American mind"—it was not until the stock market crash in the spring of 1837 that he understood the full force of that remark. Yet if the squalor of the spectacle was depressing, it was in another sense liberating. In part, the internal collapse of the "prudential" world freed Emerson from feeling that he needed to justify his more radical assertions to the skeptical eye of common sense. "Behold the boasted world has come to nothing. Prudence herself is at her wits' end. Pride, and Thrift, & Expediency, who jeered and chirped and were so well pleased with themselves and made merry with the dream as they termed it, of Philosophy & love,—behold they are all flat, and here is the Soul erect and unconquered still."

But the financial catastrophe did more than arouse prophetic glee at the failure of the sinful world. It revealed to Emerson something essential about the nature of the mind's relation to reality, about its secret hungers, its periodic crises of self-distrust, its immense capacity for symbolization. The banker who speculates in titles to parcels of western land he will never see looks like a madman to the eye of reason, and at first Emerson cannot understand what motivated apparently "solid" men to risk security and reputation in pursuit of more profits than any of them could comfortably dispose of in a lifetime. Yet he gradually came to understand that their aims were not so far from his own as they might appear to an objective observer; tycoons were poets who chose to write their epics in cash.

Martineau was surprised to discover that the European stereotype of Americans as exclusively "practical" in their interests was almost the reverse of the truth. The American people were so highly imaginative that they reminded her constantly of the Irish, and even their undoubted fascination with ways of making money had little to do with anything a European would recognize as greed. W. H. Auden makes a similar point when he observes that "what an American values . . . is not the possession of money as such, but his power to make it as a proof of his manhood; once he has proved himself by making it, it has served its function and can be lost or given away. In no society in history have rich men given away so large a part of their fortunes." And he closes his little postscript on the Almighty Dollar by predicting that few Americans will be found among the Avaricious in Dante's Purgatory, but that the Prodigals "may be almost an American colony."[15] Americans did not really need to be weaned from an overly strong attachment to the things of this world; the aims of even the shoddiest speculator were in the deep sense *otherworldly* to begin with. He did not really want money, but the sense of self-esteem its possession would confer. His aims were not in themselves vicious; he had merely chosen to pursue them with inappropriate means. He was (not that he realized it) attempting to satisfy the demands of the Reason with trophies won in the world of the Understanding.

For it is beginning to dawn on Emerson that this supposedly "philosophical" distinction between two faculties of the mind was perhaps only a way of expressing the fact that each man finds himself simultaneously enmeshed in two contradictory systems—one ethical, poetic, concerned with infinite desires and the infinite satisfactions they predict; the other limited, amoral, concerned with local gratifications that can generally be achieved only at someone else's expense. No man, the Bible warns, can serve two masters, yet every man spends his life trying to work out some compromise between the contradictory laws of poetry and economics, the pleasure principle and the reality principle, the gay science and the dismal one.

If a recognition of this fact placed the possibility of a final apocalypse like the one promised at the end of *Nature* forever out of reach, and forced Emerson to replace his relatively traditional myth of the Fall as it is given in the two Orphic chants (Creation-Fall-Redemption) with the endlessly dialectical versions of "The Protest" and "Circles," the change has its benefits as well as its obvious disadvantages. If apocalypse is never final, neither is defeat; and the soul's inability to keep the heights it is competent to gain can be balanced by a faith that each temporary depression of the soul will be overcome by a new pulsation of energy from the central heart of human desire. The single thing that had previously restrained Emerson from preaching a full reliance on the inner life—its disturbing alternation between states of ecstasy and desolation, "poverty" and "affluence" (to use the names he often gives them)—is shown to be at least no worse than the boom-and-bust cycles inherent in the structure of capitalism, and in one respect better: spiritual capital, unlike the tangible kind, returns eventually of its own accord. And so Emerson is able for the first time to see his anthems to Reason as the soundest kind of practical advice:

> Fall back on the simplest sentiment, be heroic, deal justly, walk humbly, & you do something and do invest the capital of your being in a bank that cannot break & that will surely yield ample rents—

> Here is always a certain amount of truth lodged as intrinsic
> foundation in the depths of the soul, a certain perception of ab-
> solute being, as justice, love, & the like, natures which must be
> the God of God, and this is our capital stock.

Moreover, reliance upon this inner capital offered a way out of
the chief spiritual malady from which the nation suffered: its terror of Opinion. For really, what was producing that terror—besides the normal human desire to belong to the majority in any
area of dispute, that is? Chapman is probably right when he locates the cause not in democracy but in commerce: the sense that
each person has that his economic well-being is bound up with
the workings of a vast system that is at once omnipotent and ex-
tremely fragile. "Reform," if it threatens profits and jobs, is hated
not only for the actual sufferings it might cause among those
whose economic situation is marginal but also for menacing the
only shared standard from which most people can derive a sense
of self-esteem. The reason young Bostonians were willing to hold
a rally in defense of slavery in Faneuil Hall had little to do with
slavery itself; it was owing to the fact "that Beacon Street was
trading with South Carolina."[16] By contrast, the orthodox farm-
ers of the hinterlands were militant Abolitionists from the beginning. The situation was not without its ironies, as Daniel Walker
Howe has observed: "the Unitarian believers in free will were af-
flicted with a complacent fatalism at the very time in history
when many professing loyalty to predestination were girding
themselves to do battle for the Lord."[17] Was it then true, as the
orthodox argued, that those who refused to abase themselves before God would inevitably find themselves bowing down before
Mammon? Or was it possible to be a liberal and remain a Man?

Emerson's entire career was devoted to answering that latter
question in the affirmative. But he realized that he needed a far
deeper understanding of the relationship between the individual
and his social and economic system than he had ever bothered to
acquire. And it was just this kind of knowledge that the sudden
collapse of the economy promised to provide. Hence the exultant
tone of the journal passages written during the summer of 1837,
as Emerson records his gratitude at the revelatory merits of the
catastrophe:

What was, ever since my memory, solid continent, now yawns apart and discloses its composition and genesis. I learn geology the morning after an earthquake. I learn fast on the ghastly diagrams of the cloven mountain & upheaved plain and the dry bottom of the Sea. The roots of orchards and the cellars of palaces and the cornerstones of cities are dragged into melancholy sunshine. I see the natural fracture of the stone. I see the tearing of the tree & learn its fibre & rooting. The Artificial is rent from the eternal.

What is remarkable about this passage is the way it combines the language of traditional apocalyptic with the language of the science whose authority was busily destroying the ontological foundations of Biblical revelation: geology. What Emerson suggests by its use here is that he suddenly sees the social and economic not as a given, something solid and inescapable, but as the end product of forces extending back into the unimaginable past.

In a way the crisis changed Emerson's vision of the social world as his response to Charles' death had changed his vision of the natural one: the fallenness of the world is now seen as something requiring historical explanation, and Emerson suddenly finds himself thrust into the prophet's role.

I see a good in such emphatic & universal calamity as the times bring, that they dissatisfy me with society. Under common burdens we say there is much virtue in the world & what evil coexists is inevitable. I am not aroused to say, 'I have sinned; I am in the gall of bitterness, & bond of iniquity'; but when these full measures come, it then stands confessed—Society has played out its last stake; it is checkmated.

In the quoted words Emerson is paraphrasing St. Peter's denunciation of Simon the magician of Samaria, who, in trying to *buy* from Peter the power to confer the Holy Spirit through the laying on of hands, lent his name to the sin that had such importance in giving birth to the Protestant Reformation. In one sense, poor Simon has merely made an honest mistake (the sort of mistake Emerson saw the capitalists of his own society as making too): he sees Peter's power as a thing greatly to be desired, and offers for it the only valuable thing he knows. Peter is kind enough to retain him in the community, but rebukes him severely: "Repent therefore of this thy wickedness, and pray God, if perhaps the thought of thine heart may be forgiven thee. For I perceive that thou art in the gall of bitterness, and in the bond of iniquity."[18]

In playing Peter to his own Simon, Emerson is rebuking himself for a fault almost diametrically opposed to the Samarian magician's: not of confusing the realms of money and grace, but of accepting so great a division between them that he had unwittingly played into the hands of those who were debasing men to a level below the human:

> The present generation is bankrupt of principles & hope, as of property. I see man is not what man should be. He is the treadle of a wheel. He is a tassel at the apron string of Society. He is a money chest. He is the servant of his belly.

This is the *real* bankruptcy, or, as he calls it, the "causal" bankruptcy, from which the inflations and collapses of the visible economy grow—"that the ideal should serve the actual; that the head should serve the feet." He is overcome with remorse that it has taken so great a jolt to shake him loose from his complacency, to make him "inquire if the Ideal might not also be tried." But that only makes the prophetic mission more urgent.

> I acknowledge that as far back as I can see the winding procession of humanity the marchers are lame & blind & deaf; but, to the soul, that whole past is but the finite series in its infinite scope. Deteriorating ever and now desperate. Let me begin anew. Let me teach the finite to know its Master. Let me ascend above my fate and work down upon my world.

In one sense, of course, there is nothing new about this resolution; it merely continues the project begun in the closing chapters of *Nature*. Yet the rough way the "real" world had just taken to bring itself to his attention revealed the central flaw in the vision of redemption that closes that book—its lack of a social dimension. Emerson had originally planned a manual for the private use of the would-be Idealist, not a vision of collective redemption. The apocalyptic closing chapters were added in haste and under great pressure, and Emerson himself was less than satisfied with his success at resolving the difficulties that blending had created. But though some of those difficulties were discussed in the last chapter, one particularly glaring one remains to be considered. An epiphany is a private affair; so is an ascent into Idealism. But an apocalypse can hardly take place without involving everybody.

Even if we grant Emerson his rather formidable premise—that "the problem of restoring to the world original and eternal beauty is solved by the redemption of the soul" and that a self-healed spirit would by some mysterious influence produce a "correspondent revolution in things"—we will doubtless feel that he has failed to dispose of the problem that naturally occurs to anyone reading the book. How can this spiritual revolution effect the renovation of nature unless it occurs in everyone simultaneously? If *my* spirit quits its earth while yours remains fallen, will the "disagreeable appearances—swine, spiders, pests," etc.—merely scurry out of my field of vision and into yours, as they do in Christopher Cranch's sketch? And how many people could Emerson actually hope to reach with his oracular, anonymously published little book, anyway? In "The Transcendentalist" he gently mocks the pretensions of "the good, the illuminated" who think that they have only to censure the vices of society to make "the very brokers, attorneys, and congressmen" see the error of their ways and flock to the virtuous for counsel. That is not how life works. "The good and the wise must learn to act, and carry salvation to the combatants and demagogues in the dusty arena below."

It is unlikely that Emerson himself was ever so naïve as to imagine that brokers or congressmen would seek out his advice; *Nature* had been intended rather for his natural audience, the lonely and idealistic young people who might respond to his exhilarating vision exactly as he himself had responded to Coleridge's *Aids to Reflection* or Sampson Reed's *The Growth of the Mind.* But the events of 1837 had made that selective kind of preaching seem almost criminal in its negligence. Emerson saw very clearly what was wrong with the society in which he lived, and he had the moral, economic, and emotional independence from that society to castigate it with impunity. Partly by accident and partly by choice he had become, as Chapman says, the freest man in America. Did he have the right *not* to speak out? The story of Jonah in the Bible exists as a warning to those who would try to refuse the burden of prophecy. And so in the summer of 1837 he slowly and reluctantly faced about, as Maurice Gonnaud puts it, "and began a long tussle with reality."[19]

His first opportunity to speak out came almost immediately. The Harvard chapter of the Phi Beta Kappa Society, disappointed in its attempts to secure the Rev. Dr. Jonathan M. Wainwright as orator at its annual academic exercises, had turned to Emerson. It suddenly occurred to him that two of the traditional topics for such orations—the place of the scholar in a commercial society, the embarrassing nonexistence of American literature—could be discussed as manifestations of a single, underlying problem: fear, or, as he often calls it, "self-distrust." The timidity of intellectuals confronting a vast economy upon which they are dependent yet which seems to have no room for them could easily serve as a synecdoche for the much larger problem faced by every would-be artist who must confront the intimidating richness of past tradition. To this double problem Emerson now turned.

Tradition and the Individual Talent: The American Scholar

The *literary* problem Emerson confronted was not, of course, peculiar to America; it was rather a special offshoot of that larger cultural problem recent critics have taught us to call the Burden of the Past or the Anxiety of Influence—the artist's fear that his great predecessors have exhausted the possibilities of his art, that the intimidating richness of past tradition has effectively rendered fresh creation impossible. Like all aspiring young authors, Emerson showed a gloomy consciousness of the difficulties he faced. Already during his college years he worried that he was "Late in the World too late perchance for fame," and occasionally expressed envy for antediluvians like Noah, who—whatever his other burdens—was at least not "dinned to death with Aristotle & Bacon & Greece & Rome."

If Emerson had been writing at the turn of the century instead of in the 1820s, he might at least have consoled himself with the notion that his plight was part of a general European decline. In *The Burden of the Past and the English Poet*, Walter Jackson Bate has described the specter that haunted much eighteenth-century theorizing about the history of the arts: the fear that poetry had already exhausted itself, that there was nothing left for the new poet to do. The injunction laid upon each succeeding generation of artists to be "original," i.e., different from the poets who have come before them, leaves them nothing to do but refine, polish, and finally trivialize the grand truths and bold metaphors of bards who were lucky enough to have lived when time was young and society heroic. Each culture progresses, it was assumed, through a similar life cycle; first a primitive, or Iron Age, when savage vigor predominates; then a Golden Age, where strength and sweetness are in perfect balance; then a Silver Age, of more polish than energy; and finally an age of decadence, imitation, and ultimately silence. Whether or not the arts could ever hope to revive in a place where they had once declined, no one knew, though most theorists were inclined to be pessimistic. Indeed, one of the reasons for the interest English writers of the era had taken in America's possible cultural flowering lay in their fear that the genius of English literature had exhausted itself in the mother country, and that a new Renaissance, if it ever occurred, would need virgin soil.

But by the 1830s it had become apparent that the predictions of the cultural historians had been wrong on both counts: the arts had *not* taken root in America, and in England they had gloriously revived. The great English Romantic writers had struggled with the same creative anxieties their American counterparts faced; they had, in addition, to overcome the dejection created by the defeat of their political hopes. Yet somehow in the midst of these blighting forces they had still managed to create a poetry of such originality and power that Emerson, despite his lifelong distaste for Wordsworth's "slipshod newspaper style," was led to rank Wordsworth above even Milton in his private poetic pantheon.

The great Romantics had broken out of the eighteenth-century

impasse partly by discovering new *materia poetica* in the forms
of external nature and in the unexplored complexities of the
human mind. Wordsworth, late in life, recalled that a sudden
epiphany he had experienced during a walk one evening when he
was about fourteen had helped to give him courage to pursue a
poetic career. The sight of oak boughs gradually turning black
against a sunset sky made him aware of "the infinite variety of
natural appearances which had been unnoticed by the poets of
any age or country" and left him resolving "to supply, in some
degree, the deficiency."[20]

Wordsworth dictated this note to Isabella Fenwick in 1843; it
is remarkable how closely it resembles Emerson's own advice to
the young men of Dartmouth in the address "Literary Ethics"
(1838), a later and milder version of *The American Scholar*.
"Whilst I read the poets, I think that nothing new can be said
about morning and evening," Emerson said.

> But go into the forest, you shall find all new and unattempted.
> The honking of the wild geese flying by night; the thin note of
> the companionable titmouse, in the winter day; the fall of
> swarms of flies, in autumn, from combats high in the air, pat-
> tering down on the leaves like rain; the angry hiss of the wood-
> birds; the pine throwing out its pollen for the benefit of the
> next century; the turpentine exuding from the tree;—and, in-
> deed, any vegetation; any animation; any and all, are alike un-
> attempted.

This little set piece, designed to function both as thesis and illustration, represents a technique and subject matter Emerson was
largely content to leave to younger writers like Thoreau. But that
he even advocated such a stratagem for overcoming creative paralysis shows how far Emerson had come from the Neoclassical
notions of decorum that had dominated his youth and had led (at
first) to his puzzled and hostile response to Wordsworth's poetry, whose "direct pragmatical analysis of objects" struck him as
ludicrous and perverse. The great poets of the past touched natural objects gently, as illustration or ornament; Wordsworth, he
complained, "mauls the moon & the waters & the bulrushes as
his main business."

In part Emerson's change of opinion may merely reflect the

change in literary fashion—a change that Wordsworth, of course, had largely been responsible for bringing about. The notion that it was the business of poetry to devote itself to describing "the infinite variety of natural appearances," which would have seemed incredible to Dr. Johnson, had by the mid-thirties swept the field so completely that it was in danger of becoming a new cliché. (As Lowell complained, things were getting so bad that he expected any day to find John Smith taking out a legal advertisement in the paper to announce "that he is not the J.S. who saw a cow-lily on Thursday last, as he never saw one in his life, would not see one if he could, and is prepared to prove an alibi on the day in question."[21]) But there were obvious reasons why the doctrine should have appealed to an American writer. *Our* "natural appearances" were indisputably untouched. "Nature," in America, is something quite different from the humanized, history-ridden landscape of Europe. In its emptiness and grandeur, the American landscape offers the contemplating mind an experience of sheer otherness that even the wildest of European scenes can scarcely afford. As Bryant put it in *The Prairies*, the beauty and strangeness of the landscape make the onlooker feel that he is seeing the earth as it must have appeared before the Fall.

But Bryant's own verse provided the best proof that new poetic material was not in itself a sufficient guarantee of originality. The very poems in which Bryant himself proclaims the imaginatively stimulating virtues of the American landscape are almost embarrassingly dependent upon *Tintern Abbey* for every other detail of their construction. As the journal source of the passage makes clear, Bryant was one of the artists Emerson had in mind when he complained, in "Literary Ethics," that the chief characteristic of American artistic effort seemed to be "a certain grace without grandeur, and itself not new but derivative;—a vase of fair outline, but empty."

If Emerson had come to respect Wordsworth's fidelity to natural fact, then, he did so less for its power of generating poetic raw material than for its value as the visible sign of an inward grace far more important than copiousness, more important even than originality, since originality depends upon it. In the journal for

1838 there is the telegraphic observation: "How much self reliance it implies to write a true description of anything. For example Wordsworth's picture of skating; that leaning back on your heels & stopping in mid-career. So simple a fact no common man would have trusted himself to detach as a thought."

We meet again that complex and shifty little noun "self-reliance" (the one thing the American common reader, if he still exists, is likely to associate with Emerson's name), but in an odd context. If most people were asked to define "self-reliance" they would probably come up with something that combined the notions of independence, resourcefulness, and courage in adversity. It is not immediately apparent why these virtues should be necessary to a writer of *descriptions*. True, it requires a certain amount of fortitude to resist clichés, but something more than that seems to be meant; Wordsworth is praised for the violence which allows him to rupture the smooth stream of experience, detach a small fragment, and present it as an object of contemplation to the intellect.

"Detach" is another odd word. Detach the fragment from what? From the deadly continuity of sense impressions that Emerson describes in "Experience"? There, of the lethargy that makes us glide like ghosts through our own existence, he complains: "Sleep lingers all our lifetime about our eyes, as night hovers all day in the boughs of the fir-tree. All things swim and glitter. Our life is not so much threatened as our perception." Again, in "Demonology," he writes: "We live embosomed in sounds we do not hear, scents we do not smell, spectacles we see not, and by innumerable impressions so softly laid on that though important we do not discover them until our attention is called to them." To awaken the mind from this sleep can indeed seem a heroic task, and in praising Wordsworth for attempting it Emerson places himself in a tradition that goes back to Coleridge's account of the purpose of Wordsworth's share of the *Lyrical Ballads*:

> Mr. Wordsworth . . . was to propose to himself as his object, to give the charm of novelty to things of every day, and to excite a feeling analogous to the supernatural, by awakening the mind's attention from the lethargy of custom, and directing it to the

loveliness and the wonders of the world before us; an inexhaustible treasure, but for which, in consequence of the film of familiarity and selfish solicitude we have eyes, yet see not, ears that hear not, and hearts that neither feel nor understand.[22]

Coleridge, by the Biblical allusion in his final words—which likens the ordinary inattentiveness produced by the "film of familiarity and selfish solicitude" of men to the self-destructive blindness of the children of Israel—indicates how seriously he took Wordsworth's project of freshening perception. To see the loveliness of the ordinary world can be a religious act, one that leaves us, as Emerson put it, "glad to the brink of fear."

In Coleridge's account, poetry achieves this purging of vision by stripping away a covering film. But Emerson had just as frequently experienced the revivifying power of literature as a *clothing* of perception with a glory not its own:

> We go musing into the vault of day & night, no star shines no muse descends, the stars are but white points, the roses but brick colored leaves, & frogs pipe, mice cheep, & waggons creak along the road. We return to the house and take up Plato or Augustin & read a page or two, & lo! the air swarms with life, the front of heaven is full of fiery shapes; secrets of magnanimity & grandeur invite us on every hand.

This sudden influx of power is what constitutes "our debt to Literature," he concludes. But how can we prevent this indebtedness from becoming bankruptcy? If it is true that we can see only what we make, or what we are, and if experience teaches us that we can often see only what past writers have trained us to see, then even our apparently spontaneous perceptions become suspect, as do the "selves" they seem to emanate from. "Now shall we say that only the first men were well alive, and the existing generation is invalidated and degenerate? is all literature eavesdropping, and all art Chinese imitation? our life a custom, and our body borrowed, like a beggar's dinner, from a hundred charities?"

Not entirely. Wordsworth's example suggests that a man with the courage of his own narcissism can find a way to traffic with the wealth of past literature and still keep his identity, that small lump of individual capital that Emerson, following Sampson Reed, called the *peculium* (after the word used in Roman law to designate the sum granted by a father to his son, or a master to his slave, to keep and control).[23] Emerson did not have access to the whole text of *The Prelude* when he wrote "Spiritual Laws"; but his account of consciousness there might almost have been invented to describe Wordsworth's technique in that poem—the willingness to let apparently insignificant but strangely charged memories occupy the mind until, under the probing of a later, more analytic mind, they yield their significance.

> A man is a method, a progressive arrangement; a selecting principle, gathering his like to him, wherever he goes. He takes only his own, out of the multiplicity that sweeps and circles round him. He is like one of the booms which are set out from the shore on rivers to catch drift-wood, or like the loadstone amongst splinters of steel.
>
> Those facts, words, persons which dwell in his memory without his being able to say why, remain, because they have a relation to him not less real for being as yet unapprehended. They are symbols of value to him, as they can interpret parts of his consciousness which he would vainly seek words for in the conventional images of books and other minds.

Wordsworth's "self-reliance" consists in his willingness to trust his own instincts; what the mind italicizes must be important, even if the reasons for its importance are not immediately apparent. And so he offers an ordinary experience—the distortion of perception caused by a momentary loss of equilibrium—as a symbol of the uncanny moments when there is an interchange of power between the mind and the world it half creates and half perceives:

> Not seldom from the uproar I retired
> Into a silent bay or sportively
> Glanc'd sideway, leaving the tumultuous throng
> To cut across the image of a star
> That gleam'd upon the ice: and oftentimes
> When we had given our bodies to the wind,
> And all the shadowy banks on either side

Came sweeping through the darkness spinning still
The rapid line of motion, then at once
Have I reclining back upon my heels
Stopp'd short: yet still the solitary cliffs
Wheel'd by me even as if the earth had roll'd
With visible motion her diurnal round!
Behind me did they stretch in solemn train
Feebler and feebler, and I stood and watch'd
Till all was tranquil as a summer sea.[24]

Emerson probably encountered these lines in *The Friend*, where they were first published; their insistence upon the possibility of ecstasy in unremarkable surroundings may have influenced such widely admired sentences as the "bare common" passage in the first chapter of *Nature*. Yet the more one studies the Wordsworth lines, the more one suspects that they appealed to Emerson not only as a kind of trophy won by self-reliance, but as an allegory of its mode of operation. The boy who leaves his companions, gives up the pleasures of the chase by his sudden stop, is repaid by an uncanny or sublime moment in which the massive cliffs appear momentarily agitated; the Not-Me moves in response to a power emanating entirely from the Me, who then has the pleasure of simultaneously perceiving the effect it is creating.

This seductive reversal of the "normal" relationship (Emerson would say the "fallen" relationship) between the individual consciousness and the external world sounds, in one way, like a foretaste of the redemption promised at the end of *Nature*, where we were told that "Nature is not fixed, but fluid. Spirit alters, molds, makes it. The immobility or bruteness of nature, is the absence of spirit; to pure spirit, it is fluid, it is volatile, it is obedient." The "otherness" of nature is an illusion, which will vanish as soon as the perceiving mind recognizes that "All that you call the world is the shadow of that substance which you are, the perpetual creation of the powers of thought. . . ."

This startling "transfer of the world into the consciousness" is, as Stephen Whicher rightly observes, the "vision that charges his three challenges of the 1830's—*Nature, The American Scholar,* the Divinity School *Address*—with their immense store of force."[25] In *Nature* the transfer is accomplished with some violence to commonsense perceptions of "reality," perhaps, but with no real cruelty to the transferred objects, since the objects of the phenomenal world do not occupy the same ontological level as the human consciousness, and may indeed be grateful for the translation that liberates them into full intelligibility. Emerson remarks at one point that in certain moods all animals remind him of enchanted beings in fairy tales, waiting for their destined human deliverer; in another place he says that the very stars in heaven long to "republish themselves in more delicate form than that they occupy."

But can this transfer of the world into the consciousness take place if the Not-Me assumes the shape, not of sensible objects, but of a prior *text?* After Oedipus solved the riddle of the Sphinx, he still had to contend with Laius, who was not so easily disposed of. The objects of the natural world may thank us for our translating zeal, but no prior text wishes to be reduced to the status of brute prefiguration. When such a reduction does occur—as in the "hermeneutical fiat" that turned the Torah of the Jews into the Old Testament of the Christians—it cannot be accomplished without violence.[26] For a prior *text* is the product of a consciousness exactly as central to itself as ours is to us, and what it demands from us is not interpretation but submission. If it is, from our point of view, a part of the Not-Me, it is nonetheless a Not-Me with a voice, a Not-Me that *speaks,* and—what is worst of all—says precisely those things I wished to say, was about to say.

At times these voices *ab extra* can serve to reinforce a wavering conviction in the face of timidity or prudential objections, and then Emerson can compose a little hymn of praise "To him who said it before": "And thou good ancient brother, who to ancient nations, to earlier modes of life & politics & religion, didst utter this my perception of today, I greet thee with reverence. . . ." But this idealizing view of belatedness is as rare as the flowery language in which it is couched. The curt saying of Aelius Donatus he copied into his journal a few months later is closer to his habitual sentiment: *Pereant qui ante nos nostra dixerunt.*

Emerson gives the reason for his resentment in the central aphorism of *The American Scholar:* "Genius is always sufficiently the enemy of genius by over-influence." The inspiring author entering the world finds that the great tycoons who have come before him have monopolized the market *and* the means of production; there is nothing left for him to do but take a menial position as a clerk in a thriving firm: "The English dramatic poets have Shakespearized now for two hundred years." It is enough to turn the meekest reader into an anarchist. "One would rather be 'A pagan, suckled in a creed outworn,' than to be defrauded of his manly right in coming into nature and finding not names and places, not land and professions, but even virtue and truth foreclosed and monopolized."

In the late essay "Quotation and Originality" Emerson considers the melancholy conclusions to which a study of literary history is likely to drive one. "Our debt to tradition through reading and conversation is so massive, our protest or private addition so rare and insignificant . . . that, in a large sense, one would say there is no pure originality. All minds quote." For a moment he confesses to discouragement as he contemplates the spectacle. "There is something mortifying in this perpetual circle. This extreme economy argues a very small capital of invention." Does this mean that there is nothing left for us to do but translate or imitate, no posture left for us but the extravagant humility toward the ancients which Chaucer, for instance, expresses at the end of his *Troilus and Criseyde*?

> But litel book, no makyng thou n'envye,
> But subgit be to alle poesye,
> And kis the steppes, wher as thou seest pace
> Virgile, Ovide, Omer, Lucan, and Stace.[27]

Not necessarily. Emerson suggests a different way of regarding the matter, one more appropriate to the cheerfully capitalistic spirit of the American freeman. "This vast mental indebtedness has every variety that pecuniary debt has,—every variety of merit. The capitalist of either kind is as hungry to lend as the consumer to borrow; and the transaction no more indicates intellectual turpitude in the borrower than the simple fact of debt involves bankruptcy." Emerson has observed that, if we need past literature, it also needs us. A book only "exists" in the consciousness of each reader as he is reading; if it fails to find new readers, it dies. This fact alters the balance of power between text and reader considerably; it means that tradition is less like a landed estate that we may, if we are lucky, inherit than like a lump of capital we can, if we are enterprising, learn to manipulate.

But we still need to be told how we are to go about becoming independent entrepreneurs, using our small *peculia* to gain control of vast sums of literary wealth. In *The American Scholar* Emerson says firmly that "undoubtedly there is a right way of reading"—but his declaration of faith necessarily implies that there are wrong ways of reading as well, perhaps more wrong ways than right ones. We need some understanding of the kinds of reading there are, some understanding of the instinctual dynamics of the reading process, before we can understand how to prescribe the cure for creative paralysis.

Emerson was uniquely suited for this task, since he was both a passionate reader and a cool analyst of his own responses. Very early in life he came to recognize that the encounter between reader and text was as charged with intensities of love and hatred as any other intimate relationship. Because reading itself was for him both a chief source of gratification and a chief avenue of escape, a "world elsewhere" into which he could retreat, he made the discovery that all the phenomena of imaginative projection whose operations the Romantic poets loved to trace in the mind's relationship to the landscape could be discovered as well in the mind's relationship to texts. "We attach in our kindly hours a life to every thing around us," he once observed. "What man of feeling ever passed from school without personifying his tenses, loving one aorist & hating another?" But he was also aware that the process worked (or seemed to work) the other way as well, that written texts could "people the mind with forms sublime or fair" with the same sort of "extrinsic passion" Wordsworth found in Nature's dealing with the growing boy.[28]

This influx from without was far more disturbing, since it called into question the very notion of individual identity. One can see Emerson worrying about this problem in a journal passage written as early as March 1834—two years, that is, before he completed the first sections of *Nature*.

> The subject that needs most to be/presented/developed is the principle of Self reliance, what it is, what is not it, what it requires, how it teaches us to regard our friends. It is true that there is a faith wholly a man's own, the solitary inmate of his own breast, which the faiths of all mankind cannot shake, & which they cannot confirm. But at the same time useful, how indispensable has been the ministry of our friends to us, our teachers—the living & the dead.

This is musing rather than exposition, yet even in this sketchy meditation we can discern the shapes of the opponents—Tuition and Intuition—whose warfare he was to investigate with such consuming interest for the rest of his career. To say "trust thyself," as he eventually will in the essay "Self-Reliance," not only creates some obvious ethical dilemmas (suppose our "friends" and our inner promptings are radically at odds?); it also raises some even more perplexing psychological questions. What do we mean by a "self," anyway? How do we acquire a sense of self, if a great part of what we think of as constituting our selves is derived—by imitation, incorporation, distortion, or even outright reversal—from the people or the texts that surround us? Is there anything we can call wholly our own, and upon which we can base opposition, when opposition is necessary, to the world of other selves? As Emerson observed, it is not possible to inquire into the reason for self-trust without raising the question: "Who is the Trustee?"

Becoming a self is no easier in literature than it is in life. The developing Reading Ego (as Freud might have called it) endures as many threatening vicissitudes as the real one. Our earliest kind of reading may seem unambivalent, purely gratifying; in the sentences from "Quotation and Originality" cited in an earlier chapter Emerson compares this sort of reading to an infant's sucking at the breast. We never outgrow our capacity for this kind of reading (indeed, most of our reading hours most of our lives are spent in this pleasant form of dissipation, as Emerson, an inveterate book browser, well knew), but if we never acquire a talent for any other kind of reading we remain in a state of dependence in which the question of original creation can hardly arise. "In every kind of parasite, when Nature has finished an aphis, a teredo, or a vampire bat,—an excellent sucking-pipe to tap another animal, or a mistletoe or dodder among plants,—the self-supplying organs wither and dwindle, as being superfluous." A reader who never progresses beyond the oral stage of literary assimilation matures—if we can use the word—into one of the "restorers of readings, the emendators, the bibliomaniacs of all degrees" dismissed with such contempt at the opening of *The American Scholar.*

If Emerson were really writing about scholarship, it would be hard to defend him from the charge of callowness here; but, as O. W. Firkins remarked long ago, the title of the address is a "double misnomer,"[29] since what Emerson is really concerned with has nothing to do with scholarship and is not restricted to America. He is concerned to describe the kinds of reading (and the dangers attendant upon those kinds) practiced by potential creators: American poets, not American scholars. Such readers will be far more selective than the omnivorous infants of the first stage, who can be pleased with anything in print—a history of Washington's campaigns, a Life of Brant. Only certain books, and only certain passages in those books, will be interesting to potential poets. But the force of these passages, their parental or paternal authority, will be immediate and overwhelming. They aim to "occupy" us, and demand nothing short of "an abdication of all our past & present empire."

A temporary surrender to such invasions is both inevitable and necessary; "for good reading, there must be, of course, a yielding, sometimes entire, but always some yielding to the book." If, however, this posture of surrender is maintained too long, if the mind remains content to "receive always from another mind its truth, though it were in torrents of light," then a "fatal disservice" is done. The reader may not be reduced quite to the status of parasite, but his power of independent creation will have been taken away. So powerful is the impress of the "father's" mind, so deeply is his way of seeing and saying internalized, that even the apparently spontaneous gestures of the "son" will compulsively repeat his style and manner. And this, in Emerson's view, was what had happened to American poets. "Our poetry," he once said, "reminds me of the catbird.... Very sweet & musical! very various! fine execution!... *not a note is his own,* except at last, *miow miow.*"

There have been ages in which imitation was a respectable form of both literary and spiritual activity, but Emerson's was not one of them. If a single theme unites the essays and addresses of this period of challenge (from *The American Scholar* through *Essays: First Series*), it is the insistence, first announced here in *The American Scholar,* that "the one thing in the world, of value, is the active soul." *Active* means *creative,* and *creative* means *original;* hence anything purely or merely repetitive belongs to the death instinct, and "imitation is suicide." Emerson is as ferocious as Blake in insisting that the one division in the universe that matters is the division between Prolific and Devourer, between whatever fans and whatever seeks to extinguish that central spark of energy upon which all life depends.

This view of things raises some genuinely disturbing questions, as essays like "Self-Reliance" and "Circles" will make abundantly clear. I do not agree with Winters that Emerson in those essays is advocating (intentionally or unintentionally) incest, arson, or murder, but Winters is perfectly right to raise the question, since the realignment of values Emerson insists is necessary confounds traditional ethical categories and raises the specter of moral anarchy. Here, since Emerson is talking only of that milder form of disorder a self-reliant reader creates in the midst of literary tradition, the specter he raises is not quite so terrifying—that of the self-indulgent undergraduate, say, who uses aphorisms like "Books are for the scholar's idle times" as an excuse to cut class on sunny days, or cites Emerson's advice to reject even from Plato and Shakespeare all but the "authentic utterances of the oracle" as a justification for skipping anything he finds tedious.

Allowances should be made for Emerson's rhetoric here; parts of *The American Scholar* might aptly be subtitled "The Bored Student's Revenge." That he had not been very happy during his college days is clear from the analogy he once chose to express his sense of the stupendous inefficiency of experience as a producer of wisdom. "Is not life a puny unprofitable discipline whose direct advantage may be fairly represented by the direct education that is got at Harvard College? As is the real learning gained there, such is the proportion of the lesson in life." If Emerson's own encounter with the institutional guardians of tradition had been more satisfying, he might not have been so quick to list "colleges" among the inevitable enemies of "Man Thinking," or to compare scholars whose only source of inspiration is "the printed page" to starving wretches who have tried to sustain life on "boiled grass and the broth of shoes."

But there is more than insouciance in his derogation of tradition. To place the supreme value on the active *principle* in the soul—rather than on any of the products of its activity—radically alters one's attitude toward any fixed form the creative impulse has produced. The assets of the past are only valuable if they are liquid, convertible by the "active soul" into funding for new production, turned into a form of portable property. "The scholar is that man who must take up into himself all the ability of the time, all the contributions of the past, all the hopes of the future."

In the early portions of the address Emerson is less concerned to explain the mechanism of conversion than to lure his auditors with a sense of the vast profits to be realized from the venture. Become an independent entrepreneur, he suggests, and the "torrents of light" that once threatened to blast you with their excess will be found instead to be emanating from you: "When the mind is braced by labor and invention, the page of whatever book we read becomes luminous with manifold allusion." From this state of affluence the mighty figures who once intimidated us appear as humble suitors for our approval. "We then see, what is always true, that as the seer's hour of vision is short and rare among heavy days and months, so is its record, perchance, the least part of his volume. The discerning will read, in his Plato or Shakespeare, only that least part,—only the authentic utterances of the oracle;—all the rest he rejects, were it never so many times Plato's and Shakespeare's."

This promise certainly sounds enticing, yet an acute listener might wonder whether Emerson's hopeful advice is not in danger of dissolving, upon closer inspection, into the melancholy but familiar truth that in this life only the rich get richer. One must, he says, already *be* an inventor to read well.

But there may be a way out of this circular trap. If we look closely at the four paragraphs beginning with the one that contains the aphorism about the dangers of overinfluence and ending with the one counseling rejection of "inauthentic" portions of Plato and Shakespeare, we will see that they contain not two, but three models of the reading process. In addition to the depressive vision that sees all wealth vested in the past and the manic one that sees all wealth vested in the self, there lies a more balanced view, symbolized by a pair of proverbs that seem to imply reciprocal exchange. "A fig tree, looking on a fig tree, becometh fruitful," and "He that would bring home the wealth of the Indies, must carry out the wealth of the Indies." It is true that the fertilizing or capitalizing power must still begin on one side or the other, but text and reader are now implicitly equal in size and strength, less like father and son than like Narcissus and his reflection.

For genuine reading, after all, is always a form of self-recognition. In an early journal Emerson had written: "What can we see, read, acquire, but ourselves? Cousin is a thousand books to a thousand persons. Take the book, my friend, & read your eyes out; you will never find there what I find." He returned to the same theme early in 1837, when a traveler's account of a South Sea Islander suggested an analogy for one aspect of aesthetic psychology:

> It occurred last night in groping after the elements of that pleasure we derive from literary compositions, that it is like the pleasure which the prince LeBoo received from seeing himself for the first time in a mirror,—a mysterious & delightful surprise. A poem, a sentence causes us to see ourselves. I be & I see my being, at the same time.

But this mysterious and delightful surprise is potentially dangerous, since it tempts the reader to remain, like Narcissus, perpetually fixed in a communion that starves by oversatisfying. Emerson's chief contribution to the psychology of influence anxiety lies in his recognition that in our wrestling matches with the mighty dead, our greatest enemy is not his strength, nor even our weakness, but our own omnivorous narcissism:

> Who forbade you to create? Fear. & who made fear? Sin; Inaction; Ignorance. What is this astounding greatness of other men that they should be as God to you? Why, it is two things. First, your littleness which makes them seem so large; & second, your identity with them which makes them delightful to you as the colossal portrait of yourself.

This curious emotion, in which self-aggrandizement expresses itself in self-abasement, is the secret of the power by which the great writers of the past hold us in thrall—and, if it comes to that, is the secret of the mechanism that allows us to tolerate any kind of inferiority whatever. "What a testimony—full of grandeur, full of pity, is borne to the demands of his own nature, by the poor clansman, the poor partisan, who rejoices in the glory of his chief. . . . They sun themselves in the great man's light, and feel it to be their own element."

Fortunately, the emotions of joy and surprise are not the only ones that attend the moment of self-recognition. There is also a mixture of the feeling Emerson calls "awe" and associates with the uncanny and the daemonic. It is not merely my surprise that a man who lived two hundred, or two thousand, years ago says something that "lies close to my own soul," something I myself was on the verge of saying. That can be easily enough explained by "the philosophical doctrine of the identity of all minds." No, the peculiar shudder that accompanies our pleasure in the portions of a text that speak to us with authority is caused by the fact that the precursor poet appears to know *more* about us than we knew about ourselves, or at least recognized consciously. "Other men are the lenses through which we read our own minds." Our "selves," upon closer analysis, are at least double: there is the small, conscious ego, accessible to introspection; and there is the much larger entity upon which that ego rests. "A man finds out that there is somewhat in him that knows more than he does,"

Emerson noted in his journal. "Then he comes presently to the curious question, who's who? which of these two is really me? the one that knows more, or the one that knows less? the little fellow, or the big fellow?"

That question might be easier to answer if we knew exactly what "the big fellow" contained, what his limits were. And that is really the question Emerson is attempting to answer in the portions of the address that purport to consider what he calls the "influences" on the scholar.

The first of these sections, devoted to considering the influence of "nature," simply repeats the conclusions of Emerson's first book: the natural world itself is like a vast unconscious Self whose content we must gradually translate into intelligibility by study and insight. "So much of nature as he is ignorant of, so much of his mind does he not yet possess." The third of the sections, devoted to "action," treats the scholar's life in the world in much the same way. "The world,—this shadow of the soul, or *other me*,—lies wide around. Its attractions are the keys which unlock my thoughts and make me acquainted with myself." Like Oscar Wilde, who protested that he could not know what he thought till he heard what he said, Emerson's scholar is to treat himself like an unknown substance in chemistry, and his life as an experiment to discover its properties. In words that doubtless had a profound effect upon the listening Thoreau, Emerson encourages action as an alternate route to self-knowledge. "The preamble of thought, the transition through which it passes from the unconscious to the conscious, is action. Only so much do I know, as I have lived."

In the same way, reading—that encounter with the most important of the "influences" Emerson considers in this address—is also a form of "self-recovery." We discover in our reading portions of our self that would otherwise have remained subliminal; my attraction to certain texts, and to certain specific passages within those texts, is the key that unlocks my thoughts and makes me acquainted with myself. This in turn means that the precursor's text can be treated as if it were a part of *my* unconscious, into which I have repressed the thoughts that are now returning.

Or, as Emerson will ultimately put it in the beautifully audacious opening paragraph of "Self-Reliance": "In every work of genius we recognize our own rejected thoughts; they come back to us with a certain alienated majesty." The foreignness of past texts is an illusion merely, a fiction created by the "fear" that is the shrunken ego's form of self-distrust, a self-distrust that is only an inverted or parodic form of self-love. As soon as the ego, by stopping on its heels in mid-career, performs the exhilarating reversal that inverts the relative values of "outer" and "inner," then the prior text, instead of appearing an invader, demanding an abdication of all that we have believed, becomes rather like a sympathetic psychotherapist who helps us bring to consciousness repressed thoughts we had never dared avow openly, and hence to recover energy previously wasted in repression. And with this surplus charge of energy we can break free of the very texts that have so aided us.

> The books which once we valued more than the apple of the eye, we have quite exhausted. What is that but saying that we have come up with the point of view which the universal mind took through the eyes of one scribe; we have been that man, and have passed on. First one, then another, we drain all cisterns, and waxing greater by all these supplies, we crave a better and more abundant food. The man has never lived that can feed us ever.

Metaphors of oral aggression, which accompany the rebirth of desire, are always a sign of recovered self-confidence in Emerson, as is the volcano imagery he uses for his final refutation of the "mischievous notion" that genius could ever be foreclosed or monopolized by any past writer, however great:

> The human mind cannot be enshrined in a person who shall set a barrier on any side to this unbounded, unboundable empire. It is one central fire which flaming now out of the lips of Etna, lightens the capes of Sicily; and now out of the throat of Vesuvius, illuminates the towers and vineyards of Naples. It is one light which beams out of a thousand stars. It is one soul which animates all men.

The Divinity School Address

The central fire at the core of Emerson's soul was soon to be given another chance to erupt, and the aftereffects of that eruption were to have far-reaching consequences for the shape of his career and the contours of his thought. Indeed, they were to provide him with a new understanding of the dialectics of history and a radically new way of explaining the Fall of Man.

Not that any of this was apparent to him in advance. When Emerson accepted the invitation from the senior class of the Harvard Divinity School to deliver their graduation address, it seemed to him as if he were merely being asked to continue the discourse of the previous summer, explaining the decline of American piety as he previously had explained the nonexistence of American literature. Both stemmed, in his view, from a similar error: the "capital mistake of the infant man," as he would term it in the *Address*, "who seeks to be great by following the great, and hopes to derive advantages *from another.*" And both were to be remedied by the same variety of exhortation, one that would show the infant man that the "fountain of all good" was "in himself" and convince him "that he, equally with every man, is an inlet into the depths of Reason." That last image, recalling in a milder form the volcano / central-fire image of *The American Scholar*, shows how closely the two topics were related in Emerson's mind.

Many sentences from each oration could be transferred to the other without creating an incongruity. If I met the following sentences out of context—"Imitation cannot go above its model. The imitator dooms himself to hopeless mediocrity"—I would be inclined to guess that they came from *The American Scholar*. It comes as a bit of a shock to realize that they are actually from the Divinity School *Address*, and that the imitation Emerson is warning us against is not the imitation of Shakespeare but the imitation of Christ. Traditional or "historical" Christians, in Emerson's view, were making the same mistake made by the post-Shakespearean English dramatic poets, except that in the case of Christianity the mistake had lasted much longer and was much less forgivable. Poetic genius may enjoy the prospect of monopolizing inspiration; perhaps each great poet secretly hopes he will be the last, or at least that he will be so great that subsequent poets will be intimidated by him as he was intimidated by his own precursors. But Jesus, in Emerson's view, had come to preach against self-distrust, against all excessive reverence for the merely traditional. He had come to preach the divinity of man, not his own divinity. Hence the misinterpretation of his teachings is as perverse as if someone had attempted to twist the anarchic literary advice of *The American Scholar* into the Neoclassical pieties of the *Essay on Criticism*.

The result is a religion built on a radical contradiction, an entire culture founded on an intellectual mistake. As Emerson was to explain it in the central passage of the *Address*:

> Jesus Christ belonged to the true race of prophets. . . . Alone in all history he estimated the greatness of man. . . . He saw that God incarnates himself in man, and evermore goes forth anew to take possession of his world. He said, in this jubilee of sublime emotion, "I am divine. Through me, God acts; through me, speaks. Would you see God, see me.". . ." But what a distortion did his doctrine and memory suffer in the same, in the next, and the following ages! There is no doctrine of the Reason that will bear to be taught by the Understanding. The understanding caught this high chant from the poet's lips, and said, in the next age, "This was Jehovah come down out of heaven. I will kill you, if you say he was a man." The idioms of his language and the figures of his rhetoric have usurped the place of his truth; and churches are built not on his principles, but on his tropes.

There are two things to be observed about this passage: one, that it has not lost its power to shock; and two, that Emerson, when he delivered it, had no idea just how shocking he was in fact being. Although he later came to suspect that he must on some level have wanted to provoke the reaction he got, his immediate response to the storm of criticism that broke over his head after the *Address* was one of surprise.

He had, of course, intended a provocative attack on what he regarded as the current corruptions of preaching and religious life. Conrad Wright has shown that many sections of the *Address* reflect Emerson's own acute misery as the member of a congregation subjected to the wretched preaching of one Barzillai Frost.[30] And he felt free to mention in passing several topics of debate within Unitarian circles: the Lord's Supper, which Emerson was not alone in thinking an embarrassment in a religion generally hostile to symbolism and ritual; and the proper way of regarding Jesus' miracles, which Emerson thought were too frequently treated in ways ultimately degrading to Jesus himself. But though a discussion of these matters might identify him as a controversialist, it would hardly have been sufficient to brand him a heretic.

Indeed, as several writers have pointed out (both in Emerson's day and in ours), the theology of Emerson's *Address* does not differ in most important respects from the positions advanced by Channing in the famous Baltimore sermon, that central document of American Unitarianism. Channing had there reminded his hearers that liberal Christians looked upon the Scriptures as the record of God's *successive* revelations to mankind, growing in maturity as the human race progressed—"the dispensation of Moses, compared with that of Jesus, we consider as adapted to the childhood of the human race, a preparation for a nobler system, and chiefly useful now as serving to confirm and illustrate the Christian scriptures." And he urged his hearers to take upon themselves the burden of continuing the work of reform.

> To all who hear me I would say, with the Apostle, Prove all things, hold fast to that which is good. Do not, brethren, shrink from the duty of searching God's word for yourselves, through fear of human censure and denunciation. Do not think you may innocently follow the opinions which prevail around you, without investigation, on the ground that Christianity is now so purified from error as to need no laborious research.[31]

And searching God's words for oneself meant occasionally having to reinterpret not only the Old Testament but the New; even Jesus' own words occasionally require "translation." Channing points out that this liberty is something all Protestants must take—for if the orthodox Congregationalists really adhered, as they claimed to, to the literal sense of Scripture, how could they possibly avoid accepting the Catholic doctrine of Transubstantiation?

For Unitarians, of course, the passages most in need of interpreting away were the apparently Trinitarian ones. They did this by adapting from the "higher criticism" then flourishing in Germany the principle that texts cannot be understood apart from the traditions and styles of the peoples to whom they were originally addressed. Hence many of Jesus' claims to possess a divinity equal to that of the Father are to be understood as hyperboles; he had simply adopted the glowing, bold, and figurative style of the Hebrew Scriptures. When Jesus said "I and my Father are one," what he really meant, according to Andrews Norton, was "I am fully empowered to act as his representative."[32]

When Emerson attacked rituals like the Lord's Supper, then, he could legitimately see himself as continuing the work of reformation encouraged by Channing; when he "translated" the words of Jesus, and argued that the existing Christian churches were founded not on Jesus' principles, but on his tropes, he was practicing Biblical criticism in the style of Norton. Channing, closing his Baltimore sermon with an allusion to Ezekiel, had urged his audience to pray to God that "He will overturn, and overturn, and overturn the strongholds of spiritual usurpation, until HE shall come whose right it is to rule the minds of men; that the conspiracy of ages against the liberty of Christians may be brought to an end; that the servile assent so long yielded to human creeds may give place to honest and devout inquiry into the Scriptures. . . ."[33] Emerson recalled these words after composing a long and important journal passage (in 1834) attempting to work out for the first time some arguments that would later be used in the Divinity School *Address*. But the passage shows that Emerson was already carrying the principle of perpetual spiritual revolution to lengths Channing could hardly have sanctioned:

> They have said in churches in this age "Mere Morality." O God they know thee not who speak contemptuously of all that is grand. It is the distinction of Christianity, that it is moral. All that is personal in it is nought. When any one comes who

speaks with better insight into moral nature he will be the new gospel; miracle or not, inspired or uninspired, he will be the Christ.

Unitarians were willing to see history as containing successive waves of revelation. As the Mosaic dispensation was a vast improvement over paganism, so the Gospel of Jesus was a vast improvement over the Mosaic dispensation. But no Unitarian was willing to agree that Jesus' gospel might itself be superseded. When Channing urges a continuing reformation of the church he is not suggesting that anything be *added* to the New Testament. Like all Protestant reformers since Luther himself, he is claiming that the work of reform will carry believers back to the original sense of the gospels; that the church, purged of the last remnants of Papist corruption, will finally exist in the form Jesus originally intended.

Now in the Divinity School *Address* Emerson is traditional enough (or perhaps merely strategic enough) to claim to find support for his central belief that "the soul of man does not merely, as had long been taught, contain a spark or drop or breath or voice of God; it *is* God"[34] in Jesus' own teachings. But if Emerson is right, then we must say of Christianity what Whitman later said of Emersonianism: that it breeds the giant that destroys itself. For each newly incarnated Deity will have as much right to criticize the previous scriptures as Jesus had to criticize the ones he had inherited.

The consequences of this doctrine were put into practice as early as 1832, when Emerson preached his discourse on "The Lord's Supper" to his Boston congregation. Celebration of the communion ritual had long been something of an anomaly in a church that denied not only the doctrine of Transubstantiation but also the divinity of Jesus; in the Divinity School *Address* Emerson reminds his audience of newly approbated ministers that few practicing clergymen dare face a man of wit and energy with an invitation to this anachronistic rite. In 1832 his own discomfort with the ceremony had grown to such proportions that he informed his congregation that he could no longer bear celebrating it in its present form (a note by Edward Emerson tells us that Emerson had proposed doing away with the bread and wine altogether and celebrating the rite, if at all, as purely commemorative). And he preached a sermon to support his argument that Jesus had never intended to establish a permanent ritual. The sermon begins with a careful marshalling of historical and exegetical evidence, which Edward Emerson suggests was borrowed from Emerson's brother William; the latter had gone to study theology in Germany, but had found his faith so shaken by the ideas he encountered there that he had abandoned the ministry for the law. But these learned arguments do not get close to the real source of Emerson's intransigence. What that source was he makes clear only toward the end of the sermon, in a passage more shocking, in its quiet way, than anything in the later *Address*. His real reason for opposing the Lord's Supper was simple:

> This mode of commemorating Christ is not suitable to me. That is reason enough why I should abandon it. If I believed it was enjoined by Jesus on his disciples, and that he even contemplated making permanent this mode of commemoration, every way agreeable to an Eastern mind, and yet on trial was disagreeable to my own feelings, I should not adopt it. I should choose other ways which, as more effectual upon me, he would approve more.

William Hutchison, in his study of church reform in the New England Renaissance, remarks that a genuine reformer would be likely to make such a sensation the beginning rather than the end of his protest, and that from the point of view of such a reformer "Emerson's position could be thought a supine and even an irresponsible one."[35]

Hutchison's remark introduces an important distinction. I have been calling Emerson a reformer, but he would have rejected the label if it suggested that his zeal was directed at changing institutions rather than individual behavior. In his biography of Emerson Rusk dryly entitles his chapter on the Lord's Supper incident "Theses Nailed to the Church Door," but Emerson was very far from thinking himself a Luther. He declared himself perfectly content that the ritual he opposed should stand till the end of the world, so long as *he* were excused from celebrating it. If he ever thought of himself as a reformer, it was only in the sense implied by the remark he once made that the logical conclusion of the Reformation would be a state in which there were as many churches as there were believers: a church apiece. A similar conclusion about the nature of Protestantism eventually drove Orestes Brownson, once an enthusiastic Transcendentalist, into the arms of the Roman Catholic Church.

Emerson himself was not insensible to the charms of Catholicism, a religion that made tradition itself the arbiter of truth. His grim Puritan forebears would doubtless have been shocked, but on a visit to Baltimore in 1843 he went to hear Mass celebrated in the cathedral, and wrote to Margaret Fuller, in a burst of affection for the "dear old Church," that it was "dignified to come where the priest is nothing, & the people nothing, and an idea for once excludes these impertinences." In such a mood he could "detest the Unitarians and Martin Luther and all the parliament of Barebones" and sympathize with those dissatisfied Protestants who embraced the Roman faith.

But if the Roman Church possessed for Emerson all the attractions of Romance, it also suffered from that genre's chief deficiency: he was unable to believe that its doctrines, however beautiful, were *true*. In this he resembles the speaker of Stevens' *Owl's Clover*, who remarks that the Catholic "Heaven of Europe" is "empty, like a Schloss/ Abandoned because of taxes," and contrasts it with the only heaven for which he can feel genuine nostalgia, the Protestant one, described in highly Emersonian terms as the place where

> each man
> Through long cloud-cloister-porches walked alone
> Noble within perfecting solitude,
> Like a solitude of the sun, in which the mind
> Acquired transparence and beheld itself
> And beheld the source from which transparence came;
> . . . .
> The temple of the altar where each man
> Beheld the truth and knew it to be true.[36]

"God offers to every mind the choice between truth and repose," Emerson asserted flatly in "Intellect." "Take which you please,—you can never have both." And if the pursuit of truth carried him beyond the last frontiers of institutional Christianity, he could legitimately claim to be merely carrying on the antitraditional tradition established by Jesus himself:

> He felt respect for Moses and the prophets; but no unfit tenderness at postponing their initial revelations to the hour and man that now is; to the eternal revelation in the heart. Thus he was a true man. Having seen that the law in us is commanding, he would not suffer it to be commanded. Boldly, with hand, and heart, and life, he declared it was God. Thus is he, as I think, the only soul in history who has appreciated the worth of a man.

But if Emerson is happy to agree that Jesus is so far the best prophet we have had, he is not willing to see him as the last. Any religion that declares its canon of sacred books closed, that places all contact with the Divine in the past, dooms itself to the same variety of death-by-entropy that eventually afflicts a literary tradition built on the premise that nature and Homer are the same. And this, in Emerson's view, was what was happening to contemporary religion. "Men have come to speak of the revelation as somewhat long ago given and done, as if God were dead."

He knows that his own attempt to show "that God is, not was; that He speaketh, not spake" will sound to some like madness, but he could advance the same defense of his theology that he later advanced for his theory of literature. It was not, he insisted, in a "bragging spirit" that he argued that "the reader of Shakespeare is also a Shakespeare or he could find no joy in the page." No, this manner of considering the mighty dead "leaves in the pupil as much veneration for Shakespeare & Homer as before; only they are made still alive, their power still accessible & not a sepulchre to him." The last sentence, recalling as it does the opening sentences of *Nature*, suggests why Emerson thought his radical insistence on the wealth of the Self was necessary. The pious spirits in the church or academy who hope to make contact with the power of the past by bringing tribute to its sepulchers will inevitably discover that the spirit they wish to honor has departed; like the women who come to the tomb of Jesus on Easter morning, they will receive only the news: "He is not here: for he is risen."[37]

The women received this news as a joyful revelation, and Emerson suggests that we do the same, looking forward to the New Teacher (or, as he was later to call him, the Central Man) instead of back regretfully at the past. For really, was there not much for a New Teacher to accomplish? We need a new faith that can transcend, or subsume, the destructive skepticisms of the modern world—textual criticism, empirical science, and all the rest—not one that merely tries to ignore them or explain them away in apologias that deceive no one and satisfy no one. The old theme of the *translatio studii*, the gradual Westering of imagination, which had led Bishop Berkeley to hope for such great things from American bards, is invoked by Emerson in a final, audacious prayer for a *prophet* of our own:

> I look for the hour when that supreme Beauty, which ravished the souls of those Eastern men, and chiefly of those Hebrews, and through their lips spoke oracles to all time, shall speak in the West also. The Hebrew and Greek Scriptures contain immortal sentences, that have been bread of life to millions. But they have no epical integrity; are fragmentary; are not shown in their order to the intellect. I look for the new Teacher, that shall follow so far those shining laws, that he shall see them come full circle; shall see their rounding complete grace; shall see the world to be the mirror of the soul; shall see the identity of the law of gravitation with purity of heart; and shall show that Ought, that Duty, is one thing with Science, with Beauty, and with Joy.

The Universal Grudge: "The Protest" and "Circles"

It is not entirely clear what response, if any, Emerson was expecting to his *Address*. By mid-October, when the controversy had been raging for three months, he could declare proudly and defiantly in his journal that "he saw well enough before he spoke the consequence of his speaking, that up there in his silent study by his dim lamp he fore-heard this Babel of outcries." But the evidence from journals and letters closer to the event is more ambiguous, and suggests a blending of surprise and distress. Of course Emerson knew that he was being deliberately provocative when he entered the heated Unitarian controversy over the miracles of Jesus with declarations that "the word Miracle," as pronounced by contemporary Christian churches, is "Monster"—a judgment that resembles J. H. van den Berg's remark that a miracle in a Cartesian universe is nothing more than a "spoiled fact."[38] But Emerson had hurled bolts of defiance at conservative powers before and gotten away with it. As Perry Miller points out, much of *The American Scholar* would have struck a contemporary audience as a studied insult to the Harvard faculty before whom it was delivered—yet at the postlecture dinner Emerson heard himself flattered by his old idol, Edward Everett, and toasted by another man as "The Spirit of Concord" who "makes us all of one mind."[39]

But if Emerson anticipated a similar response to his Divinity School *Address*, he must have been rudely shocked; he had overnight become something much closer to a Spirit of Discord. An entry he made in his journal after he had attended the Phi Beta Kappa festivities of 1838 suggests how agitated he was at the reception he encountered there. "Yesterday at Φ.B.K. anniversary. Steady, steady.... The young people & the mature hint at odium, & aversion of faces to be presently encountered in society." Only four days earlier he had been savagely attacked in an article (by Andrews Norton, as Emerson discovered later) in the public newspaper. Emerson was discovering that it was one thing to attack Cicero or Locke; quite another to launch an assault on the tenets of revealed religion. "See how quickly the whole community is touched by an academical discourse on theism," he noted wonderingly in his journal. "At an imagined assault of a cardinal truth, the very mud boils." Touching the whole community with his eloquence had of course been one of Emerson's boyhood dreams; he had succeeded, but in a way he would hardly have chosen.

Emerson was not seriously worried about the "decorous & limitary" rage of the cultivated classes. But it was more difficult to remain calm "when the ignorant and the poor are aroused, when the unintelligent brute force that lies at the bottom of society is made to growl & mow." There is no evidence that Emerson was ever hooted in the public streets, as Alcott had been when another Boston newspaper, again quoting Norton, had described Alcott's *Conversations with Children on the Gospels* as "one third . . . absurd, one-third blasphemous, and one-third obscene."[40] Yet the experiences Emerson had were evidently unsettling enough to make him realize that he needed more than "nerve" to oppose the public rage. Only a man who had attained the "heights of magnanimity and religion," he decided, could treat it "godlike," as "a trifle of no concernment."

Had Emerson attained such heights? He apparently preserved his outward calm; his wife wrote to her sister: "I do not know that he has felt a moment's uneasiness on his own account."[41] But the journals tell a different story. Though Emerson had a permanent income from his first wife's estate, and hence did not face ruin even if his sudden unpopularity should end his budding career as a lecturer, he was still struck by the irrational power the controversy possessed to blacken his moods and disturb his equilibrium. "A man writes a book which displeases somebody who writes an angry paragraph about it in the next newspaper. That solitary paragraph whilst it stands unanswered seems the voice of the world. . . . What was yesterday a warm, convenient, hospitable world soliciting all the talents of all its children looks bleak & hostile & our native tendency to complete any view we take carries the imagination out at once to images of persecution, hatred, & want."

Emerson could laugh himself out of such exaggerated terrors easily enough. What was more difficult to endure was the sudden loss of that atmosphere of sympathy in which, he discovered, his powers unfolded most easily. Unlike Thoreau, who "did not feel himself except in opposition," Emerson throve best when he and his audiences were in harmony. His vision of "perfect eloquence," after all, was one in which the hearer "would lose the sense of dualism; of hearing from another; would cease to distinguish between the orator & himself; would have the sense only of high activity & progress." Sympathy was a "supporting atmosphere"; a climb into "this thin iced difficult Andes of reform" exposed a man to hatred so unsettling that, in spite of his best resolutions, he will find it difficult to keep from losing "his sweetness & his flesh."

Yet if Emerson was chagrined to discover previously unsuspected weaknesses in himself, he also was finding the experience profoundly instructive. The pattern of assertion-and-retreat he could trace in the whole affair was beginning to suggest some new explanations for that central mystery his first book had spent such effort attempting to unravel: the fallenness of the world. In *Nature* the chief sorrows of man seem to be his alienation from nature and the instability of his joy, afflictions Emerson accounted for in the complementary myths of *contraction* (the Orphic chants) and *dislocation* (the axis-of-vision passage). As Emerson shifts his attention from the natural to the social world, the chief evil men face seems to be the universal human preference for the familiar, the customary, the traditional, which manifests itself (as Emerson had discovered) in virulent opposition to reform. To account for the perplexing fact that in a world where each individual is "born sane" the society these individuals compose is a dismal affair, a poor-spirited thing that "desponds; sneers; serves; sits," that "talks from the senses and not from the soul," Emerson is forced to invent a new myth of the Fall, one that combines the Orphic poet's sense that the Fall results from some failure of outflowing energy with the axis-of-vision passage's insistence that our life manifests a bewildering alternation of fallen and unfallen states. This new myth, which we may call the myth of *ossification*, Emerson first introduces in a lecture of 1839 entitled "The Protest" and brings to final perfection in the essay "Circles."

"The Protest" was part of a course of lectures on "Human Life" that Emerson delivered in the winter of 1839–1840; Joel Porte is surely right to see in it a recasting of the events of the previous turbulent year.[42] In it Emerson asks: "What is the front the world always shows to the young spirit?" and immediately answers: "Strange to say, the Fall of Man." This fact of individual experience is echoed in the oldest traditions of every nation, which inevitably contain a "dark legend" about the "depravation of a once pure and happy society." Why do these legends exist? What do they signify? "What but this that it is an universal fact that man is always in his actual life lapsing from the commandments of the Soul?"

Yet the curious thing about Emerson's vision of these lapses is that he does not see them as the result of depravity so much as of a kind of lassitude. "There is somewhat infirm and retreating in every action; a pause of self-praise; a second thought. He has done well and he says I have done well and lo! this is the beginning of ill." It must seem at first to each generous youth who confronts the entrenched forces of conservatism with his schemes of reform as if his adversaries belong to a different species from himself; but if he attends to the motions of his own soul, he will realize that their rigid resistance to change is only the outward and visible counterpart of the emotions that beset his own soul when each sally of the spirit has exhausted itself. With advancing age this tendency to rest becomes something actively pernicious, and what was first a momentary lull in the outward flow of spirit becomes a formidable barrier opposing it. "This old age; this ossification of the heart; this fat in the brain; this degeneracy; is the Fall of Man." Against this petrifaction Emerson opposes the zeal that lies "lodged in the heart of Youth." Yet to be generally effective this power must not be confined to protesting one specific evil: slavery, private property, the oppression of women, domestic service. It must instead ripen into something Emerson calls, in a memorable phrase, a "deeper and universal grudge."

But with that phrase Emerson has moved beyond any description of recognizable political phenomena and on to something much more abstract: an attempt to identify the opposing principles whose interaction shapes the contours of social and political history. He has arrived, in fact, at something very like what Blake scholars call the Orc cycle—a vision of human history that sees it as a ceaseless dialectic generated by the opposing powers of order and energy. Emerson's version of this story is given its fullest exposition in one of his shortest and most explosive essays, "Circles."

All of the other essays in Emerson's first book of essays have titles that identify some specific entity or virtue as the focus of the essay's concern: the over-soul, spiritual laws, prudence, heroism. But the title of "Circles" suggests that Emerson wishes here to identify a peculiar pattern that manifests itself in every kind of human activity or speculation. If, as Emerson asserts in "History," the same human mind that wrote history must also read it—"The Sphinx must solve her own riddle"—then the pattern Emerson is at such pains to identify in "Circles" must be regarded as the second of his attempts to answer the riddle of a sphinx.

He goes out of his way, in the very first paragraph of the essay, to suggest that his interest, like the scientist's or speculative historian's, is only in accurate description, not in praise or condemnation. The first paragraph ends with the assertion that "our life is an apprenticeship to the truth, that around every circle another can be drawn; that there is no end in nature, but every end is a beginning; that there is always another dawn risen on mid-noon, and under every deep a lower deep opens." The final clauses of the sentence splice together Adam's joyous description of Raphael's approach with Satan's lament on Mt. Niphates; they constitute a sort of *Marriage of Heaven and Hell* on the level of the sentence. And, like Blake's little book, "Circles" deliberately confounds traditional ethical categories with its insistence that "nothing is secure but life, transition, the energizing spirit. No love can be bound by oath or covenant to secure it against a higher love. No truth so sublime but it may be trivial tomorrow in the light of new thoughts." And the conclusion inevitably following from such a premise? "People wish to be settled: only as far as they are unsettled, is there any hope for them."

Emerson's insistence upon the redemptive values of instability and the deadliness of consistency derive largely from his own recent experiences with the Unitarian establishment. These men had been in their own youth the liberal wing of New England Congregationalism; their behavior now led Emerson to the conclusion that there was something in the very essence of reforming zeal that inevitably generated, or rather declined into, its opposite. He gives expression to this centrally important notion in a paragraph close to the beginning of the essay:

> The life of man is a self-evolving circle, which, from a ring imperceptibly small, rushes on all sides outward to new and

larger circles. The extent to which this generation of circles, wheel without wheel will go, depends on the force or truth of the individual soul. For, it is the inert effort of each thought having formed itself into a circular wave of circumstance,—as, for instance, an empire, rules of an art, a local usage, a religious rite,—to heap itself on that ridge, and to solidify, and hem in the life. But if the soul is quick and strong, it bursts over that boundary on all sides, and expands another orbit on the great deep, which also runs up into a high wave, with attempt to stop and to bind.

The remainder of the essay may be regarded as an attempt to assess the implications of this vision for the individual and for society as a whole. These implications are indeed *unsettling*, to use the word Emerson prefers in the essay. Chief among them is the notion that no truth is permanent: the boldest speculation of one era becomes the reactionary obstruction of the next. Lockean empiricism had been a liberating philosophy once, but in clinging to it blindly now the Harvard Establishment was contributing to the backwardness of the university and the decline of the church.

The only way that the individual can avoid becoming transformed from a youthful Orc to an aging Urizen is by "preferring truth to his past apprehension of truth" (an idea to be explored even more fully in "Self-Reliance"). He must acquire the "intrepid conviction that his laws, his relations to society, his christianity, his world, may at any time be superseded and decease." He must learn the hard lesson that "there is no virtue which is final; all are initial. . . . The terror of reform is the discovery that we must cast away our virtues, or what we have always esteemed such, into the same pit that has consumed our grosser vices."

Is there any way, though, to distinguish genuine intrepidity from a mindless glorification of change for change's sake? Any way to distinguish a formula like "the virtues of society are the vices of the saint" from a thoroughgoing skepticism that ends in universal doubt? The very fact that we are able to pose the question should, Emerson insists, reassure us, for "this incessant movement and progression, which all things partake, could never become sensible to us, but by contrast to some principle of fixture or stability in the soul." If we were really nothing more than creatures of the flux, we would never know it; that we *are* aware of some ultimate fixture, some "flying Perfect" that all our generated circles are attempts to encompass, proves the existence of something unchanging at our centers.

What is the nature of this "principle of fixture?" Emerson is as chary of naming or defining it as the Hebrews were of pronouncing the name of God. The closest he will come to characterizing it is through analogy; the essay's final sentences list parodic forms—inverted analogies or resemblances—that tell us, at least, what this center is *like*. "Dreams and drunkenness, the use of opium and alcohol are the semblance and counterfeit of this oracular genius, and hence their dangerous attraction for men. For the like reason, they ask the aid of wild passions, as in gaming and war, to ape in some manner these flames and generosities of the heart." From this we can infer that the central principle, however fixed or stable, is neither rigid nor motionless; its stability is alive with all the energy of desire.

In a recent essay on Emerson Stanley Cavell draws a suggestive contrast between a European philosopher like Heidegger, for whom thinking is a kind of dwelling or inhabitation, and Emerson, for whom thinking is a kind of abandonment. "The idea of abandonment contains what the preacher in Emerson calls 'enthusiasm' or the New Englander in him calls 'forgetting ourselves' . . . together with what he calls leaving or relief or quitting or release or shunning or allowing or deliverance, which is freedom . . . , together further with something he means by trusting or suffering (as in the image of the traveler—the conscious intellect, the intellect alone—'who has lost his way, [throwing] his reins on the horse's neck, and [trusting] to the instinct of the animal to find his road' . . .)."[43] When Emerson says, "The way of life is wonderful: it is by abandonment," he is punning, for abandonment pertains in different ways to the center and to the circumference. The way of life requires abandonment *of* the ossified circumference of past thought in favor of the new truth rupturing and pushing beyond it; it requires abandonment *to* that central principle of life, higher than reason or even faith, which in its first protests against all forms of limitation "already tends outward with a vast force, and to immense and innumerable expansions."

"Self-Reliance"

To learn how to achieve this double abandonment we must turn to the best known of Emerson's essays, "Self-Reliance." If "Circles" was an attempt to discern the general laws governing human behavior, "Self-Reliance" is an attempt to formulate a code of conduct for the individual believer, to answer the question: "What shall *I* do to be saved?"

Emerson had always conceived of the principle of self-reliance as an answer to the problem of individual salvation; one of his earliest explorations of the topic, a sermon entitled "Trust Yourself," was preached as a commentary upon Matthew 16:26: "For what is a man profited, if he shall gain the whole world, and lose his own soul?" In it Emerson had used a passage from an early journal that already contains the essence of the later doctrine:

> Every man has his own voice, manner, eloquence, & just as much his own sort of love & grief & imagination & action. Let him scorn to imitate any being, let him scorn to be a secondary man, let him fully trust his own share of God's goodness, that correctly used it will lead him on to perfection which has no type yet in the Universe save only in the Divine Mind.

It was the gospel he had been sent that he might preach, the good news he had been chosen to proclaim. The topic was never far from his thoughts. In 1835, when he was chiding himself for his lack of literary productivity, listing things he felt were peculiarly his own, one of the topics was "the sublimity of Self-reliance." As his thought widened and matured, his conception of the principle grew likewise, until it came to signify everything praiseworthy in the universe. If the "universal grudge" was Emerson's term for the spirit behind every scheme of reform, self-reliance was the name he used to designate the means by which all schemes of reform were to be accomplished. "It is easy to see that a greater self-reliance must work a revolution in all the offices and relations of men," he argues in the essay, "in their religion; in their education; in their pursuits; their modes of living; their association; in their property; in their speculative views." (That Emerson conceived of self-reliance as a *revolutionary* principle is particularly important to remember now, when his attacks on "miscellaneous popular charities" are in danger of making him sound like the most reactionary politicians. The latter should ponder the implications of Emerson's closing remarks—that "the reliance on Property, including the reliance on governments which protect it, is the want of self-reliance" before rushing to claim Emerson as one of their own.) Every subject that had attracted Emerson's attention in the turbulent years just past—the imitativeness of American literature, the "terror of opinion" that made Americans moral cowards, the reliance upon property that engendered that terror, the futility of preaching that teaches the soul to look for help anywhere other than within itself, the necessity of training the soul to conceive of life as a perpetual process of abandonment—can all be treated under the general rubric of self-reliance. The essay as it stands is a kind of gigantic coda to the work of Emerson's decade of challenge. Some have found its very variousness distracting; Firkins, who concedes the essay's greatness, nevertheless complains that it lacks "tone"; there is in the essay "a singularly mixed effect of anthem, eclogue, sermon, and denunciation." Yet he admits that "no essay of Emerson contains so many phrases that are at the same time barbed and winged."[44]

In fact, the success of those phrases in establishing themselves as proverbial may be the greatest obstacle to the enjoyment of the contemporary reader, who may feel at first as though he is thumbing through a particularly worn copy of *Bartlett's Familiar Quotations*. Yet to the reader willing to look beyond the familiar phrases, attentive to the interplay of Emerson's many voices and to the startling redefinition of familiar terms those voices proclaim, the essay will shortly come to seem as strange and difficult as it really is.

It begins with a restatement of themes made familiar by *The American Scholar*: the self-reliant man who has the courage to make his own spontaneous impressions into universal symbols (as Wordsworth had done) will find himself triumphing over the tyranny of time. "Speak your latent conviction and it shall be the universal sense; for the inmost in due time becomes the outmost,—and our first thought is rendered back to us by the trumpets of the Last Judgment." Hence Emerson's First Commandment: "Trust thyself: every heart vibrates to that iron string." What Emerson means by self-trust is given to us, as usual, not by definition but by analogy: it is something like the pure self-centeredness of infancy, something again like the "nonchalance of boys who are sure of a dinner." It is action without self-consciousness, action without concern for (or even awareness of) consequences—the sort of thing Blake had in mind when he praised Jesus as one who "acted from impulse, not from rules."[45]

Unfortunately, this kind of self-trust is nearly impossible for a grown man to achieve; a grown man is "clapped into jail by his consciousness. As soon as he has once acted or spoken with eclat"—and Emerson is surely thinking here of his own experience after the Divinity School *Address*—"he is a committed person, watched by the sympathy or the hatred of hundreds whose affections must now enter into his account. There is no Lethe for this." The point is not that the man is incapable of telling the truth after once speaking with éclat; merely that he can never recapture that purer kind of innocence that consists in being *unaware* of the consequences. An orator who could somehow manage to free himself from this jail of self-consciousness, and "having observed, observe again from the same unaffected, unbiassed, unbribable, unaffrighted innocence," would make himself formidable; his opinions "would sink like darts into the ear of men, and put them in fear."

That Emerson is describing not himself but his possible hero, the figure he will later call the Central Man, is apparent from his use of the conditional mood; his own journals were there to remind him how far he was from his own ideal. One is inclined to suspect that his private chagrin is partly responsible for the uncharacteristic bitterness of the attack he now launches on the chief obstacle to self-trust. "Society everywhere is in conspiracy against the manhood of every one of its members. Society is a joint-stock company in which the members agree for the better securing of his bread to each shareholder, to surrender the liberty and culture of the eater." Hence Emerson's Second Commandment: "Whoso would be a man must be a nonconformist."

What follows this assertion is a violent and disturbing paragraph that seems to have been designed to contain something to offend everyone. Emerson begins by advocating, like Yeats, the casting out of all remorse. Later on in the essay he will define "prayer" as "the soliloquy of a beholding and jubilant soul"; he here advances the same startling conception of penitence: "Absolve you to yourself, and you shall have the suffrage of the world." From these sublime heights of self-reliance he grandly condescends to answer the objections of the "valued adviser" who used to importune him with the "dear old doctrines of the church. On my saying, What have I to do with the sacredness of traditions, if I live wholly from within? my friend suggested— 'But these impulses may be from below, not from above.' I replied, 'They do not seem to me to be such; but if I am the Devil's child, I will live then from the Devil.' "

The logic of this answer is like the logic of Blake's famous Proverb of Hell: "Sooner murder an infant in its cradle than nurse unacted desires."[46] Emerson is not advocating diabolism any more than Blake is advocating infanticide; the hyperbole is a way of suggesting the real ugliness of the alternative—in Emerson's case, maintaining a dead church, contributing to a dead Bible-society, worshipping a dead God. The word that needs stressing in Emerson's reply is not "Devil" but the verb "live": it is better to live from the Devil than die with the church. "For to him that is joined to all the living there is hope," as Ecclesiastes puts it in a verse Emerson might have cited here, "for a living dog is better than a dead lion."[47]

Harriet Martineau had been impressed with the remarkable good-humor Americans displayed, their kindness and courtesy toward one another. She did not connect this quality, which she admired, with the want of moral independence she deplored, but Emerson did. "In this our talking America we are ruined by our good nature and listening on all sides." "Check this lying hospitality and lying affection." Self-reliance is impossible without honesty, and honesty sometimes entails a willingness to be rude. Emerson cannot yet claim that he has this willingness; "every decent and well-spoken individual affects and sways" him more than is right. But he indulges in a fantasy of rudeness, imagines himself being able to speak the "rude truth" first to a proselytizing Abolitionist, then to members of his own family. "I shun father and mother and wife and brother, when my genius calls me. I would write on the lintels of the door-post, *Whim.* I hope it is somewhat better than whim at last, but we cannot spend the day in explanation." The sentences are discreetly blasphemous: they allude both to Jesus' command to leave father and mother for his sake, and to God's directive to the children of Israel to mark with blood the lintel of the doorway, that the Angel of Death might pass over their houses and spare their firstborn. Emerson's redeemer is his genius (a theme he will develop with more explicitness later in the essay); his saving sign is a confession of irresponsibility and even triviality, designed to make the serious men—the controversialists, the paragraph writers—pass over his house as something beneath contempt. It resembles a similar passage in "Circles" in its blend of irony and affected innocence:

> But lest I should mislead any when I have my own head, and obey my whims, let me remind the reader that I am only an experimenter. Do not set the least value on what I do, or the least discredit on what I do not, as if I pretended to settle anything as true or false. I unsettle all things. No facts are to me sacred; none are profane; I simply experiment, an endless seeker, with no Past at my back.

Whim is only a provisional term; we hope that it will be replaced by something better than whim at last (what we hope it will be is the force he will later call Spontaneity or Instinct—though these terms are hardly more likely to recommend him to the orthodox) but we cannot spend the day in explanation, for the same reason that the children of Israel could not tarry to leaven their bread when Pharaoh finally agreed to let them go. As Cavell says, Emerson, in writing *Whim* upon the lintels, is "taking upon himself the mark of God, and of departure. . . . This departure, such setting out is, in our poverty, what hope consists in, all there is to hope for; it is the abandoning of despair, which is otherwise our condition."[48]

But leaving the dead institutions of society behind is only half the task of departure. Our own past acts, as "Circles" points out, are governed by the same law of ossification visible in history as a whole. And leaving behind our own past insights may be even harder than rejecting the counsels of society, for we naturally possess a greater affection for our own past thoughts. Then, too, there is the fear that inconsistency will expose us to ridicule, that hardest of all crosses to bear. Emerson gave evidence early that he was not to be scared from self-trust by the hobgoblin of foolish consistency; the editor of his sermons tells of an incident in which Emerson interrupted his delivery of a sermon to say quietly to the congregation: "The sentence which I have just read I do not now believe,"[49] and then went on to the next page.

Such determination to prefer truth to his past apprehension of truth also governs the choice of the example Emerson now inserts into "Self-Reliance" to illustrate what he means by having the courage to risk self-contradiction. He had always objected strongly to any Theism that described God as a Person. "I deny Personality to God because it is too little not too much," he wrote in his journal. "Life, personal life is faint & cold to the energy of God." This denial of personality to God was one of the things his auditors had found most offensive about the Divinity School *Address*. The sermon his former colleague at the Second Church, Henry Ware, Jr., had preached in objection to Transcendentalist ideas in September 1838 was called "The Personality of the Deity"; it regarded attempts to reduce God to an abstract set of laws or moral relations as "essentially vicious." The *Christian Examiner* reviewed Emerson's address and Ware's sermon together, greatly to the detriment of the former.[50]

Emerson's doctrine of Divine Impersonality had angered a whole community; the *Address* had helped end his career as a supply preacher in Unitarian pulpits, and for all he knew at the time, it might have ended his career as a lecturer. Yet now, in "Self-Reliance," he warns himself against making an idol of his own theology: "In your metaphysics you have denied personality to the Deity; yet when the devout motions of the soul come, yield to them heart and life, though they should clothe God with shape and color. Leave your theory, as Joseph his coat in the hand of the harlot, and flee." It is only after describing how these menaces to self-trust or abandonment are to be overcome that Emerson will consider the question posed by the trusted adviser whose earlier warnings he had scorned. "The magnetism which all original action exerts is explained when we inquire the reason of self-trust. Who is the Trustee? What is the aboriginal Self on which a universal reliance may be grounded?"

The answer he gives, though, concerns not persons but powers: a "deep force" he calls by the triple name of Spontaneity, Instinct, and Intuition. "Gladly I would solve if I could this problem of a Vocabulary," Emerson groaned after the Divinity School *Address;* he knew very well that his effort to topple "the idolatry of nouns & verbs" in which the Deity had been so long addressed would not be easy. It is easy to object to the terms Emerson chooses, particularly easy for those readers to whom the *instinctual* suggests something bestial, the *spontaneous* something irresponsible, and the *intuitive* something irrational. But the risk of being misunderstood is one Emerson will have to run (anyway, "to be great is to be misunderstood") if he expects to find words in any vocabulary that will suggest a *force* felt by the individual as proceeding from within, yet somehow connected to the larger forces of nature, forces that are prior to reflection, self-consciousness, and the sallies of the will, prior even to that primary fall into division that created him as a separate being. "For the sense of being which in calm hours rises, we know not how, in the soul, is not diverse from things, from space, from light, from time, from man, but one with them, and proceeds obviously from the same source whence their life and being also proceed." To explain what he means by this Emerson offers this quiet prose summary of the Orphic chants of *Nature:* "We first share the life by which things exist, and afterwards see them as appearances in nature, and forget that we have shared their cause." What defines us as individuals is that act of forgetting; hence the paradox that intuition is a better pipeline to truth than conscious reflection. "When we discern justice, when we discern truth, we do nothing of ourselves, but allow a passage to its beams. If we ask whence this comes, if we seek to pry into the soul that causes, all philosophy is at fault. Its presence or absence is all we can affirm."

But here, at the heart of the essay, the reader is likely to be troubled by a contradiction. Emerson began by urging us to insist on ourselves, to express what is absolutely peculiar to us as individuals; he now makes it a defining characteristic of the state of true vision that in it "we do nothing of ourselves" but merely "allow a passage to its beams." This is evidently a paradox; it is one that is as central to Emerson's faith as the Incarnation was to traditional Christianity. Indeed, it is a resemblance Emerson acknowledges later on in the essay with his unobtrusive little epigram: "a man is the word made flesh." *Any* man is the word made flesh, the incarnation of the universal in the particular. "It seems to be true," Emerson had written in that early journal passage concerning self-trust, "that the more exclusively idiosyncratic a man is, the more general & infinite he is, which though it may not be a very intelligible expression means I hope something intelligible. In listening more intently to our own reason, we are not becoming in the ordinary sense more selfish, but are departing more from what is small, & falling back on truth itself & God."

Here Quentin Anderson (with whom, for once, I find myself in complete agreement) makes an important distinction. It is true that Emerson believes in the existence of a realm of spiritual laws that serves as a base for independent moral vision. "But what the early radical Emerson was excited about was not the existence of the base, but the discovery of the primacy of the individual, who can alone realize the claims of spirit." And he concludes: "There is something inclusive that justifies his activity—this is a statement which quickly leads us away from Emerson: *only the activity uniquely mine can manifest the inclusive*—this is a statement which leads us toward an understanding of him."[51]

Emerson, in other words, is less interested in inquiring into the nature of that Aboriginal Self on whom we can rely than in the nature of the procedures the individual must follow in order to open himself, if only momentarily, to that *power* he regarded as the essence of divinity. When he was only nineteen he wrote in his journal that "the idea of *power* seems to have been every where at the bottom of theology"; in another place he noted that power enters "somewhat more intimately into our idea of God than any other attribute." Power is "a great flood which encircles the universe and is poured out in unnumbered channels to feed the fountains of life and the wants of Creation, but every where runs back again and is swallowed up in its eternal source. That Source is God."

In the highest moments, when we are for a moment the channel through which absolute power is flowing, the petty dialectic of self and society, self and past acts of the self, fades away into insignificance; until Emerson can turn on his own vocabulary with withering contempt. "Why then do we prate of self-reliance? Inasmuch as the soul is present, there will be power not confident but agent. To talk of reliance is a poor external way of speaking." The term "self-reliance" implies dualism, disunion, a poor frightened individual attempting to rely *on* that Aboriginal Self presumed to be within. If this were really the new religion Emerson had come to preach, it would be no better than the one it replaced. In fact, it would remind us of nothing so much as the ruinous narcissism of Blake's Albion, who loses the Divine Vision when he turns his eyes toward his "Self" or Shadow and makes that his God:

> Then Man ascended mourning into the splendors
>   of his palace
> Above him rose a Shadow from his wearied intellect
> Of living gold, pure, perfect, holy: in white linen
>   pure he hover'd
> A sweet entrancing self delusion....[52]

When the soul is really present, Emerson insists, all *sense* of dualism ceases; one does not feel like a little self worshipping or trusting or relying on a bigger Self, but like a power open to that "great flood which encircles the universe." Self-reliance is not an attitude or a virtue; it is a way of acting, and can only be manifested through action. "Speak rather of that which relies, because it works and is." The distinction is made clearer in the section of the essay concerning the application of self-reliance to prayer: Emerson commends "the prayer of the farmer kneeling in his field to weed it, the prayer of the rower kneeling with the stroke of his oar," but lashes out at the kind of prayer that "looks abroad and asks for some foreign addition to come through some foreign virtue" not only because such prayer for a private end seems to him "meanness and theft" but because it "supposes dualism and not unity in nature and consciousness." True prayer knows no such dualism, even in its contemplative phase. Then it is merely "the soliloquy of a beholding and jubilant soul. It is the spirit of God pronouncing his works good."

In a pair of terse epigrams Emerson condenses the wisdom he has acquired in the turbulent years just passed. "Life only avails, not the having lived," is one; it is an admonition not to look for power in the sepulchers of past literature or past religion or past forms of social organization. "Power ceases in the instant of repose" is the second; it warns us that the divinity within us can only be manifested during those brief moments in which the soul, overcoming the deadliness of the past (including its own past), manages to shoot the gulf, dart to a new aim—manages to do this despite its knowledge that the new aim will someday be as deadly as the old. "This one fact the world hates, that the soul *becomes;* for, that forever degrades the past, turns all riches to poverty, all reputation to a shame, shoves Jesus and Judas equally aside."

The really formidable difficulty of this enterprise suggests why Emerson felt it necessary to invoke Instinct and Intuition as the only forces that can still put us in contact with our own divinity. The conscious intellect, the intellect alone, could draw only one lesson from Emerson's myth of ossification: that all action is the vanity of vanities. Successful creation is a momentary circumventing of that conscious intellect, which will reassert itself soon enough; the real danger for Americans was not that a surrender to Instinct would plunge them into a maelstrom of uncontrollable passions but that even the wildest impulses can scarcely overcome for a moment the national tendencies to caution, imitativeness, and dissimulation. Hence Emerson's insistence upon the necessity of "surprise," as in the closing paragraph of "Circles"—"The one thing which we seek with insatiable desire, is to forget ourselves, to be surprised out of our propriety, to lose our sempiternal memory, and to do something

without knowing how or why; in short, to draw a new circle"—
or in the poem "Merlin":

> "Pass in, pass in," the angels say
> "In to the upper doors,
> Nor count compartments of the floors,
> But mount to paradise
> By the stairway of surprise."

The man who has perfected the art of abandonment has acquired the only kind of affluence that Fate cannot menace. He has acquired "living property, which does not wait the beck of rulers, or mobs, or revolutions, or fire, or storm, or bankruptcies, but perpetually renews itself wherever the man breathes."

The Curse of Kehama

How shall we face the edge of time? We walk
In the park. We regret we have no nightingale.
We must have the throstle on the gramophone.
Where shall we find more than derisive words?
When shall lush chorals spiral through our fire
And daunt that old assassin, heart's desire?
Wallace Stevens, "A Duck for Dinner"

"Experience"

Emerson's final version of the Fall story is his shortest and most epigrammatic. It is remarkable not so much for its content as for its tone, and the startling nature of the "facts" it is invented to explain. The voice we hear in "Experience" has neither the rhapsodic intensity of the Orphic chants, nor the chill impersonality of the axis-of-vision formula, nor the militancy of "The Protest" or "Circles." It is instead the voice of a man of the world: urbane, rueful, a little weary. "It is very unhappy, but too late to be helped, the discovery we have made that we exist. That discovery is called the Fall of Man."

Equating self-consciousness with the Fall is of course one of the commonest Romantic ways of allegorizing the story of Genesis. And the myth of ossification, with its insistence that the conscious intellect was the enemy of that central power accessible only by surprise or abandonment, may be regarded as containing or at least implying this final myth (which we may call the myth of *reflection*).

But this new version differs from its predecessors in two significant respects. It is considerably more pessimistic in its implications (there is no suggestion that the catastrophe of self-consciousness is either potentially or temporarily reversible), and the evidence adduced to support it is more shocking, in its quiet way, than anything Emerson had ever written. In *Nature* he had based his argument for the original divinity of the Self on its surviving capacity for ecstasy; in "Circles," on its refusal to accept limitation. In "Experience" what is taken as proof of the "ill-concealed Deity" of the Self is neither its joy nor its zeal but simply its ruthlessness:

> There are moods in which we court suffering, in the hope that here at least we shall find reality, sharp peaks and edges of truth. But it turns out to be scene-painting and counterfeit. The only thing grief has taught me, is to know how shallow it is. That, like all the rest, plays about the surface, and never introduces me into the reality, for contact with which we would even pay the costly price of sons and lovers.

> We believe in ourselves as we do not believe in others. We permit all things to ourselves, and that which we call sin in others is experiment for us. It is an instance of our faith in ourself that men never speak of crime as lightly as they think; or that every man thinks a latitude safe for himself which is nowise to be indulged to another. . . . No man at last believes that he can be lost, or that the crime in him is as black as in the felon.

Emerson had once wanted to write a book like the Proverbs of Solomon; "Experience" sounds more like the *Maxims* of La Rochefoucauld.

The necessary ruthlessness of the Self had been a corollary of the doctrine of self-reliance from the beginning, of course; it is implicit in Emerson's exhortation to "shun father and mother and wife and brother" when genius calls, even if it causes them pain. And it is avowed even more frankly in "Circles," where Emerson argues that "men cease to interest us when we find their limitations. The only sin is limitation. As soon as you once come up with a man's limitations, it is all over with him." As individuals, we are always in the position of the disappointed child in "Experience" who asks his mother why the story he enjoyed yesterday fails to please him as much the second time around. And the only answer Emerson can give us is the one he offers the child: "will it answer thy question to say, Because thou wert born to a whole and this story is a particular?" This information is hardly an unmixed blessing. If our hunger for "sphericity" is on the one hand the only defense we have against the soul's tendency to ossification, it is on the other hand the restlessness that "ruins the kingdom of mortal friendship and of love."

Emerson's deliberate emphasis in essays like "Circles" and "Experience" on the ruthlessness and secret cruelty of the Self shocks us, and is meant to. It is not merely (as Firkins guesses) "that a parade of hardness may have seemed to him a wholesome counterpoise to the fashionable parade of sensibility,"[1] though that was doubtless an added attraction. Emerson says these unpleasant things chiefly because he thinks they are true. Of course it would be easier for us and for society as a whole if they were *not* true, if there were some way of living without the ruinous ferocity of desire, which never ceases to torment us in thought, even if our outward behavior is decorous. Our mortal condition would be easier to endure if the divine Providence had *not* "shown the heaven and earth to every child and filled him with a desire for the whole; a desire raging, infinite; a hunger, as of space to be filled with planets; a cry of famine, as of devils for souls"— as Emerson puts it in a memorable passage in "Montaigne." That desire sends us off on a perpetual quest through the world of experience, and at the same time foredooms the quest to failure, since each particular satisfaction can only frustrate a being whose desire is for the whole. As questers, we are partly like Tennyson's Ulysses—

> . . . . all experience is an arch wherethrough
> Gleams that untravelled world whose margin fades
> For ever and for ever when I move . . .[2]

but even more like Tennyson's Percivale—

> "Lo, if I find the Holy Grail itself
> And touch it, it will crumble into dust."[3]

Romance—the glamour or beauty that could transmute life's baser metals into gold—is always somewhere else, somewhere just beyond our grasp. "Every ship is a romantic object, except that we sail in. Embark, and the romance quits our vessel and hangs on every other sail in the horizon." Or, as he had put it in the earlier essay "Love": "each man sees his own life defaced and disfigured, as the life of man is not, to his imagination."

Sensible people, hearing these confessions of frustration and despair, counsel renunciation of the Self's imperial ambitions. But Emerson denies that any permanent renunciation is possible. For one thing, that glimpse of the whole we were granted as children survives in adult life as more than a memory. Just when we have, as we think, managed to adjust our desires to reality, the old vision reappears to tantalize us:

> How easily, if fate would suffer it, we might keep forever these beautiful limits, and adjust ourselves, once for all, to the perfect calculation of known cause and effect. . . . But ah! presently comes a day, or is it only a half-hour, with its angel-whispering,—which discomfits the conclusions of notions and years!

And this reminder, while it distresses us, calls to our attention something we cannot safely ignore. The desire that torments us is also the only "capital stock" we have to invest in the actions and relationships of life. The man who tried to conduct his business on the principles of common sense alone "would quickly be bankrupt. Power keeps quite another road than the turnpikes of choice and will; namely the subterranean and invisible tunnels and channels of life."

These meditations on power and ruthlessness are an important part of the essay "Experience." They constitute a sort of ground bass heard at intervals beneath the constantly varying melodies of the essay, and contribute not a little to the impression of toughness it makes on the reader's mind. Yet toughness is hardly the essay's most significant characteristic. What is strikingly new about "Experience" is the voice that is heard in its opening paragraph, a voice neither powerful nor ruthless, but instead full of bewilderment, exhaustion, and despair:

> Where do we find ourselves? In a series of which we do not know the extremes, and believe that it has none. We wake and find ourselves on a stair; there are stairs below us, which we seem to have ascended; there are stairs above us, many a one, which go upward and out of sight. But the Genius which according to the old belief stands at the door by which we enter, and gives us the lethe to drink, that we may tell no tales, mixed the cup too strongly, and we cannot shake off the lethargy now at noonday. Sleep lingers all our lifetime about our eyes, as night hovers all day in the boughs of the fir-tree. All things swim and glitter. Our life is not so much threatened as our perception. Ghostlike we glide through nature, and should not know our place again.

When Dr. Beard, in his *American Nervousness*, wanted a phrase that would convey to a popular audience an accurate sense of the new disease he had identified and named *neurasthenia*, he instinctively chose a metaphor Emerson would have admired: "nervous bankruptcy."[4] In the peculiar lassitude of the prose here—so different from the militant assertiveness of "Circles" or "Self-Reliance"—Emerson has managed to create a stylistic correlative to the "Feeling of Profound Exhaustion" Dr. Beard found characteristic of the nervously bankrupt.[5] Insufficiency of vital force is in fact Emerson's chief complaint in this opening passage.

> Did our birth fall in some fit of indigence and frugality in nature, that she was so sparing of her fire and so liberal of her earth that it appears to us that we lack the affirmative principle, and though we have health and reason, yet we have no superfluity of spirit for new creation? We have enough to live and bring the year about, but not an ounce to impart or invest. Ah that our Genius were a little more of a genius! We are like the millers on the lower levels of a stream, when the factories above them have exhausted the water. We too fancy that the upper people have raised their dams.

No reader of Emerson's journals can be unfamiliar with the mood described here. Recurrent laments over want of stamina and of animal spirits, over feelings of exhaustion and despair, punctuate the earliest notebooks. "I have often found cause to complain that my thoughts have an ebb & flow," he noted in one of them. "The worst is, that the ebb is certain, long, & frequent, while the flow comes transiently & seldom." A few pages earlier, a pious composition intended as a meditation "Upon Men's Apathy to their Eternal interests" turns into a meditation upon apathy of a more personal sort—a meditation whose systematic hopelessness, coming from a youth of nineteen, almost raises a smile:

> In the pageant of life, Time & Necessity are the stern masters of ceremonies who admit no distinctions among the vast train of aspirants.... And though the appetite of youth for marvels & beauty is fain to draw deep & strong lines of contrast between one & another character we early learn to distrust them & to acquiesce in the unflattering & hopeless picture which Experience exhibits.

This grim lesson Emerson hastens to apply to his own disappointing life:

> We dreamed of great results from peculiar features of Character. We thought that the overflowing benevolence of our youth was pregnant with kind consequences to the world; that the agreeable qualities in the boy of courage, activity, intelligence, & good temper would prove in the man Virtues of extensive & remarkable practical effect.

The passage is revealing; it provides a glimpse of what Emerson's boyhood ambition had really been—not to become a reclusive scholar and occasional lecturer, but to be a public figure, an eloquent mover of men, like his hero Daniel Webster. The disinterest of his elders in his visionary schemes of regeneration had not dampened his personal ambitions; if anything, it had increased them. "The momentary ardour of childhood found that manhood & age were too cold to sympathise with it, & too hastily inferred that its own merit was solitary & unrivalled & would by and by blaze up, & make an era in Society." But this childhood ardor, like Wordsworth's "visionary gleam," eventually died away of its own accord:

> Alas. As it grew older it also grew colder & when it reached the period of manhood & of age it found that the waters of time, as

they rolled had extinguished the fire that once glowed & there
was no partial exemption for itself. The course of years rolls an
unwelcome wisdom with them which forcibly teaches the vanity of human expectations.

And he concludes: "The dreams of my childhood are all fading
away & giving place to some very sober & very disgusting views
of a quiet mediocrity of talents & condition."

The intellectual revolution of the early 1830s—the discovery
of the God within—liberated Emerson from the hopelessness
that had oppressed his young manhood, but it could not do much
for his stamina. He circumvented the limitations of his constitution by carefully husbanding his time and strength, and he
learned to make the best of his alarming *"periods* of mentality"
("one day I am a doctor, & the next I am a dunce") by means of
the unique method of composition he had already perfected by
the mid-thirties. He spent his mornings barricaded in his study,
writing isolated paragraphs in his journal when the spirit was
upon him. When a longer composition was needed—a sermon or
a lecture—he quarried in these journals for material and, as
Chapman says, "threw together what seemed to have a bearing
on some subject, and gave it a title." Chapman adds, correctly, I
think, that what keeps this method from resulting in an "incomprehensible chaos" is Emerson's single-mindedness:

> There was only one thought which could set him aflame, and
> that was the unfathomed might of man. This thought was his
> religion, his politics, his ethics, his philosophy. One moment of
> inspiration was in him own brother to the next moment of in-
> spiration, although they might be separated by six weeks.[6]

What keeps this procedure from resulting in monotony for the
reader, is first, the sheer power and felicity of Emerson's prose;
next, the perpetual surprise of his observations (who else would
have thought of comparing readers at the Boston Athenaeum to
flies, aphids, and sucking infants?); and finally, his unflinching
honesty, which will not let him rest until he has subjected his
claim for the unfathomed might of man to every shred of negative
evidence that can reasonably be urged against it. The combina-

tion of his single-mindedness and his insistence upon recognizing all the "opposite negations between which, as walls, his being is swung" is responsible for the curious fact about his work noticed long ago by Firkins. "Emerson's wish to get his whole philosophy into each essay tended toward sameness and promiscuity at once; it made the *essays similar* and the *paragraphs diverse.*"[7] (It is also responsible for the fact that while his paragraphs are extraordinarily easy to remember word for word, they can be almost impossible to locate. Anything can be anyplace. The most time-consuming feature of being a student of Emerson is the necessity it places one under of repeatedly rereading half the collected *Works* and *Journals* in the maddening pursuit of some paragraph one can remember but not find.)

But his habits of composition, though they enabled him to produce a body of written work that would be remarkable enough for even a vigorous man, probably contributed to his sense of the unbridgeable gap between the life of the soul and the life of the senses, between the Reason and the Understanding. His ecstasies were carefully reserved for his study; the price he paid for them was an abnormally lowered vitality for the acts and perceptions of everyday life. He repeatedly complains of the "Lethean stream" that washes through him, of the "film or haze of unreality" that separates him from the world his senses perceive. How to transfer "nerve capital" (as a follower of Dr. Beard termed it[8]) from the column of the Reason to the column of the Understanding seemed to him life's chief insoluble problem. In "Montaigne" he writes:

> The astonishment of life is the absence of any appearance of reconciliation between the theory and practice of life. Reason, the prized reality, the Law, is apprehended, now and then, for a serene and profound moment amidst the hubbub of cares and works which have no direct bearing on it;—is then lost for months and years, and again found for an interval, to be lost again. If we compute it in time, we may, in fifty years, have half a dozen reasonable hours. But what are these cares and works the better? A method in the world we do not see, but this parallelism of great and little, which never discover the smallest tendency to converge.

Or, as he had once laconically observed: "Very little life in a life-time."

Yet despite this discouraging arithmetic Emerson had always refused to abandon his insistence that the visionary moments constituted our *real* life, the one in which we felt most truly ourselves. This insistence is not quite as suicidal as it sounds, for the visionary moments, however brief they may be when measured by the clock, have a way of expanding while they are occurring into an eternal present that makes a mockery of duration. In a paragraph of "Circles" that looks forward to Thoreau's parable of the artist of Kouroo, Emerson had written:

> It is the highest power of divine moments that they abolish our contritions also. I accuse myself of sloth and unprofitableness, day by day; but when these waves of God flow into me, I no longer reckon lost time. I no longer poorly compute my possible achievements by what remains to me of the month or the year; for these moments confer a sort of omnipresence and omnipotence, which asks nothing of duration, but sees that the energy of the mind is commensurate with the work to be done, without time.

With this proviso in mind it is easier to understand why Emerson could speculate in his journal that "in the memory of the disembodied soul the days or hours of pure Reason will shine with a steady light as the life of life & all the other days & weeks will appear but as hyphens which served to join these."

In "Experience" Emerson tries for the first time in his career to describe life as it looks from the standpoint of the hyphens rather than the heights, from the "waste sad time" (as Eliot calls it) separating the moments of vision rather than from the moments themselves. It is his attempt to confront the only form of suffering he recognized as genuinely tragic, because it was the only one for which his imagination could discover no answering compensation—the haze of unreality that sometimes suggested to him that we were "on the way back to Annihilation."

Emerson had originally planned to call the essay "Life." At first glance the difference between the two titles does not seem very great. Everthing that happens in life can be described as an experience: a visionary moment as much as a bump on the head.

Emerson himself uses the word this way in "The Transcendentalist" when he says that a transcendentalist's faith is based on a "certain brief experience" that surprises him in the midst of his everyday worries and pursuits.

Yet the word "experience" also had a technical meaning in empirical philosophy, where it refers to that portion of the world accessible to the senses, the world of time and space. This is the meaning it has in the works of Hume, whose skepticism had provoked the young Emerson into his first spiritual crisis during the decade of the 1820s. "Experience" is the weapon Hume uses to demolish belief in miracles and the argument for God's existence based on inferences from the evidence of design in the universe. If one accepted Hume's thesis—that "we have no knowledge but from Experience"—it was difficult to avoid his conclusion—that "we have no Experience of a Creator & therefore know of none." Hume could also use arguments from experience to shake belief in more fundamental assumptions: in the existence of matter, in the relationship of cause and effect, in the stability of personal identity. Emerson puzzled over these problems. In a high-spirited letter to his Aunt Mary written in 1823 he confessed that the doubts raised by this "Scotch Goliath" were as distressing to him as worries about the origin of evil or the freedom of the will. "Where," he asked rhetorically, "is the accomplished stripling who can cut off his most metaphysical head? Who is he that can stand up before him & prove the existence of the Universe, & of its Founder?" All the candidates in the "long & dull procession of Reasoners that have followed since" only proved, by their repeated attempts to confute Hume, that Hume had not been confuted.

Here, it is evident, Emerson is still accepting his teachers' argument that an attack on the existence of the material universe led inevitably to an attack on the existence of God. Whicher points out that "though Berkeley had denied the existence of matter independent of perception to confute sceptical materialism," to the Scottish Realists whose philosophical works dominated the Harvard scene in Emerson's youth, "the end product of the Ideal Theory was the scepticism of Hume."[9]

Emerson's discovery of "the God within" released him from

the necessity of clinging to proofs of the existence of matter, since once the confirmation of the truths of religion had been made a purely intuitive affair, no longer dependent for its ratification on miracles perceivable by the senses, the "Ideal Theory" no longer seemed dangerous. The endless, fussy debates about whether we could trust the testimony of the Apostles who claimed to have witnessed the miracles of Jesus, about how the immutable laws of nature could have been temporarily suspended (e.g., whether Jesus made the water he walked on temporarily solid or himself temporarily weightless), about whether the gospels in which these events were recorded were genuine or spurious, neutral historical records or (as the German Higher Critics alleged) legendary or mythological narratives, could all be dispensed with in one liberating gesture. "Internal evidence outweighs all other to the inner man," Emerson wrote in 1830. "If the whole history of the New Testament had perished & its teachings remained—the spirituality of Paul, the grave, considerate, unerring advice of James would take the same rank with me that now they do." It is the truth of the doctrine that confirms the truth of the miracle, not the other way round. If it were not so, Emerson frankly confesses, he would probably "yield to Hume or any one that this, like all other miracle accounts, was probably false."

Hume's argument against the possibility of miracles had rested on the observation that our opinions about the reliability of testimony and about the probability of matters of fact are both drawn from experience. We usually believe the testimony of honorable witnesses, because we have found from experience that such men usually tell the truth. But we also form our opinions about the probability of matters of fact from our experience: whether it is likely to snow in July, whether a man can walk on water or rise from the dead. "The reason, why we place any credit in witnesses and historians, is not derived from any *connexion*, which we perceive *a priori*, between testimony and reality, but because we are accustomed to find a conformity between them. But when the fact attested is such a one as has seldom fallen under our observation, here is a contest of two opposite experiences; of which the one destroys the other, as far as its force goes, and the superior can only separate on the mind by the force, which remains."[10]

Emerson's mature position can best be characterized by saying that he accepts Hume's argument but reverses his conclusions. When the testimony involved is not the testimony of witnesses but the testimony of consciousness, the "superior force" clearly belongs to consciousness. Experience and consciousness are indeed in perpetual conflict: "life is made up of the intermixture and reaction of these two amicable powers, whose marriage appears beforehand monstrous, as each denies and tends to abolish the other." When an irreconcilable conflict occurs, it is consciousness, not experience, whose testimony we believe. Hence Emerson's delight in the "scientific" equivalent to this assertion: the law he attributed to the Swiss mathematician Euler and quoted in the "Idealism" chapter of *Nature*. "The sublime remark of Euler on his law of arches, 'This will be found contrary to all experience, yet it is true;' had already transferred nature into the mind, and left matter like an outcast corpse."

Idealism had always held a secret attraction for Emerson, which had survived unchanged even during the years when his teachers were telling him to regard it as dangerous. In a letter to Margaret Fuller in 1841 he writes: "I know but one solution to my nature & relations, which I find in the remembering the joy with which in my boyhood I caught the first hint of the Berkleian philosophy, and which I certainly never lost sight of afterwards." What Emerson means by the "Berkleian philosophy," as Whicher notes, is not Berkeley's particular system but

> simply the "noble doubt . . . whether nature outwardly exists."
> The seductive reversal of his relations to the world, with which
> the imagination of every child is sometimes caught, transfer-
> ring his recurrent sense of a dreaminess in his mode of life to
> outward nature, and releasing him in his imagination into a sol-
> itude peopled with illusions, was scepticism of a special kind—

but a kind that increasingly seemed not the murderer of faith but rather its midwife.[11] The man who believes that the mind alone is real, matter only a phenomenon, is easier to convince of spiritual realities than the empiricist who continually demands sensible proofs. "Idealism seems a preparation for a strictly moral life & so skepticism seems necessary for a universal holiness," Emerson noted in an early journal. Indeed, if what he asserts in "Montaigne" is correct—that "belief consists in accepting the affirmations of the soul; unbelief, in denying them"—it is the empiricist, not the idealist, who deserves the title of skeptic. With this in mind, the history of philosophy begins to look very different. The classical skeptics no longer look frightening—Emerson quotes with approval de Gerando's opinion that Sextus Empiricus' skepticism had been directed only at the external world, not at metaphysical truths. Even the Scotch Goliath begins to look less formidable. "Religion does that for the uncultivated which philosophy does for ~~Hume~~ Berkeley & Viasa;—makes the mountains dance & smoke & disappear before the steadfast gaze of Reason." Emerson crossed out Hume's name (enlisting Hume as an ally of religion was presumably too radical an idea for Emerson at this point in his career, though the Emerson of "Circles" would have found it plausible), but that he thought of Hume in context at all is significant enough.

But Idealism as a doctrine was more than philosophically important to Emerson; it was emotionally important as well. *Nature* as originally planned was to have ended with the chapter "Idealism"; and in that chapter he suggests some of the chief attractions the doctrine possessed. When "piety or passion" lifts us into the realm of Ideas, "we become physically nimble and lightsome; we tread on air; life is no longer irksome, and we think it will never be so. No man fears age or misfortune or death in their serene company, for he is transported out of the region of change." "The best, the happiest moments of life are these delicious awakenings of the higher powers, and the reverential withdrawing of nature before its God."

No wonder Emerson seized eagerly upon every philosopher whose system tended toward idealism of one kind or another: Plato, Plotinus, Berkeley, Kant, Fichte, Schelling. Religious doctrines, too, he tends to judge by their approximations to idealism. In an early journal he notes with approval that idealism seems to be a primeval theory, and quotes from the Mahabharata (one of the sacred books of India) a sentence that neatly inverts the Peripatetic formula (*nihil in intellectu quod non ante fuerit in sensu*) upon which Locke had based his philosophy. "The senses are nothing but the soul's instrument of action; *no knowledge can come to the soul by their channel*" (emphasis added).

I have made this digression into Emerson's philosophical interests for a reason: the essay "Experience" cannot, I think, be fully understood without some grasp of the metaphorical ways in which he employs the technical vocabulary of epistemology to talk about things like grief, guilt, ruthlessness, and isolation. Stanley Cavell sees in Emerson the only thinker who can be said to have anticipated the Heidegger of *Being and Time* in an attempt "to formulate a kind of epistemology of moods":

> The idea is roughly that moods must be taken as having at least as sound a role in advising us of reality as sense-experience has; that, for example, coloring the world, attributing to it the qualities "mean" or "magnanimous," may be no less objective or subjective than coloring an apple, attributing to it the colors red and green. Or perhaps we should say: sense-experience is to objects what moods are to the world.[12]

What makes this difficult subject more complicated still is Emerson's own recognition that the various epistemological theories proposed by every philosopher from Plato to Kant might themselves be little more than metaphorical equivalents of moods or habitual ways of taking the world. "I fear the progress of Metaphysical philosophy may be found to consist in nothing else than the progressive introduction of apposite metaphors," Emerson had dryly remarked in an early journal. "Thus the Platonists congratulated themselves for ages upon their knowing that Mind was a dark chamber whereon ideas like shadows were painted. Men derided this as infantile when they afterwards learned that the Mind was a sheet of white paper whereon any & all characters might be written." The real difficulty in arriving at an epistemology of moods is that moods are likely to dictate beforehand the shape of one's epistemology. A soul in a state of exaltation will instinctively incline to the mystical idealism of the Mahabharata; a soul in a state of depression, to the skepticism of Hume.

A healthy but nonreflective man might find the epistemology of the Scottish Realists sufficiently convincing; a more introspective man might not rest content until he had seen the relation between subject and object given transcendental ground in the philosophy of Kant.

Words like "experience" and "idealism" have different meanings in each of these systems, and different from any are the meanings they have acquired in popular use, where "idealism" is taken to mean any rosy or elevated estimate of human possibilities, and "experience" the process by which that estimate is lost. In "Experience" Emerson does not so much attempt to introduce order into this confusion as to exploit its ironies. If the essay, like life itself, is a "train of moods" or succession of "many-colored lenses which paint the world their own hue," each showing only what lies in its focus, then one of the chief ways of arriving at an epistemology of moods is by studying the shadings these words take on as the paragraphs pass by. From some moods within the essay, "experience" looks like a neutrally descriptive word; from others, a term of bitterness or contempt; from others still, the most savage of ironies. And the same thing holds true for "idealism," as one can see from the sentence (which may be the bitterest Emerson ever wrote) taken from the paragraphs of the essay that deal with the death of his son: "Grief too will make us idealists."

From the beginning of the essay the concept of experience is already involved in ironies. The opening image, which compares life to the climbing of an endless staircase, has reminded more than one critic of a Piranesi engraving, and Porte has pointed out that Emerson's references to "lethe" and "opium" recall a passage in DeQuincey's *Confessions of an English Opium-Eater*, where Piranesi's *Carceri d'Invenzione* is explicitly mentioned.[13] But DeQuincey was describing dreams induced by an actual drug; Emerson is describing the ordinary waking consciousness, life as it presents itself to the senses.

Hume, who thought that all knowledge came through experience, divided the contents of the mind into "IMPRESSIONS and IDEAS," the former derived from sensation (whether from external nature or the passions themselves), the latter the "faint images" of the former.[14] Since the two are different not in kind but only in degree, he pauses at the beginning of the *Treatise of Human Nature* to consider whether the two can ever be confused. He admits that in madness or fever or dreams ideas may become almost as lively as impressions, and that conversely there are some states in which "it sometimes happens, that our impressions are so faint and low, that we cannot distinguish them from our ideas."[15] What Emerson suggests in the opening paragraph of "Experience" is that the state Hume admitted as exceptional is in fact closer to being the norm: our impressions are most of the time as faint as our ideas, and a system of philosophy that separated one from the other according to the "degrees of force and liveliness, with which they strike upon the mind"[16] would very shortly lose the power to tell reality from phantasmagoria. The first irony we can record about experience is that it chiefly menaces the very philosophical system supposed to revere it. The exhaustion that attends it numbs the mind so that all the things we perceive "swim and glitter" like apparitions—a condition that, as Emerson accurately says, threatens not so much our life as our perception.

The second paragraph of the essay lodges a different complaint: the fact that experience and whatever wisdom can be derived from it are never coincident. Our life becomes meaningful only retroactively. "If any of us knew what we were doing, or where we are going, then when we think we best know! We do not know to-day whether we are busy or idle. In times when we have thought ourselves indolent, we have afterwards discovered that much was accomplished and much was begun in us." The most valuable experiences Wordsworth discovered in his childhood as he looked back on it were not the incidents a biographer would be likely to record but rather certain uncanny moments of heightened perception that occurred unexpectedly in the midst of ordinary childish sports—ice skating, robbing birds' nests, going for a night ride in a stolen boat—just as the most significant experience during the European tour he made as a young man turned out to be not the visions of sublime Alpine scenery but the vague feeling of depression that had succeeded the peasant's revelation that he and his companion had passed the highest point on their Alpine journey without recognizing it. Life and the meaning of life can never be apprehended simultaneously; like Pandarus in *Troilus and Criseyde* we can all justly complain "I hoppe alwey byhynde."[17]

Nor can any illumination ever prove final. "What a benefit if a rule could be given whereby the mind could at any moment *east* itself, & find the sun," Emerson had written in his journal. "But long after we have thought we were recovered & sane, light breaks in upon us & we find we have yet had no sane moment. Another morn rises on mid-noon." That final Miltonic allusion (along with its demonic counterpart, "under every deep a lower deep opens") may be regarded as a slightly more cheerful version of the staircase image that opens "Experience": it combines the suggestion of interminability with the suggestion that with each new layer of experience there is at least a widening of circumference or gain in wisdom. As Emerson says later on in the essay, "the years teach much that the days never know." Unfortunately, this wisdom clarifies only the past; each new situation finds us blundering like novices. "The individual is always mistaken." This melancholy but resigned conclusion resembles the opinion Yeats expresses in *Per Amica Silentia Lunae*, that since no disaster in life is exactly like another, there must always be "new bitterness, new disappointment";[18] it is perhaps even closer to the remark made by a contemporary Zen master, Shunryu Suzuki, to the effect that the life of a Zen master in pursuit of enlightenment "could be said to be so many years of *shoshaku jushaku* —'to succeed wrong with wrong,' or one continuous mistake."[19]

It is important to realize that at this point in the essay Emerson is *not* contrasting the wisdom that comes from experience with the higher wisdom that comes from consciousness. He is exploring a curious paradox that exists within experience itself. "All our days are so unprofitable while they pass, that 'tis wonderful where or when we ever got anything of this which we call wisdom, poetry, virtue. We never got it on any dated calendar day." The contrast between the pettiness of our daily lives and the accumulated wisdom that somehow results from them is so vast that even a resolute empiricist will be driven to mythology or fiction to account for it. "Some heavenly days must have been intercalated somewhere, like those that Hermes won with the dice of the Moon, that Osiris might be born."

Yet the cruelest feature of experience is the power it possesses of alienating us not only from our perceptions and our interpretations but even from our own sorrows:

> What opium is instilled into all disaster! It shows formidable as we approach it, but there is at last no rough rasping friction, but the most slippery sliding surfaces; we fall soft on a thought; *Ate Dea* is gentle,—
>
> > "*Over men's heads walking aloft,*
> > *With tender feet treading so soft.*"
>
> People grieve and bemoan themselves, but it is not half so bad with them as they say. There are moods in which we court suffering, in the hope that here we shall find reality, sharp peaks and edges of truth. But it turns out to be only scene-painting and counterfeit. The only thing grief has taught me, is to know how shallow it is. That, like all the rest, plays about the surface, and never introduces me into the reality, for contact with which we would even pay the costly price of sons and lovers. Was it Boscovich who found out that bodies never come in contact? Well, souls never touch their objects. An innavigable sea washes with silent waves between us and the things we aim at and converse with. Grief too will make us idealists. In the death of my son, now more than two years ago, I seem to have lost a beautiful estate,—no more. I cannot get it nearer to me. If to-morrow I should be informed of the bankruptcy of my principle debtors, the loss of my property would be a great inconvenience to me, perhaps, for many years; but it would leave me as it found me,—neither better nor worse. So it is with this calamity; it does not touch me; something which I fancied was a part of me, which could not be torn away without tearing me nor enlarged without enriching me, falls off and leaves no scar. It was caducous. I grieve that grief can teach me nothing, nor carry me one step into real nature. The Indian who was laid under a curse that the wind should not blow to him, nor fire burn him, is a type of us all. The dearest events are summer-rain and we the Para coats that shed every drop. Nothing is left us now but death. We look to that with a grim satisfaction, saying, There at least is a reality that will not dodge us.

I have quoted the whole of this magnificent passage because it is chiefly in its cumulative force that it achieves its great and disturbing power over us. I have never yet read a commentary on it that I thought did justice to the peculiar kind of shock it administers to the reader who is encountering the essay for the first time. The casual brutality of the sentence in which Emerson introduces the death of his son *as an illustration* is unmatched by anything I know of in literature, unless it is the parenthetical remark in which Virginia Woolf reports the death of Mrs. Ramsay in the "Time Passes" section of *To the Lighthouse.*

Not that the unreality or numbness Emerson reports is itself shocking. Many writers before and after Emerson have said as much. A similar experience forms the subject of Dickinson's chilling lyric, "After great pain, a formal feeling comes"; it is also analyzed in a passage of Sir Thomas Browne's *Hydrotaphia* from which Emerson had copied sentences into one of his early journals. "There is no antidote against the *Opium* of time," Browne reminds us, and then goes on to say:

> Darknesse and light divide the course of time, and oblivion shares with memory a great part even of our living beings; we slightly remember our felicities, and the smartest stroaks of affliction leave but short smart upon us. Sense endureth no extremities, and sorrows destroy us or themselves. To weep into stones are fables. Afflictions induce callosities, miseries are slippery, or fall like snow upon us, which notwithstanding is no unhappy stupidity. To be ignorant of evils to come, and forgetfull of evils past, is a mercifull provision in nature, whereby we digest the mixture of our few and evil dayes, and our delivered senses not relapsing into cutting remembrances, our sorrows are not kept raw by the edge of repetitions.[20]

The whole passage, even down to the details of its tactile imagery, is a striking anticipation of "Experience." Yet the differences are as noteworthy as the similarities. The slipperiness of misery, which Browne calls a "mercifull provision in nature," is for Emerson "the most unhandsome part of our condition." And this is so because Emerson, unlike Browne, sees in the unreality of grief only an intensification of our normal state of alienation or dislocation from the world our senses perceive. This distance—

the "innavigable sea" that washes between us and the world—is the real torture. If grief could relieve it, if suffering could introduce us to the reality behind the glittering and evanescent phenomena, we would welcome it. For contact with that reality we would be *willing* to pay (as Emerson says in what is surely the most chilling of all his hyperboles) "even the costly price of sons and lovers."

But grief proves to be as shallow as everything else. In a letter written a week after the death of his son Emerson laments: "Alas! I chiefly grieve that I cannot grieve; that this fact takes no more deep hold than other facts, is as dreamlike as they; a lambent flame that will not burn playing on the surface of my river. Must every experience—those that promised to be dearest & most penetrative,—only kiss my cheek like the wind & pass away? I think of Ixion & Tantalus & Kehama." "Kehama" is an allusion to Robert Southey's long narrative poem *The Curse of Kehama*, in which a virtuous character named Ladurlad is laid under a curse by the wicked ruler Kehama, who, though himself a mere mortal, has learned to wrest such power from the gods that he is able to send a burning fire into Ladurlad's heart and brain, and at the same time order the elements to flee from him. As Ladurlad laments:

> The Winds of Heaven must never breathe on me;
> The Rains and Dews must never fall on me;
> Water must mock my thirst and shrink from me;
> The common earth must yield no fruit to me;
> Sleep, blessed Sleep! must never light on me;
> And Death, who comes to all, must fly from me,
> And never, never set Ladurlad free.[21]

Ladurlad is the "Indian" mentioned in "Experience": in making him a "type of us all" Emerson gives us his grimmest assessment of the human condition: an endless, goalless pilgrimage, driven by an inner but unquenchable fire through a world that recedes perpetually before the pilgrim. The bitter lesson we learn from experience is the soul's imperviousness to experiences. The traumas are not traumatic. "The dearest events are summer-rain, and we the Para coats that shed every drop." If we look forward with a "grim satisfaction" to death, it is because it is the one event in life that we can be sure will not slip through our fingers. "There at least is a reality that will not dodge us."

Yet the central portion of the passage is the most explicitly self-lacerating. In observing that grief, like poetry or religion, convinces us of the insubstantiality of the phenomenal world, in offering as evidence for this assertion his own imperviousness to the death of his son, whose loss he likens, with deliberate vulgarity, to the loss of an estate, Emerson is indulging in a candor so "dreadful" (as Bishop puts it) that it has driven more than one critic to suppose that he either did not mean what he said or else was unaware of his meaning.[22]

Part of the problem comes from the difficulty of determining Emerson's tone in the passage. Bishop has pointed out Emerson's fondness for what he calls "tonal puns." He instances a sentence from *The Conduct of Life:* "Such as you are, the gods themselves could not help you." Bishop says: "One can hear a voice that says this insultingly and another voice, intimate and quiet, that says it encouragingly."[23] But he confesses that sentences like "*Ate Dea* is gentle" and "Grief too will make us idealists" and "I cannot get it nearer to me" leave him puzzled. Are they straightforward or ironical, desperate or resigned?[24] The answer, I think, is that we *can* imagine a voice that says all of these things with bitter irony, but that we can also imagine them being said in a voice as toneless and detached as that of a witness giving evidence in a war crimes trial, or that of the wasted and suffering discharged soldier whom Wordsworth questions about his experiences in Book IV of *The Prelude:*

> ... in all he said
> There was a strange half-absence, as of one
> Knowing too well the importance of his theme
> But feeling it no longer.[25]

Emerson is driven to offer his testimony by an inner necessity. I admire Maurice Gonnaud's fine remark about this compulsion: "The greatness of an essay like 'Experience' lies, I suggest, in our sense of the author's being engaged in a pursuit of truth which has all the characters of faith except its faculty of radiating happiness."[26]

What sharpens the sting of the revelations is Emerson's tacit acknowledgment, through his phrasing and imagery, that fate itself has retroactively conferred upon some brave assertions of the past the one kind of irony it was beyond his power to intend. Thus "grief too will make us idealists" both echoes and answers a journal entry of 1836 in which Emerson was working out the concepts that later became part of the sixth chapter of *Nature*: "Religion makes us idealists. Any strong passion does. The best, the happiest moments of life are these delicious awakenings of the higher powers & the reverential withdrawing of nature before its god." His remark that his relationship to his son proved to be "caducous" recalls a happy declaration, made after the departure of some friends in August of 1837, that he had faith in the soul's powers of inifinite regeneration: "these caducous relations are in the soul like leaves ... & how often soever they are lopped off, yet still it renews them ever." Even more chilling is the prophetic remark he made to Jones Very during the latter's visit in 1838: "I told Jones Very that I had never suffered, & that I could scarce bring myself to feel a concern for the safety & life of my nearest friends that would satisfy them: that I saw clearly that if my wife, my child, my mother, should be taken from me, I should still remain whole with the same capacity of cheap enjoyment from all things." There is a kind of self-contempt in this passage; Emerson had already survived so many losses that he felt confident in predicting his response to more. But this passage was written when little Waldo was barely two. In the intervening years— years in which Emerson had delightedly recorded his small son's doings and sayings in his otherwise austerely intellectual journal—he had evidently come to hope that this relationship was somehow different, that it was something that "could not be torn away without tearing me nor enlarged without enriching me."

Alas. Though Elizabeth Hoar's brother Rockwood "was never more impressed with a human expression of agony than by that of Emerson leading the way into the room where little Waldo lay dead,"[27] Rusk tells us, Emerson discovered to his sorrow that the prophecy he had made in 1838 was true. In his young manhood he had been greatly stirred by the remark of a Methodist farmer he worked with one summer that men were always praying and that their prayers were always answered. "Experience" records Emerson's grim awareness that the price you pay for invulnerability is invulnerability.

The passages here recanted were all confined to Emerson's private journals—a fact that helps explain why the opening pages of "Experience," almost alone among Emerson's works, give the impression of being not heard but overheard. But these privately recorded passages are not the only ones to be so retracted. Nearly every critic of the essay has pointed out the connection between some detail of its imagery or argument and those of an earlier work that it systematically recants or retracts. Thus the opening question—"Where do we find ourselves?"—when compared to the boldness of *Nature*'s opening—"Let us inquire, to what end is nature?"—suggests the bewilderment that has overtaken this latter-day Oedipus as he turns from riddle solving to self-examination. The opening image of an endless staircase recalls the "mysterious ladder" of "Circles," but where the latter saw a new prospect of power from every rung, "Experience" sees only repetition and exhaustion. Idiosyncrasy or subjectivity, which in "Self-Reliance" was felt to be the source of one's chief value, now becomes part of the limitation of temperament, which shut us out from every truth our "colored and distorting lenses" cannot transmit. The horizon that in "Circles" was a promise of perpetual expansion has now become merely a metaphor for frustration: "Men seem to have learned of the horizon the art of perpetual retreating and reference." In *Nature* Emerson was a Transparent Eye-ball; in "Experience" he is shut in "a prison of glass which [he] cannot see." The "noble doubt" whether nature outwardly exists, the exhilarating suggestion that perhaps the whole of the outward universe is only a projection from the apocalypse of the mind, has become in "Experience" the Fall of Man.[28]

But if "Experience" is in one way a palinode, it is in another way a continuation, under grimmer conditions, of the faith Emerson had never relinquished. That faith first enters the essay only as a kind of recoil against the reductiveness of the argument in the section devoted to temperament. Life is a string of moods, each showing only what lies in its focus; temperament is the iron wire on which these beads are strung. "Men resist the conclusion in the morning, but adopt it as the evening wears on, that temper prevails over everything of time, place, and condition, and is inconsumable in the flames of religion."

Yet in the midst of this determinism Emerson suddenly pauses to note the "capital exception" every man makes to general or deterministic laws—that is, himself. Although every man believes every other to be "a fatal partialist," he never sees himself as anything other than a "universalist." (In a similar passage later on in the essay Emerson will observe that we make the same exception to moral laws, which is why no man can believe that "the crime in him is as black as in the felon.") In "Circles" Emerson had noted that "every man supposes himself not to be fully understood; and if there is any truth in him, if he rests at last on the divine soul, I see not how it can be otherwise. The last chamber, the last closet, he must feel was never opened; there is always a residuum unknown, unanalyzable. That is, every man believes he has a greater possibility." However much we may appear to one another as creatures limited by a given temperament, bound by the "links of the chain of physical necessity," the very fact that our consciousness rebels utterly at such a description of *ourselves* is the best evidence we have of the falsity of the doctrine. On its own level—the level of nature, of experience—temperament may be final, relativism inescapable.

> But it is impossible that the creative power should exclude itself. Into every intelligence there is a door which is never closed, through which the creator passes. The intellect, seeker of absolute truth, or the heart, lover of absolute good, intervenes for our succor, and at one whisper of these high powers we awake from our ineffectual struggles with this nightmare. We hurl it into its own hell, and cannot again contract ourselves to so base a state.

Yet this recovery, though it suggests the direction the essay will take, is by no means a final triumph over the lords of life. After Temperament there is Succession, by which Emerson means both the succession of "moods"—which he has already discussed—and the succession of "objects." The succession of moods is something we suffer; the succession of objects is something we choose. "We need change of objects." Our hunger for the whole keeps us restlessly searching through the world of experience in pursuit of a final consummation forever denied us. But if there are no final satisfactions, there are at least partial ones. In *The American Scholar* Emerson had compared inspiration to the "one central fire which flaming now out of the lips of Etna, lightens the capes of Sicily; and now out of the throat of Vesuvius, illuminates the towers and vineyards of Naples." The image he uses in "Experience" is considerably less apocalyptic, but the faith it expresses is the same: "Like a bird which alights nowhere, but hops perpetually from bough to bough, is the Power which abides in no man and no woman, but for a moment speaks from this one, and for another from that one."

The essay by this point seems to have established a pattern—a dip into despair, followed by a recoil of hope. But suddenly and unexpectedly Emerson turns on himself and his method: "what help from these fineries or pedantries? What help from thought? Life is not dialectics." This yawing back and forth between despair and hope is not, after all, how we spend most of our time. "Life is not intellectual or critical, but sturdy." Some way must be found to redeem the time, to treat it as something other than an emptiness separating moments of vision. "To fill the hour,— that is happiness; to fill the hour and leave no crevice for a repentance or an approval. We live amid surfaces, and the true art of life is to skate well on them." In these sentences we hear a different voice emerging, a voice that will become stronger in "Montaigne" and dominant in a book like *English Traits*. It is the voice of strong common sense, giving a view of the world Emerson had indeed expressed earlier, in things like the "Commodity" chapter of *Nature* and in essays like "Prudence" and "Compensation," but had never before offered as a serious *alternative* to the world of Reason. Now, for the first time, he proposes the "mid-world" as something other than a step on the way to vision.

Yet the mid-world offers no permanent anchorage either; moments of illumination *will* return whether we want them to or not, upsetting all our resolutions to keep "due metes and bounds." "Underneath the inharmonious and trivial particulars, is a musical perfection, the Ideal journeying always with us, the heaven without rent or seam." This region is something we do not make, but find, and when we find it all the old exhilaration returns. We respond with joy and amazement to the opening of "this august magnificence, old with the love and homage of innumerable ages, young with the life of life, the sunbright Mecca of the desert. And what a future it opens! I feel a new heart beating with the love of the new beauty. I am ready to die out of nature and be born again into this new yet unapproachable America I have found in the West."

For a vision of life that assessed man only from the platform of "experience" would leave out half his nature. "If I have described life as a flux of moods, I must now add that there is that in us which changes not and which ranks all sensations and states of mind." This something is the "central life" mentioned at the end of "Circles," the center that contains all possible circumferences. "The consciousness in each man is a sliding scale, which identifies him now with the First Cause, and now with the flesh of his body; life above life, in infinite degrees." Different religions have given this First Cause different names—Muse, Holy Ghost, *nous*, love—but Emerson confesses that he likes best the one ventured by the Chinese sage Mencius: "vast-flowing vigor." Asked what he means by this, Mencius describes it as the power that can "fill up the vacancy between heaven and earth" and that "leaves no hunger." With this definition we have come as far as possible from the terminal exhaustion and depletion of the essay's opening paragraphs: "we have arrived as far as we can go. Suffice it for the joy of the universe that we have arrived not at a wall, but at interminable oceans. Our life seems not so much present as prospective; not for the affairs on which it is wasted, but as a hint of this vast-flowing vigor."

But if this is the end of the dialectic, it is not the end of the essay, which—like life itself—will not let us remain in any state of illumination for long. We are brought back to the mid-world in a paragraph that summarizes all that has come before:

> It is very unhappy, but too late to be helped, the discovery we
> have made that we exist. That discovery is called the Fall of
> Man. Ever afterwards we suspect our instruments. We have
> learned that we do not see directly but mediately, and that we
> have no means of correcting these colored and distorting lenses
> which we are, or of computing the amount of their errors. Per-
> haps these subject-lenses have a creative power; perhaps there
> are no objects. Once we lived in what we saw; now, the rapa-
> ciousness of this new power, which threatens to absorb all
> things, engages us. Nature, art, persons, letters, religions, ob-
> jects, successively tumble in, and God is but one of its ideas.

As Michael Cowan notes, this investigation of Subjectiveness in
some ways "represents a spiralling back to the lord of Illusion,
but now seen from the viewpoint of the saved rather than the
damned imagination."[29] What has made the difference is the discovery that there is an irreducible something in the soul that
rebels fiercely at any attempt to reduce it to a mere "bundle of
perceptions," and that is hence the best proof that any such definition is false. Knowing that the soul retains even in in its grimmest moments "a door which is never closed, through which the
creator passes" is the saving revelation that transforms the hell of
Illusion into the purgatory of Subjectiveness. We are still unable
to transcend the limitations of our vision, but now we seem not so
much cut off from the real as the unconscious progenitors of it.
Our "subject-lenses," unlike the object-lenses of a telescope or
microscope, do not merely magnify reality, they determine its
characteristics: "the chagrins which the bad heart gives off as
bubbles, at once take form as ladies and gentlemen in the street,
shopmen or bar-keepers in hotels, and threaten or insult whatever is threatenable or insultable in us." This is a trivial example
of a principle, anything but trivial, whose gradual triumph one
can witness in the history of the race. Realism is the philosophical system of every primitive tribe, but as civilization advances,
men come gradually to suspect that as it is the eye that makes the
horizon, so it is the beholder who creates the things he perceives.

It is not to be denied that there is something melancholy about
such self-awareness. In a lecture entitled "The Present Age," delivered in 1837, Emerson expresses the traditional Romantic envy
of those luckier ages that lived in what they saw:

> Ours is distinguished from the Greek and Roman and Gothic ages, and all the periods of childhood and youth by being the age of the second thought. The golden age is gone and the silver is gone—the blessed eras of unconscious life, of intuition, of genius.... The ancients were self-united. We have found out the difference of outer and inner. They described. We reason. They acted. We philosophise.

The act of reflection severs us as with an "innavigable sea" from the "things we aim at and converse with," and at the same time plants in our minds the suspicion that these things, which *feel* so distant, may not be "out there" at all. On this point modern empiricism and idealism coincide. Hume wrote: "Let us fix our attention out of ourselves as much as possible: Let us chace our imagination to the heavens, or to the utmost limits of the universe; we can never really advance a step beyond ourselves, nor can conceive of any kind of existence, but those perceptions, which have appear'd in that narrow compass."[30] As Emerson remarked of a similar passage from the materialist Condillac, "what more could an idealist say?"

This imprisonment has some lamentable consequences, as Emerson is the first to acknowledge, for the kingdoms of mortal friendship and of love. "Marriage (in which is called the spiritual world) is impossible, because of the inequality between every subject and every object.... There will be the same gulf between every me and every thee as between the original and the picture." For the soul, though it incarnates itself in time as an ordinary mortal with ordinary limitations, is in fact "of a fatal and universal power, *admitting no co-life*" (emphasis added). To say this is to push one's philosophy considerably beyond antinomianism; it ought logically to lead to a state in which everything—theft, arson, murder—is permitted. Emerson does not attempt to refute this objection. Instead (in what is surely one of the more audacious gestures in American literature) he coolly embraces it. That crime occurs at all is the best evidence we have of our unshakable belief in the divinity of the self. "It is an instance of our faith in ourselves that men never speak of crime as lightly as they think.... Murder in the murderer is no such ruinous thought as poets and romancers will have it; it does not unsettle him or fright him from his ordinary notice of trifles; it is an act quite easy to be contemplated." Our reasons for abstaining from murder are (by a nice irony) purely empirical, derived from experience: "in its sequel [murder] turns out to be a horrible confounding of all relations." Emerson's own version of the categorical imperative derives from the same ontology. Just as the highest praise we can offer any artist is to think that he actually possessed the thought with which he has inspired us, so the highest tribute we can pay to a fellow human being is to assume that his exterior—which must remain to us merely a part of the phenomenal—conceals a Deity as central to itself as our own. "Let us treat the men and women well; treat them as if they were real; perhaps they are."

We have here reached the shadowy ground where philosophy and psychology merge. In the letter to Margaret Fuller quoted earlier Emerson had claimed that the Berkleian philosophy was the clue to his nature *and relations*. Idealism as a philosophical doctrine appealed to him partly because it offered a credible way of accounting for the loneliness and isolation to which he felt temperamentally condemned. In 1851, after a rambling talk with Thoreau in which both of them had "stated over again, to sadness, almost, the Eternal loneliness," Emerson exclaimed, "how insular & pathetically solitary, are all the people we know!" We are inclined to try to find excuses for our separation from others, but in more honest moments we admit the grimmer truth: "the Sea, vocation, poverty, are seeming fences, but Man is insular and cannot be touched. Every man is an infinitely repellent orb, and holds his individual being on that condition." Existence for each of us is a drama played out in a private theater that admits only one spectator:

> Men generally attempt early in life to make their brothers first, afterwards their wives, acquainted with what is going forward in their private theater, but they soon desist from the attempt on finding that they also have some farce or perhaps some ear- & heart-rending tragedy forward on their secret boards on which they are intent, and all parties acquiesce at last in a private box with the whole play performed before him *solus*.

The same haunting notion prompts the question that closes this section of "Experience": "How long before our masquerade will end its noise of tambourines, laughter and shouting, and we will find it was a solitary performance?"

It is true, as Emerson says, that the muses of love and religion hate these developments. But our inescapable subjectivity has its own compensations. The "sharp peaks and edges of truth" we had hoped to find in reality we discover at last in the soul. God himself is "the native of these bleak rocks," an insight that "makes in morals the capital virtue of self-trust. We must hold hard to this poverty, however scandalous, and by more vigorous self-recoveries, after the sallies of action, possess our axis more firmly. The life of truth is cold and so far mournful; but it is not the slave of tears, contritions, and perturbations. It does not attempt another's work, nor adopt another's facts." As James Cox notes, "if 'Self-Reliance' was a ringing exhortation to trust the self, 'Experience' turns out to disclose that, after the last disillusion, there is nothing to rely on *but* the self."[31]

And the sunbright Mecca of the West? The New Jerusalem, the kingdom of man over nature? What has become of it? In a journal Emerson had once noted sadly that "it takes a great deal of elevation of thought to produce a very little elevation of life. . . . Gradually in long years we bend our living to our idea. But we serve seven years & twice seven for Rachel." In "Experience" Emerson admits that he has served his time—"I am not the novice I was fourteen, nor yet seven years ago"—and still must be content only with Leah. "Let who will ask, Where is the fruit? I find a private fruit sufficient." This private fruit is, as Yoder says, "consciousness without correspondent results"[32]—but I think it is not quite true to say that it is the only paradise offered us after the circuitous journey of "Experience." The view from Pisgah is as clear as it ever was.

In a letter to Margaret Fuller written to mark the second anniversary of his son's death Emerson declared himself no closer to reconciling himself to the calamity than when it was new, and compared himself to a poor Irishman who, when a court case went against him, said to the judge, "I am not satisfied." The senses have a right to perfection as well as the soul, and the soul will never rest content until these "ugly breaks" can be prevented. The attitude of defiance and the feeling of impotence recall a famous journal entry written a few months after his son's death. Speaking of Christ's sacrifice, he says:

> He did well. This great Defeat is hitherto the highest fact we have. But he that shall come shall do better. The mind requires a far higher exhibition of character, one which shall make itself good to the senses as well as the soul. This was a great Defeat. We demand Victory.

If it is not clear how long we will have to wait for this victory, how wide is the distance between ourselves and the Promised Land, Emerson refuses to give up hope. "Patience and patience, we shall win at the last." Experience may counsel only despair, "but in the solitude to which every man is always returning" there is a "sanity" that gives a very different kind of advice. "Never mind the ridicule, never mind the defeat; up again, old heart!—it seems to say." The "romance" that fled from our ship at the beginning of "Experience" returns at the end to become the goal of our weary but still hopeful pilgrimage. The "true romance which the world exists to realize"—the point at which desire and fact, the pleasure principle and the reality principle, will coincide—"will be the transformation of genius into practical power."

Yet the ending of "Experience," if it restates the old hope—or at least restates the impossibility of giving it up—hardly leaves us cheered. As Firkins says, "the victory is gained in the end, idealism is reëstablished, but the world in which its authority is renewed looks to the common eye like a dismantled, almost a dispeopled, universe."[33] After such knowledge, what consolation?

Emerson develops two main answers to his question in the decade of the 1840s, one of them given in "The Poet," the other in "Montaigne." Both are attempts to find some sort of "paradise within" to compensate the individual for his loss of Eden and for his failure to reach the New Jerusalem. One is designed to satisfy the Reason, the other the Understanding. (The very fact that this distinction still remains is a sign that the consolations offered are clearly thought of as *second bests*.[34]) And both essays, in their imagery and structure, show that by now Emerson's four fables—contraction, dislocation, ossification, and reflection— have become a system of significances as useful to him as the Biblical stories had been to his ancestors: a series of types or analogies by which the chaotic impressions of experience could be ordered and understood.

The Adequate Genesis: "The Poet"

It may sound odd at first to call "The Poet" the affirmation of a second best, since the praise offered the poet there is nearly unqualified. Emerson's later essays, Yoder points out, generally move by "balanced antitheses or counterstatements" and hence tend to appear as "stalemates, games of rhetoric played with mellowed detachment in place of imaginative zeal."[35] But "The Poet" is a single high-pitched rhapsody of praise. Not until the "Preface" to the 1855 edition of *Leaves of Grass* will there be comparable claims made for the poet's importance. Indeed, "The Poet" is clearly one of the essays that brought the simmering Whitman to a boil. In it Emerson portrays himself as a John the Baptist, looking for "the timely man, the new religion, the reconciler, whom all things await." And he continues, in a passage that obviously caught the eye of the younger man:

> Dante's praise is that he dared to write his autobiography in colossal cipher, or into universality. We have yet had no genius in America, with tyrannous eye, which knew the value of our incomparable materials, and saw, in the barbarism and materialism of the times, another carnival of the same gods whose picture he so much admires in Homer. . . . Our log-rolling, our stumps and their politics, our fisheries, our Negroes and Indians, our boats and our repudiations, the wrath of rogues and the pusillanimity of honest men, the northern trade, the southern planting, the western clearing, Oregon, and Texas, are yet unsung.

Yet most of "The Poet" urges a kind of poetic activity very different from this blending of local color with the egotistical sublime. The old hope that poetry is the revelation of "the double meaning, or shall I say the quadruple or the centuple or much more manifold meaning, of every sensuous fact," and that the poet can become a liberating god through the practice of his art, returns to haunt Emerson with all its intensity as his earthly hopes fade.

In the late essay "Poetry and Imagination" there is the beautiful (and very Stevensian) sentence: "The poet is representative,—whole man, diamond-merchant, symbolizer, emancipator; in him the world projects a scribe's hand and writes adequate genesis." The "adequate genesis" is the belief in "the essential dependence of the material world on thought and volition" that had first been affirmed in the final chapter of *Nature* and that now, at the beginning of "The Poet," theologians and intellectual men are taken to task for not sufficiently crediting. "Theologians think it a pretty air-castle to talk to the spiritual meaning of a ship or a cloud, of a city or a contract, but they prefer to come again to the solid ground of historical evidence." What they fail to realize is that "things admit of being used as a symbol, because nature is a symbol, in the whole, and in every part." And what does it symbolize? The truth given form in the Orphic chants of *Nature*. "The Universe is the externization of the soul. Wherever the life is, that bursts into appearance around it." The true poem, the "adequate genesis," would be the revelation of this truth, but the individual poems we presently have are only fragments of it.

> For all poetry was written before time was, and whenever we are so finely organized that we can penetrate into that region where the air is music, we hear those primal warblings and attempt to write them down, but we lose ever and anon a word or a verse and substitute something of our own, and thus miswrite the poem.

The highest truth, Emerson had said in "Self-Reliance," can never be told, for all that we say is "the far off remembering of the intuition." Yet a little further on in "The Poet" we are left to wonder whether the faultiness of memory is really to blame for the miswritten poems, or whether language itself is hostile to imagination. "Language is fossil poetry," Emerson tells us in "The Poet"; but he also implies that poetry is fossil language:

> . . . . the quality of the imagination is to flow, and not to freeze. The poet did not stop at the color or the form, but read their meaning; neither may he rest in this meaning, but he makes the same objects exponents of his new thought. Here is the difference betwixt the poet and the mystic, that the last nails a symbol to one sense, which was a true sense for a moment, but soon becomes old and false. For all symbols are fluxional; all language is vehicular and transitive, and is good, as ferries and horses are, for conveyance, not as farms and houses are, for homestead.

We meet again here Emerson's insistence that thinking is not inhabitation but abandonment, and see again the anxiety that gave rise to it: the tremendous fear that the soul's natural tendency to ossification will transform the purest truth into the deadliest falsehood. Emerson sees all religion as poetry—"the religions of the world are the ejaculations of a few imaginative men"—but his own experience with Christianity had shown him how easy it was to mistake the figurative for the literal. In the Divinity School *Address* he had complained that the churches were built not on Jesus' principles but on his tropes; he now extends the observation to religion in general. "The history of hierarchies seems to show that all religious error consisted in making the symbol too stark and solid, and was at last nothing but an excess of the organ of language." Bigotry is frozen poetry.

The greatest contributor to the process of ossification—if not indeed its sole cause—is reflection, self-consciousness, that slight pause of self-praise that makes us too enamored of our past thoughts to shoot the gulf to new ones. In a journal passage written after Emerson had challenged the claims of some friends who had aspired to being judged "substantial & central," he reveals how closely his later explanation of the Fall ("the discovery we have made that we exist") fits in with his earlier one (the fable of dislocation). Emerson tells his friends that they are "intellectual," and hence only "the scholars, or the learned, of the Spirit or Central Life." If they had been more like the young mystic Jones Very, who had visited Emerson for some days in 1838, "if the centres of their life were coincident with the Centre of Life," he would gladly bow the knee and accept all they said without contradiction. But instead he feels in them "the slight dislocation of these Centres which allowed them to stand aside & speak of these facts *knowingly.*" To be self-conscious is to be dislocated, or fallen; it is to have one's center *not* coincident with that "central life" that, in "Circles," is named as the only generator of new circles.

This linking of intellectuality and loss of power is also made in the charge Emerson levels at Plato in *Representative Men.* Most of the essay is a rhapsody of praise: Plato is the balanced soul, blender of Asian vastness and European logic, consummate rhetorician and yet lover of the One. Emerson can think of only one serious deduction from his merit. "He is intellectual in his aim; and therefore, in expression, literary.... His writings have not,—what is no doubt incident to this regnancy of intellect in his work,—the vital authority which the screams of prophets and the sermons of unlettered Arabs and Jews possess."

The question of authority—the relationship between the speaker's character and his rhetoric—was one with which Emerson, as a pulpit and lyceum orator, had long been preoccupied. In an early journal he alludes to Matthew 7:28–29: "And it came to pass, when Jesus had ended these sayings, the people were astonished at his doctrine: For he taught them as one having authority, and not as the scribes." Emerson remarks that this is "a distinction most palpable. There are a few men in every age I suppose who teach thus."

Authority is derived from character; but Emerson meant much more by "character" than the classical rhetorical theorists had meant by *ethos* (though Emerson's concept includes theirs). "Character is higher than intellect," he wrote in 1837, "and Character is what the German means when he speaks of the Daimonisches." Character is "a reserved force, which acts directly by presence and without means. It is conceived of as a certain undemonstrable force, a Familiar or Genius, by whose impulses the man is guided, but whose counsels he cannot impart." It is, in other words, the same force Socrates called his *daimon*.

Emerson had been interested in Socrates' *daimon* from an early age. One of his prize essays in college was "A Dissertation on the Character of Socrates," and the concept of the *daimon* continued to fascinate him long after he left college. He identified it, not surprisingly, with the Christian conscience. In a journal passage from the year 1828 he records several anecdotes of Socrates' obedience to the advice of his *daimon* and concludes: "I suppose that by this Daemon, Socrates designed to describe by a lively image the same judgment which we term conscience. We are all attended by this daemon. We are acquainted with that signal which is as the voice of God." But the *daimon* appealed to Emerson because it was more than an "inner check"; it was (to borrow a phrase from Bishop) more like an "initiating inward force."[36] It told one not only what to abstain from, but what to do. In 1834 Emerson had been greatly excited by a conversation with a Quaker lady who had learned, as she said, to have *no choice*.

> Can you believe, Waldo Emerson, that you may relieve yourself of this perpetual perplexity of choosing? & by putting your ear close to the soul, learn always the true way. I cannot but remark how perfectly this agrees with the Daimon of Socrates, even in that story which I once thought anomalous, of the direction as to the two roads.

In the last sentence Emerson is alluding to a story from Plutarch: "Socrates, warned by his Daemon to change his road, walked another way.... His friends went laughingly on but were overturned by a herd of swine."[37]

But the *daimon* was more than a guide to conduct. Emerson saw it as the source of all superlative power in human activity, whether in poetry, oratory, or political agitation. "There is no strong performance without a little fanaticism in the performer," he once wrote. "Charles King Newcomb had this Δαιμων dazzling his eyes, & driving his pen. Unweareable fanaticism, (which if it could give account of itself to itself, were lost,)—is the Troll that

'by night threshed the corn
'Which ten day laborers could not end.' ' "

The orator is the man who, above all, needs daimonic power. "What others effect by talent or eloquence, this man accomplishes by some magnetism. 'Half his strength he put not forth.' " He does not need to perform feats of strength. "He conquers because his arrival alters the face of affairs." The people who decided that Jesus spoke very differently from the scribes did not need to see him perform miracles to be convinced of the truth of his doctrines; they were convinced merely by his "authority."

Authority is in fact the point of the story Matthew tells immediately after he reports the remark of the people concerning Jesus and the scribes. A centurion with a sick servant appeals to Jesus for a cure, and Jesus agrees to go with the centurion to his house. But the centurion replies: "Lord, I am not worthy that thou shouldest come under my roof; but speak the word only and my servant shall be healed. For I am a man under authority, having soldiers under me: and I say to this man, Go, and he goeth; and to another, Come, and he cometh; and to my servant, Do this, and he doeth it."[38] Jesus marvels at the man's faith, and heals the servant by simple command.

If Jesus' authority had been extended to remove every evil from the face of the earth, his triumph would have been complete. In the gnomic verses prefixed to the essay "Character," Emerson says of the Redeemer whom he awaits: "He spoke, and words more soft than rain/ Brought the Age of Gold again." Christ's failure to inaugurate the Golden Age is what Emerson refers to when he calls Christ's death a "great Defeat" and makes the (otherwise unintelligible) remark that "the mind requires a far higher exhibition of character" than the life of either Jesus or Socrates displays. "The mind requires a victory to the senses; a force of character which will convert judge, jury, soldier, and king; which will rule animal and mineral virtues, and blend with the courses of sap, of rivers, of winds, of stars, and of moral agents."

Glimmerings of this daimonic power were what Emerson was always searching for in the poetry and oratory of his contemporaries. Such power was the rarest and most precious of gifts, and hence its prostitution was the only truly unforgivable sin in Emerson's private decalogue. His early reverence for Webster grew out of his sense that Webster possessed this power; so did his unappeasable fury after Webster had used it to help pass the Fugitive Slave Law in 1850. Only those who know how great was Emerson's reluctance to mix in political affairs and how strong was his private resolution never to attack *individuals* in his essays or addresses can understand what it meant for him (and he was then a dignified man of letters in his late forties) to take out after Webster on the campaign trail, delivering speeches in which, as Chapman says, he is "savage, destructive, personal, bent on death."[39] He was bitterer even than Whittier, who had portrayed Webster as a fallen archangel in "Ichabod," but had urged some compassion for his sin. Emerson will have none of it; he continues attacking Webster even after his death. Webster was the man who could have been what Emerson in his boyhood had wanted to be: the man who persuades the masses and the government to virtue through the sheer authority of his presence. "If his moral sensibility had been proportioned to the force of his understanding, what limits could have been set to his genius and beneficent power?" Instead, after making a few hypocritical bows to the church, Webster threw his great weight on the side of "animal good"—that is, of "property." It was as if Jesus, instead of delivering the Sermon on the Mount, had launched into a defense of the money changers in the Temple.

Daimonic power is a gift; it has nothing to do with talent. In "The Poet" Emerson records a conversation concerning a "recent writer of lyrics" (probably Tennyson, as Edward Emerson guesses) "whose head appeared to be a music-box of delicate rhythms, and whose skill and command of language we could not sufficiently praise. But when the question arose whether he was not only a lyrist but a poet, we were obliged to confess that he is plainly a contemporary, not an eternal man." Daimonic power is what makes the difference between "men of talent who sing" and those true poets who are "children of the music." (On the other hand, it is better to be a man of talent than a poet who claims an inspiration his verses do not manifest. In a letter to Elizabeth

Hoar written in 1840 Emerson complains that his attempts to remove the "bad grammar" and "nonsense" from the poetic manuscripts of William Ellery Channing the Younger before their publication in *The Dial* have been refused by the poet on the grounds that his mistakes were all "consecrated by his true *afflatus.*" Emerson asks irritably: "Is the poetic inspiration to embalm & enhance flies & spiders? As it fell in the case of Jones Very, cannot the spirit parse & spell?")

Jones Very was a young Harvard tutor whose poetry and criticism Emerson helped to publish in 1839. Very was a mystic; his exaltations had gotten him committed to the Charlestown Asylum for a brief time in 1838. Shortly after his release he visited Emerson (who was then in the midst of the controversy provoked by the Divinity School *Address*), causing the latter to remark, "I wish the whole world were as mad as he." Was Very insane? "At first sight & speech, you would certainly pronounce him so. Talk with him a few hours and you will think all insane but he." Emerson did not know whether to call his condition "monomania or mono *Sania*"; but he was impressed both with Very's perfect sincerity—he "charmed us all," Emerson says, "by telling us he hated us all"—and by the magnitude of his poetic gift. Very, in fact, may have been the one who first suggested to Emerson the inverse relationship between authority and self-consciousness. "He is sensible in me of a little colder air than he breathes," Emerson noted in his journal. "He thinks me covetous in my hold of truth, of seeing truth separate, & of receiving or taking it instead of merely obeying. The Will is to him all, as to me (after my own showing,) Truth." Very's way of soliciting the spirit was simple: "He would obey, obey." Yet the formal precision and technical brilliance of Very's mystical sonnets proved that the spirit need not express itself in incoherent rhapsodies; *daimons* could scan, as well as parse and spell.

Emerson was probably thinking of his instinctive deference to Very when he said in "Self-Reliance" that "who has more obedience than I, masters me, though he should not raise his finger." But in this crucial passage from "The Poet" he is clearly drawing on his own experience as well:

It is a secret which every intellectual man quickly learns, that beyond the energy of his possessed and conscious intellect he is capable of a new energy (as of an intellect doubled on itself), by abandonment to the nature of things; that beside his privacy of power as an individual man, there is a great public power on which he can draw, by unlocking, at all risks, his human doors, and suffering the ethereal tides to roll and circulate through him; then he is caught up into the life of the Universe, his speech is thunder, his thought is law, and his words are universally intelligible as the plants and animals. The poet knows that he speaks adequately then only when he speaks somewhat wildly, or "with the flower of the mind"; not with the intellect used as an organ, but with the intellect released from all service and suffered to take its direction from its celestial life; or as the ancients were wont to express themselves, not with the intellect along but with the intellect inebriated by nectar. As the traveller who has lost his way throws his reins on his horse's neck and trusts to the instincts of the animal to find his road, so must we do with the divine animal who carries us through this world.

For Emerson, too, had had experience of the *daimons;* they were part of his method of composition. "He was subject to ecstasies in which his mind worked with phenomenal brilliancy,"[40] as Chapman says, and in these ecstasies he indeed felt as if he were opening himself to the Power that was at once the center and circumference of the universe. And his attitude toward this inner Power was like Very's, or Jonathan Edwards's; that was why Very's answer to the problem of authority interested him. This attitude, as Whicher points out, combines "an awe at the presence of the Infinite within him; a royal pride in this guest that overbore self-distrust; a sense as well of present unworthiness, and a fresh incentive to fitting virtue and greatness."[41] Emerson's conversion to a religion based on obedience to this Power is a genuine conversion experience, and is treated by him as such. "Conversion from a moral to a religious character is like day after twilight," he had written shortly after his own dawning sense of an inner divinity had come to full day. "The orb of the earth is lighted brighter and brighter as it turns until at last there is a particular moment when the eye sees the sun and so when the soul perceives God." To know oneself fully is to understand the presence of this inner

Deity; that is why Emerson entitled the awkward little prose poem he hastily wrote down in 1831 "Gnothi Seauton":

> ... take this fact unto thy soul—
> God dwells in thee.—
> It is no metaphor nor parable
>
>   . . .
>
> Clouded & shrouded there doth sit
> The Infinite
> Embosomed in a man
> And thou art stranger to thy guest
> And know'st not what thou dost invest.
>
>   . . .
>
> Then bear thyself, o man!
> Up to the scale & compass of thy guest
> Soul of thy soul.
>
>   . . .
>
> ... if thou listen to his voice
> If thou obey the royal thought
> It will grow clearer to thine ear
> More glorious to thine eye
> The clouds will burst that veil him now
> And thou shalt see the Lord.

No one would claim that this is poetry, but after reading it one can scarcely credit Yvor Winters's assertion that for Emerson "the religious experience was a kind of good-natured self-indulgence."[42] There is in fact not much difference between the attitude expressed in this scrap of verse and the one implicit in a remark Very made to Emerson during his visit: "He felt it an honor, he said, to wash his face, being as it was the temple of the Spirit."

Nor does the resemblance end there. The discovery that God was within not only irradiated the individual, it promised to provide him with a key to the mysteries of external nature:

> Because in thee resides
> The Spirit that lives in all

And thou canst learn the laws of Nature
Because its author is latent in thy breast.

Or, as he had said in "Self-Reliance": "the sense of being which
in calm hours rises, we know not how, in the soul, is not diverse
from things, from space, from life, from time, from man, but one
with them and proceeds obviously from the same source whence
their life and being also proceed. We first share the life by which
things exist, and afterwards see them as appearances in nature,
and forget that we have shared their cause." One of Very's most
beautiful sonnets had expressed a similar belief; it is entitled
"The Lost."

> The fairest day that ever yet has shone,
> Will be when thou the day within shall see;
> The fairest rose that ever yet has blown,
> When thou the flower thou lookest on shalt be;
> But thou art far away among Time's toys;
> Thyself the day thou lookest for in them,
> Thyself the flower that now thine eye enjoys,
> But wilted now thou hang'st upon thy stem.
> The bird thou hearest on the budding tree,
> Thou hast made sing with thy forgotten voice;
> But when it swells again to melody,
> The song is thine in which thou wilt rejoice;
> And thou new risen midst these wonders live
> That now to them dost all thy substance give.[43]

This faith is the rock upon which *Nature* had been built, and it
continues to dominate Emerson's conception of the poetical character even after his theories of symbolism and poetry had under-
gone a radical shift.

For in *Nature* Emerson had thought of the material universe as
a vast picture book whose symbols poets were to collaborate at
translating into human language. "By degrees we may come to
know the primitive sense of the objects of nature, so that the
world shall be to us an open book, and every form signficant of its
hidden life and final cause." "That which was unconscious truth

becomes, when interpreted . . . a new weapon in the magazine of power." The poet's task, then, is to translate nature back into thought by interpreting as many natural phenomena as possible: to contribute to the dictionary of symbols which is at once the grand poem of mankind and the restoration of nature.

But the whole project of spiritual lexicography depends upon the answer to one important question, which was defined by W. K. Wimsatt in an article on "Two Meanings of Symbolism." The question is "whether the world and its parts have symbolic meanings that are at all strictly determinate, whether the 'book of nature' described by such authors as Saint Bonaventure in the thirteenth century and Drummond of Hawthornden in the early seventeenth, is written in one language, a scientifically specific language, or in the polysemous ambiguity of poetry itself."[44] At the time of *Nature* Emerson is thinking, or hoping, that the book of nature is written in a single tongue. But his growing dissatisfaction with the Swedenborgian theory of "correspondences"— the most fully worked out system of translation—had, by the early 1840s, made him painfully aware that, as Wimsatt remarks, "formulary or stereotyped symbolism as a creative technique is a contradiction. It has always tended to fizzle out into the quaint conceptions of bestiary, lapidary, emblem book, or the debased patristic style of the Euphuist."[45] In *Representative Men* Emerson ridicules Swedenborg for poorly tethering every natural object to a single spiritual sense: "a horse signifies carnal understanding; a tree, perception; the moon, faith; a cat means this; an ostrich that; an artichoke this other." The language of nature is infinitely polysemous: "In nature each individual symbol plays innumerable parts, as each particle of matter circulates in turn through every system. The central identity enables any one symbol to express successively all the qualities and shades of real being." But if every symbol can express all the qualities of real being, then obviously no dictionary of symbols is possible, since each symbol would require a definition infinite in length and identical, except for itself, with the definition of every other.

Hence by the early 1840s Emerson is forced to develop a different conception both of nature and of symbolism, a conception he refers to as "the metamorphosis." Nature is no longer seen as a book, but as a process, a flux, a "rushing stream." "Its smoothness is the smoothness of the pitch of the cataract. Its permanence is a perpetual inchoation." It is no longer conceived of as a veil separating man from eternity, but as a gigantic trope for eternity, in which process itself is made to represent pure stasis—as in Wordsworth's famous vision of the Gorge of Gondo:

> The immeasurable height
> Of woods decaying, never to be decayed,
> The stationary blasts of waterfalls,
> And in the narrow rent at every turn
> Winds thwarting winds, bewildered and forlorn,
> The torrents shooting from the clear blue sky,
> . . .
> Tumult and peace, the darkness and the light—
> Were all like workings of one mind, the features
> Of the same face, blossoms upon one tree;
> Characters of the great Apocalypse,
> The types and symbols of Eternity,
> Of first, and last, and midst, and without end.[46]

Yet is is perhaps not quite accurate to call Emerson's new vision of nature static, even by implication, for the old hope that "through Nature there is a striving upward" has not been extinguished, merely reformulated. In *Nature* this upward striving had manifested itself in the ascending series of "uses" to which nature could be put by man. But by the time Emerson had come to deliver an address called "The Method of Nature" in 1841 he was attributing a kind of upward mobility to nature itself. *Nature* had begun by inquiring "to what end is nature?" We now are told that nature "does not exist to any one or any number of particular ends." To all our interrogations, her only answer is "I grow, I grow."

> We can point nowhere to anything final; but tendency appears on all hands: planet, system, constellation, total nature is growing like a field of maize in July; is becoming somewhat else; is in rapid metamorphosis. The embryo does not more strive to be a man than yonder burr of light we call a nebula tends to be a ring, a comet, a globe, and parent of new stars.

This perpetual upward striving or "excess of life" is the quality "which in conscious beings we call *ecstasy*," and suggests how poetry is to be written. "As the power or genius of nature is ecstatic, so must its science or description of it be. The poet must be a rhapsodist; his inspiration a sort of bright casualty." He is to suggest nature's perpetual metamorphoses by his ceaseless proliferation of tropes; his chief virtue is what the classical theorists called *copia*. This fecundity is the quality Emerson most valued in Shakespeare; Shakespeare, he said, "suggests a wealth which beggars his own."

And the effect of this proliferation upon the listener will be to recreate in him nature's original ecstasy. For (as Emerson observes in "The Poet") "if the imagination intoxicates the poet, it is not inactive in other men. The metamorphosis excites in the beholder an emotion of joy. The use of symbols has a certain power of emancipation and exhilaration for all men. We seem to be touched by a wand which makes us dance and run about happily, like children. . . . Poets are thus liberating gods." In the late essay "Poetry and Imagination" Emerson suggests why this should be so: "the value of a trope," he says, "is that the hearer is one: and indeed Nature itself is a vast trope and all particular natures are tropes. As the bird alights on the bough, then plunges into the air again, so the thoughts of God pause but for a moment in any form."

It was a perception of this truth that entitled Swedenborg to his place in Emerson's band of poetical grandees (despite Emerson's distaste for his overly rigid system of "correspondences"). "Before him the metamorphosis continually plays. Everything on which his eye rests, obeys the impulses of moral nature. . . . When some of the angels affirmed a truth, the laurel twig which they held blossomed in their hands." In *Divine Love and Wisdom* Swedenborg records a conversation he overheard in the spiritual world between two men who in life had been presidents of the Royal Society (Swedenborg visited England several times and died in London). The two men are examining a celestial bird to see how it differs from an earthly bird of the same species. In form it does not, but the two men know that the celestial bird is "nothing but an affection of some angel represented outside the angel as a bird," and that the bird will "vanish or cease with its affection." And indeed, Swedenborg affirms, "this came to pass."[47] (The Swedish seer also thought that this principle— which was called the doctrine of the Affections Clothed—applied on earth as well, though the affections of men, unlike those of angels, are fixed into permanence by an infusion of matter. There are as many snakes in the world as there are wicked impulses, as many song birds as there are virtues. Emerson found this notion intoxicating as a young man; it probably accounts for the hope he expressed in *Nature* that "the problem of restoring to the world original and eternal beauty, is solved by the redemption of the soul." Rid the soul of wicked impulses, and the ugly phenomena will vanish of their own accord.[48])

These are the broad outlines of Emerson's ecstatic theory of poetry. What practical consequences can be deduced from them? First of all, Emerson's theory makes impossible any conception of autotelic art. The theory is mercilessly diachronic. The architectonics, the balanced stresses or structures dear to a formalist's heart, simply do not interest him. Indeed, they cannot interest him, since according to his theory of language they do not exist. Words cannot embody truth, they can only suggest it. "Power ceases in the instant of repose." The poem is true for the poet only as he is composing it, for the reader only as he is reading it. Vivian Hopkins, who in 1951 published a study of Emerson's aesthetic theories, was the first to remark that in all his statements about poetic symbols there is a certain shying away from the literary object itself. "One notices that Emerson never looks long at the object involved, but usually considers the symbol in terms of the writer's creative power . . . or in terms of its effect on the observer, as exhilaration or consolation." And she concludes, quite correctly, that in Emerson's theory "each symbol is figured merely as a stimulus to send the reader on to new intuitions."[49] Like Blake, Emerson is a "spiritual utilitarian";[50] poetic symbols are only valuable to him as conduits through which the divine electricity flows to shock men into transcendence. The notion that idea and image either can or should be fused into "inseparable unity" (that God-term of formalist criticism) is exactly what

Emerson denies. The poet, he says, "perceives the independence of the thought on the symbol, the stability of the thought, the accidency and fugacity of the symbol." The thought is the only place Emerson thinks of looking for structure rather than mere successiveness: "it is not metres, but a metre-making argument that makes a poem,—a thought so passionate and alive that like the spirit of a plant or an animal it has an architecture of its own, and adorns nature with a new thing." Yet even this new thing cannot retain its exhilarating and emancipating power forever: "the books we once valued as the apple of the eye, we have quite exhausted," Emerson reminds us in *The American Scholar*. The problem Hopkins noticed in Emerson's theory of symbols—that the material object used as a symbol "has only temporary value in objectifying spiritual intuition"—is also true of the larger entity these symbols compose. "As the spirit flows on, it leaves the object behind."[51]

The fugacity of the symbol and of the poem is repeated on a larger scale throughout literary and cultural history. *Exigi monumentum aere perennis* is the boast of the traditional poet, but Emerson had warned us in "Circles" that "permanence is but a word of degrees":

> The Greek sculpture is all melted away, as if it had been statues of ice: here and there a solitary figure or fragment remaining, as we see flecks and scraps of snow left in cold dells and mountain clefts, in June and July. For, the genius that created it, creates now somewhat else. The Greek letters last a little longer, but are already passing under the same sentence, and tumbling into the inevitable pit which the creation of new thought opens for all that is old.

This distressing doctrine is not without its cheerful side, at least for the would-be poet. If he can really convince himself that "the experience of each new age requires a new confession, and the world seems waiting always for its poet," as Whitman clearly did, it might even be thought an exhilarating one. But eventually the poems he produces will be consumed by the same process that rendered them necessary. Although Emerson in "The Poet" quotes an anonymous bard as saying that "the melodies of the poet ascend and leap and pierce into the deeps of infinite time," any reader of "Circles" will be likely to demur: even the "songs of the nations" will be at last nothing more than a few additional crumpled sheets in what Stevens calls the "trash can at the end of the world."[52]

Yet the chief difficulty with Emerson's theory of poetry is not the obsolescence to which it dooms the poem but the intolerable strain to which it subjects the poet. The poet must be a prophet; a healer, who "repairs the decays of things"; the "true and only doctor," who, by his revelation that the material universe is in essence symbolic, invites his fellow men "into the science of the real." His only way of "sharing the path or circuit of things through forms, and so making them translucid to others," is to surrender himself "at all risks" to "the divine *aura* which breathes through things" and experience in himself the flowing metamorphosis he is to describe. And his chief merit as a practicing poet will be his ability simply to keep going, to endure this *ecstasis* as long as possible and hence to suggest, through his ceaseless proliferation of tropes, the "splendor of meaning that plays over the visible world." And he must do all this without losing his capacity for joy. At the end of his essay on Shakespeare in *Representative Men* Emerson confesses his disappointment that the greatest poet in the world had used his immense genius for mere entertainment, that he "rested in [the] beauty" of his symbols and never "took the step which seemed inevitable to such genius," asking "what is that which they themselves say?" But suddenly he checks himself with the reflection that Shakespearean insights in the religious poets had not prevented their tropes from turning into fetters:

> ... other men, priest and prophet, Israelite, German, and Swede, beheld the same objects: they also saw through them that which was contained. And to what purpose? The beauty straightaway vanished; they read commandments, all-excluding mountainous duty; an obligation, a sadness, as of piled mountains, fell on them, and life became ghastly, joyless, a pilgrims' progress, a probation, beleaguered round with doleful histories of Adam's fall and curse behind us; with doomsdays and purgatorial fires and penal fires before us; and the heart of the seer and the heart of the listener sank in them.

And he concludes that the world still awaits "its poet-priest, a reconciler," who can blend the insight of the seer, the authority of the prophet, and the joy of the poet.

The problem with this task is not that it cannot be attempted—Whitman was in fact to attempt it, only eleven years after "The Poet" was published, attempt to open himself to "the afflatus surging and surging,"[53] and in passages of great delicacy and beauty proclaim the ecstatic power it has given him to realize a vision of nature's ceaseless proliferation in its minutest particulars:

Swiftly arose and spread around me the peace and joy and
    knowledge that pass all the art and argument of the earth:
And I know that the hand of God is the elderhand of my own,
     . . .
And that a kelson of the creation is love;
And limitless are leaves stiff or drooping in the fields,
And brown ants in the little wells beneath them,
And mossy scabs or the wormfence, and heaped stones,
    and elder and mullen and pokeweed.[54]

The problem is that there is a price to be paid for these ecstasies; nothing is got for nothing. In his very first sermon Emerson had told his congregation to remember that God "is not so much the observer of your actions, as he is the potent principle by which they are bound together"—a conviction that also lies behind the paradoxes of the passage in "Spiritual Laws" where we are first informed that "a man is a method, a selecting principle" and then told that he is like a boom set out to catch driftwood or a magnet among steel filings. The point is that the *contents* of the mind, empirically inspected, indeed appear random, chaotic, a Humean "bundle of perceptions." What holds them together is this "life within life, this literal Emanuel, *God within us.*"

But if the God departs? If the spirit flows on through the poet and leaves him behind like an exhausted symbol? Then you get the filings without the magnet, the driftwood without the boom, the Whitman of the "Sea-Drift" poems: "I too but signify at the utmost a little washed-up drift." The Self does not simply return to normal after an ecstasy; it disintegrates:

> Chaff, straw, splinters of wood, weeds, and the sea-gluten,
> Scum, scales from shining rocks, leaves of salt-lettuce,
>   left by the tide.[55]

You get the Whitman of the 1860 *Leaves of Grass* instead of the Whitman of 1855; the Stevens of "The Snow Man" instead of the Stevens of "Tea at the Palaz of Hoon"; the Emerson of "Experience" instead of the Emerson of "The Poet."

For the nature of my argument in this chapter has obliged me to obscure an important fact. I have been discussing "The Poet" as if it followed "Experience," but Emerson clearly meant the reader to encounter "The Poet" first. We are to go directly from the ejaculations of praise for the poet—"Thou true land-lord! sea-lord! air-lord! Wherever snow falls or water flows . . . there is Beauty, plenteous as rain, shed for thee"—to the exhaustion and depletion of the opening paragraphs of "Experience," where we are like the millers on the lower levels of a stream when the factories above them have exhausted the water.

Nor is this inverse resemblance a chance one; the repetition of phrases and metaphors in the two essays is far too systematic to have been accidental. These are only the most prominent examples:

> . . . when an emotion communicates to the intellect the power to sap and upheave nature, how great the perspective! . . . [D]ream delivers us to dream, and while the drunkenness lasts we will sell our bed, our philosophy, our religion, in our opulence.
>
> *"The Poet"*

> Dream delivers us to dream, and there is no end to illusion.
> *"Experience"*

> And this is the reward; that the ideal shall be real to thee, and the impressions of the actual world shall fall like summer rain, copious, but not troublesome to thine invulnerable essence.
> *"The Poet"*

> The Indian who was laid under a curse that the wind should
> not blow on him, nor water flow to him, nor fire burn him, is a
> type of us all. The dearest events are summer rain, and we the
> Para coats that shed every drop.
>
> *"Experience"*

There is the same relationship between "The Poet" and "Experience" as between the mystical idealism of the Mahabharata and the skeptical idealism of Hume; they are the manic and depressive sides of the same coin.

> But, as it sometimes chanceth, from the might
> Of joy in minds that can no farther go,
> As high as we have mounted in delight
> In our dejection do we sink as low....[56]

"Reading Emerson is like drinking," Alfred Kazin has remarked. "You start so high that by the end of some pieces you cannot help getting depressed."[57] "The Poet" is fatiguing in this way, I think; so is its immediate descendent, Whitman's "Preface" to the 1855 edition of *Leaves of Grass*. Both demand from the reader an *ecstasis* almost as great as the one they recommend to the poet.

Yet the danger of plunging from the emotional heights of "The Poet" to the emotional depths of "Experience" is not the greatest sadness implicit in the first essay. Whicher has pointed out that the very extravagance of Emerson's praise for the poet as the only liberator conceals "a relinquished hope of power."[58] He had once hoped for an artist who could not only "upheave and balance and toss every object in nature for his metaphor," but someday prove himself capable "of playing such a game with his hands instead of his brain." Now he is willing to rest with an *expression* of the highest truth rather than an embodiment of it. Our greater Redeemer not appearing, the poet is the closest thing we have to a liberating god, since he alone among men can submit the shows of things to the desires of the mind. But as Whicher points out, "the victory of the poet presupposes the earlier defeat. It is only because the poetic *life* is not realized, perhaps cannot be, that the poet's *prophecy* of such a life can make him a liberating god.... His reward, the reward he brings others, is not self-union, but a magic flare of imagination, without means and without issue, an intoxicating glimpse of the inaccessible ideal."[59]

"Montaigne": The Middle Way

Poetry gives us visions of the ideal world we have despaired of realizing; it "sweetly torments us with invitations to its own inaccessible homes." Its satisfactions are inseparable from its frustrations. But are there no genuine satisfactions for us in the here-and-now? Satisfactions for the Understanding, if not for the Reason? In "Experience" Emerson had reminded us that life "is not critical or intellectual, but sturdy," and had endeavored to convince us that "the mid-world is best," that "everything good is on the highway," and that "if we will take the good we find, asking no questions, we shall have heaping measures." But the dialectic in that essay, oscillating between extremes of doubt and affirmation, prevented him from resting long enough in that mid-world to make its satisfactions very credible. The opportunity of writing an essay about his old favorite, Montaigne, for *Representative Men* gave him a way to reconsider the themes of "Experience" from this middle ground and, under the aegis of Montaigne's life and personality, to claim a far wider territory for the Understanding than his own life and character would allow.

For Emerson had precisely that blend of resemblance to and difference from Montaigne to make his impersonation of the French writer interesting. On the one hand, he enjoyed with Montaigne that uncanny experience of recognition described in "Self-Reliance": in Montaigne's works he recognized his own rejected thoughts coming back with a certain alienated majesty. He tells us in "Montaigne" of the "delight and wonder" that attended his first reading of the *Essays*: "It seemed to me as if I had myself written the book, in some former life, so sincerely it spoke to my thought and experience." But Montaigne also possessed qualities Emerson feared he lacked. "Montaigne," he observed in his journal, "has the *de quoi* which the French cherubs had not when the courteous archbishop implored them to sit down." (In the story the archbishop says, *"Asseyez-vous, mes enfants"*; but the cherubs decline. *"Monsieur, nous n'avons pas de quoi."*) His own writing, he knew, was always in danger of drifting off into the vaporous; in the famous self-examination he conducted shortly before his twenty-first birthday he complained that his "want of sufficient *bottom*" made him take an awkward and apologetic attitude toward his fellow men. The sturdiness of Montaigne, the self-possession born of a life of action in the real world, were just what Emerson lacked, and what he knew was necessary for the kind of thing he now wished to recommend. For adroit as he was in creating alternative personae for himself in prose, he knew that there was a limit to the authority of a purely literary construct:

> Talent without character is friskiness. The charm of Montaigne's egotism, and of his anecdotes, is, that there is a stout cavalier, a seigneur of France, at home in his château, responsible for all this chatting.
> Now suppose it should be shown and proved that the famous *Essays* were a *jeu d'esprit* of Scaliger, or other scribacious person, written for the booksellers, and not resting on a real status picturesque in the eyes of all men. Would not the book instantly lose almost all its value?

Emerson has a right to discuss in his own person the doubts of the skeptic; he is much less certain about his right to offer Montaigne's remedy for skepticism: "Come, no chimeras! Let us go abroad; let us mix in affairs; let us learn and get and have and climb. . . . Let us have a robust, manly life; let us know what we know, for certain; what we have, let it be solid and seasonable and our own. A world in the hand is worth two in the bush." A robust, manly life, mixing in affairs, is just what Emerson's constitution and temperament denied him; in impersonating Montaigne he is able to lay claim by proxy to a range of experience much wider than his own.

The essay begins by restating, as sharply as possible, the old contrasts between the world of the senses and the world of the soul. "Every fact is related on one side to sensation, and on the other to morals. . . . Life is a pitching of this penny,—heads or tails. . . . This head and this tail are called, in the language of philosophy, Infinite and Finite; Relative and Absolute; Apparent and Real; and many fine names beside." But the very fact that

Emerson now describes these two faces as equal in importance shows how far he has come from his early confidence that the Reason always transcended and subsumed the Understanding; now, as Yoder points out, "the two are set against each other in an equitable and horizontal polarity."[60] The key strategy of classical Pyrrhonism—setting opposed dogmatisms against one another until both cancel each other out—is pursued by Emerson in the opening pages of "Montaigne" with obvious playfulness and yet genuine zeal. For his object is to introduce a new hero-type, appropriate to the mid-world of experience, to replace those earlier heroes of the world of pure Reason, the scholar and the poet.

This new hero is "the skeptic," who arises to occupy the "middle ground" between the opposing forces of the abstractionist and the materialist. "He finds both wrong by being in extremes. He labors to plant his feet, to be the beam of the balance." Dogmatists on both sides of the battlefield make themselves ridiculous by denying one-half of experience; the skeptic tries to give an opinion that acknowledges, if it cannot reconcile, both of the sides. He refuses to make himself ridiculous by philosophizing beyond his depth. "If there is a wish for immortality, and no evidence, why not just say that? If there are conflicting evidences, why not state them? If there is not ground for a candid thinker to make up his mind, yea or nay,—why not suspend the judgment?" This is the ἐποχή recommended by the skeptics of antiquity—the suspension of judgment prompted by the recognition that against every statement the contradictory may be advanced with equal reason. A truly wise man will not dogmatize. To every important question he simply replies: "There is much to say on all sides."

Emerson is careful to distinguish between this definition of the skeptic and the popular one, according to which skepticism suggests "universal denying" and even "scoffing and profligate jeering at all that is stable and good." Emerson's skeptic is rather "the considerer, the prudent, taking in sail, counting stock, husbanding his means," the man who realizes that "adaptiveness" is the distinguishing characteristic of human nature, and who recognizes that rigid maxims are useless in the ceaseless storm of elements, affecting both perceiver and perceived, that constitutes human life. In "Experience" Emerson had defined man as "a golden impossibility." He now expands this definition into one of the most haunting sentences in "Montaigne": "We are golden averages, volitant stabilities, compensated or periodic errors, houses founded on the sea."

The man fit to occupy this middle position must be a "vigorous and original thinker," one who has shown, by his own success in living, that he is "sufficiently related to the world to do justice to Paris and London" as well as to the simpler realm of the Ideal. These qualities meet in the character of Montaigne, who combines candor and earthiness in proportions that are irresistible.

> Here is an impatience and fastidiousness at color or pretense of any kind. He has been in courts so long as to have conceived a furious disgust at appearances; he will indulge himself with a little cursing and swearing; he will talk with sailors and gipsies, use flash and street ballads; he has stayed in-doors till he is deadly sick; he will to the open air, though it rain bullets. . . . He likes his saddle. You may read theology, and grammar, and metaphysics elsewhere. Whatever you get here shall smack of the earth and of real life, sweet, or smart, or stinging.

This same vigor characterizes not only Montaigne's choice of subjects but also his style. As Emerson's well-known hyperbole has it: "Cut these words and they would bleed; they are vascular and alive."

Montaigne is above all others the master of the "positive degree" Emerson so greatly admired:

> Montaigne talks with shrewdness, knows the world and books and himself . . . never shrieks, or protests, or prays: no weakness, no convulsion, no superlative: does not wish to jump out of his skin, or play any antics, or annihilate space and time, but is stout and solid. . . . He keeps the plain; he rarely mounts or sinks; likes to feel solid ground and the stones underneath. His writing has no enthusiasms, no aspiration; contented, self-respecting, and keeping the middle of the road.

He is, in other words, the antitype of the poet, who is always rising into ecstasies or sinking into depressions. But if Montaigne offers us no tantalizing glimpses of the inaccessible Ideal, his solidity and good sense perhaps can provide a better defense against the onslaughts of the "Lords of Life" Emerson had named in "Experience" than all the consolations of momentary transcendence.

For it becomes clear by the middle of the essay that Emerson intends to use Montaigne as a vantage point from which to attain a different view of the "doubts and negations" he had examined in "Experience": a view characterized by ironic distance, self-possession, and wit, as the one in the earlier essay had been characterized by a kind of desperate sincerity. The difference between the essays is evident in the way Emerson announces the seriousness of his pursuit of truth in each. "I have set my heart on honesty in this chapter," he says in "Experience." In "Montaigne" he says: "I shall not take Sunday objections, made up on purpose to be put down. I shall take the worst I can find, whether I can dispose of them or they of me." The truculence and low-keyed humor in the tone of the latter suggest the terms in which the battle is to be fought and imply as well some of the ways it can be won.

Since the ironic attitude toward the self that Emerson in "Montaigne" recommends as the best defense against "the exaggeration and formalism of bigots and blockheads" is predicated upon self-awareness, that slight dislocation of our own centers from the Center of Life that allows us to speak *knowingly* of our own enthusiasms, self-consciousness can hardly seem in "Montaigne" the evil it is represented to be in "Experience." The "levity of intellect" that makes simple piety impossible ("The dull pray; the geniuses are light mockers") may very well have been "the subject of much elegy in our nineteenth century, from Byron, Goethe, and other poets of less fame," but Emerson confesses that it is not very affecting to his imagination. "What flutters the Church of Rome, or of England, or of Geneva, or of Boston, may yet be very far from touching any principle of faith." The discovery we have made that we exist may indeed be very unhappy, but it is too late to be helped, and a wise man will content himself with the reflection that "if the ancients possessed one world, we have two." One is reminded of the gentle teasing

Emerson had administered to the conventions of Romantic melancholy in *The American Scholar:*

> Our age is bewailed as the age of Introversion. Must that needs be evil? We, it seems, are critical. We are embarrassed with second thoughts. . . . We are lined with eyes. We see with our feet. The time is infected with Hamlet's unhappiness,—
>
> "Sicklied o'er with the pale cast of thought."
>
> Is it so bad then? Sight is the last thing to be pitied. Would we be blind? Do we fear lest we should outsee nature and God, and drink truth dry?

If the Fall into self-consciousness is irreversible, it brings its own compensations, as he had pointed out in "The Present Age":

> For my part I am content there shall be a certain slight discord in the song of the morning stars, if that discord arise from my ear being opened to the undersong of spirits. What consolation, what truth, are not hereby opened to us? This insight, this introversion gives us to know that all the seeming confusion of events and voices around us, beheld from a certain elevation of thought, become orderly and musical.

"Elevation of thought" is in fact the remedy proposed for the second of the major doubts or negations Emerson examines in "Montaigne": the "power of moods, each setting at nought all but its own tissue of facts and beliefs." "Experience" had explored this negation, too; but what was there treated elegiacally has become, in "Montaigne," a subject for rueful humor:

> Our life is March weather, savage and serene in one hour. We go forth austere, dedicated, believing in the iron links of Destiny, and will not turn on our heel to save our life: but a book, or a bust, or only the sound of a name, shoots a spark through the nerves, and we suddenly believe in will: my finger-ring shall be the seal of Solomon; fate is for imbeciles; all is possible to the resolved mind. Presently . . . common sense resumes its tyranny; we say, "Well, the army, after all, is the gate to fame, manners, and poetry: and, look you,—on the whole, selfishness plants bests, prunes best, makes the best commerce and the best citizen."

It is difficult for a man to take himself very seriously when an hour, or two hours, can produce in him a complete revolution of creeds and attitudes. "Are the opinions of a man on right and wrong, on fate and causation, at the mercy of a broken sleep or an indigestion? . . . I like not the French celerity,—a new Church and State once a week." But though this second negation provides occasion for a display of that "whimsical despair"[61] Firkins noticed in many of his works, the despair is not really very deep. The "power of moods" is no greater threat to belief than the levity of intellect. "As far as it asserts rotation of states of mind, I suppose it suggests its own remedy, namely in the record of larger periods. What is the mean of many states; of all the states?" As he had said in "Self-Reliance," speaking of inconsistency: "These varieties are lost sight of at a little distance, at a little distance, at a little height of thought. One tendency unites them all. The voyage of the best ship is a zigzag line of a hundred tacks. See the line from a sufficient distance, and it straightens itself to the average tendency."

But the final negation, the "main resistance which the affirmative impulse finds," is not so easily disposed of. The "doctrine of the Illusionists"—the belief that "we have been practiced upon in all the principal performances of life, and free agency is the emptiest name"—remains to plague the most determined man of faith. What experience teaches is that the "objects" we pursue in life with such desperate zeal are largely projections from the imagination. Worse still, we gradually recognize that even in our fine renunciations we get no closer to reality; we merely exchange one bauble for another. "There are as many pillows of illusion as flakes in a snow-storm," Emerson writes in the essay "Illusion" from *The Conduct of Life*. "We wake from one dream into another dream. The toys to be sure are various, and are graduated in refinement to the quality of the dupe. The intellectual man requires a fine bait; the sots are easily amused." But no one is free from the fascination. "In the life of the dreariest alderman, fancy enters into all details and colors them with rosy hue." And if the snowstorm of illusions ceases for an instant to reveal the Reality behind it, the vision only helps to show how illusory is the "progress" the individual thinks he has made since the last moment of revelation. In a journal passage later revised for inclusion in "Montaigne" Emerson recorded one of his chief worries. "They say the Mathematics leave the mind where they found it. What if life or Experience should do the same?" Even the minimal consolation offered in the essay "Experience"—that the years teach much which the days never know, though the individual is always mistaken—sometimes gives way to a grimmer vision of human life, as in the chilling little allegory that ends "Illusions":

> Every god is there sitting in his sphere. The young mortal enters the hall of the firmament; there is he alone with them alone, they pouring on him benedictions and gifts, and beckoning him up to their thrones. On the instant, and incessantly, fall snow-storms of illusions. He fancies himself in a vast crowd which sways this way and that and whose movement and doings he must obey: he fancies himself poor, orphaned, insignificant. The mad crowd drives hither and thither, now furiously commanding this thing to be done, now that. What is he that he should resist their will, and think or act for himself? Every moment new changes and new showers of deceptions to baffle and distract him. And when, by and by, for an instant, the air clears and the cloud lifts a little, there are the gods still sitting around him on their thrones,—they alone with him alone.

But if the "absence of any appearance of reconciliation between the theory and practice of life," the frustrating "parallelism of great and little, which never react on one another, nor discover the smallest tendency to converge," is the doubt that cannot be disposed of, it is also a doubt that cannot dispose of me, since it grants me a vision of the very perfection it places forever beyond my reach, and hence revives my old hopes at the very moment it seeks to extinguish them. I agree with Maurice Gonnaud when he argues that it is a mistake to describe Emerson's later career as an expression of "resignation," which is not the same thing as "acknowledged loss of individual power."[62] The "undiminished intensity of purpose," the "majestic abstractions and the intimation of unchanging truth," are still there, even if they are now played off against an equally vivid awareness of the lessons of skepticism. Emerson's vision in these later essays has not narrowed, much less become shut in by that heaven of brass under which the unbelievers labor. "If anything, the range and depth of human experience has been increased. It now includes in tingling companionship the wildest promise and the most humiliating frustration."[63] Hence those curious and uniquely Emersonian passages in which a faith is expressed that blends in one improbable mixture the optimism of Candide and the skepticism of Voltaire. Sometimes this faith finds expression in a wistfully humorous passage, as in the essay "Worship," where an alter ego named "Benedict" asserts:

> I am never beaten until I know that I am beaten. I meet powerful, brutal people to whom I have no skill to reply. They think they have defeated me. . . . I seem to fail in my friends and clients, too. That is to say, in all the encounters that have yet chanced, I have been historically beaten; and yet I know all the time that I have never been beaten; have never yet fought, shall certainly fight when my hour comes, and shall beat.

And sometimes in a deeply moving one, as in the famous journal passage written three months after his son's death:

> There is now a sublime revelation in each of us which makes us so strangely aware & certain of our riches that although I have never since I was born for so much as one moment expressed the truth, and although I have never heard the expression of it from any other, I know that the whole is here,—the wealth of the Universe is for me. Every thing is explicable & practicable for me. And yet whilst I adore this ineffable life which is at my heart, it will not condescend to gossip with me, it will not announce to me any particulars of science, it will not enter into the details of my biography, & say to me why I have a son & daughters born to me, or why my son dies in his sixth year of joy. Herein then I have this latent omniscience coexistent with omnignorance. Moreover, whilst this Deity glows at the heart, & by his unlimited presentiments gives me all power, I know that tomorrow will be as this day, I am a dwarf, & I remain a dwarf. That is to say, I believe in Fate. As long as I am weak, I shall talk of Fate; whenever the God fills me with his fulness, I shall see the disappearance of Fate.
> I am *Defeated* all the time; yet to Victory I am born.

The riddle of the age, Emerson once said, has for each man a private solution. If his own honesty made him refuse to "lie for the right" and say "there are no doubts," it also obliges him to confess, at the end of "Montaigne," that for him personally the contest between belief and unbelief had been rigged from the beginning. "Some minds are incapable of skepticism. The doubts they profess to entertain are rather a civility or accommodation to the common discourse of their company. They may well give themselves leave to speculate, for they are sure of a return." Like the spiritual tycoon of "Self-Reliance," they have invested the capital of their being in a bank that cannot break; like the resolute pilgrim of "Experience," they arrive at the end of their quest to discover not a wall, but interminable oceans. If the universe for unbelievers is "like an infinite series of planes, each of which is a false bottom," for believers it is infinite in the opposite direction: "Once admitted to the heaven of thought, they see no relapse into night, but infinite invitation on the other side. Heaven is within heaven, and sky over sky, and they are encompassed with divinities."

Believer and unbeliever are inextricably linked, since the only kind of faith open to the unbeliever is a "reflex or parasite faith; not a sight of realities, but an instinctive reliance on the seers and believers of realities. The manners and thoughts of believers astonish them and convince them that these have seen something which is hid from themselves." But the very laws of thought that link them together ensure that their relationship will always be full of strife. The "sensual habit" of the unbeliever, his preference for the familiar and traditional, "would fix the believer to his last position, whilst he as inevitably advances; and presently the unbeliever, for love of belief, burns the believer." The implicit model for this sentence is the old myth of ossification from "Circles"; its use here shows why Emerson found his private mythology indispensable. It allowed him to explain the horror of human history without attributing essential evil to anyone, and hence enabled him to reconcile a belief in man's innocence with the unavoidable evidence of his depravity.

But a memory of "Circles" also suggests why the distinction

between "believers" and "unbelievers" (in Emerson's sense) is a more useful one than the popular distinction between believers and skeptics. Many of those who would classify *themselves* as believers are unbelievers in Emerson's system, while much of what they would condemn as skepticism he regards as the highest expression of faith. "The new statement is always hated by the old, and, to those dwelling in the old, comes like an abyss of skepticism," Emerson had said in "Circles"; he now repeats the assertion: "Great believers are always reckoned infidels, impracticable, fantastic, atheistic, and really men of no account." Jesus of Nazareth, after all, was a skeptic to the orthodox Jews of his day.

For the real target of skepticism, as Richard Popkin points out in his *History of Scepticism*, is not faith but dogmatism, "the view that evidence can be offered to establish that at least one non-empirical proposition cannot possibly be false."[64] What the skeptic questions is the ability of unaided *human* reason to attain truth. Whether absolute truth exists, and whether it is knowable through some other means (e.g., faith in Revelation), is a separate question, and thoroughgoing skeptics can be found giving diametrically opposed answers to it: Hume and Voltaire in one camp, Pascal and Kierkegaard in the other. Montaigne's great skeptical treatise, the *Apology for Raymond Sebond,* attacks every variety of dogmatic assertion in order to degrade the claims of human reason; it degrades reason in order to elevate faith. Only through faith can we attain knowledge of truth, faith freely given by God. "All that we undertake without his assistance, all that we see without the lamp of his grace, is only vanity and folly." The man who adopts the "perpetual confession of ignorance," the systematic suspension of judgment characteristic of the Pyrrhonists, is in the best position to receive the truths of Revelation: "He is a blank tablet prepared to take from the finger of God such forms as he shall be pleased to engrave upon it."[65]

Montaigne's *Apology* ends with a sudden leap into Christian faith; Emerson's essay on Montaigne concludes with the same miraculous act of levitation, a restatement of the faith that had originally guided him to the discovery of the God within, and now is discovered to remain after the last depredations of doubt:

The final solution in which skepticism is lost, is in the moral sentiment, which never forfeits its supremacy. All moods may be safely tried, and their weight allowed to all objections: the moral sentiment as easily outweighs them all, as any one. This is the drop which balances the sea. I play with the miscellany of facts, and take those superficial views which we call skepticism; but I know that they will presently appear to me in that order which makes skepticism impossible.

This belief—that "the world is saturated with deity and with law"—may be no more acceptable to the modern reader than Montaigne's, or Dante's, or Milton's; but even those who find it impossible to share Emerson's faith must admire the steadiness of vision it made possible. The faithful man "can behold with serenity the yawning gulf between the ambition of man and his power of performance, between the demand and supply of power, which makes the tragedy of all souls." This "yawning gulf" had been Emerson's chief subject from the beginning, but rarely had it been portrayed with as much ferocity as in the final pages of "Montaigne":

> Charles Fourier announced that "the attractions of man are proportioned to his destinies"; in other words, that every desire predicts its own satisfaction. Yet all experience exhibits the reverse of this; the incompetency of power is the universal grief of young and ardent minds. They accuse the divine Providence of a certain parsimony. It has shown the heaven and earth to every child and filled him with a desire for the whole; a desire raging, infinite; a hunger, as of space to be filled with planets; a cry of famine, as of devils for souls. Then for the satisfaction,—to each man is administered a single drop, a bead of dew of vital power, *per day,*—a cup as large as space, and one drop of the water of life in it. Each man woke in the morning with an appetite that could eat the solar system like a cake; a spirit for action and passion without bounds; he could try conclusions with gravitation or chemistry; but, on the first motion to prove his strength,—hands, feet, senses, gave way and would not serve him. He was an emperor deserted by his states, and left to whistle by himself, or thrust into a mob of emperors, all whistling: and still the sirens sang, "The attractions are proportioned to the destinies."

The sheer insatiability of human desire has rarely been so vividly described; it puts one in mind of the observation Emerson had entered in his journal when he was only twenty-four: "The emperor Napoleon is as much a proof of heaven & eternity as the life of St. Paul. He proves how impossible it is to satisfy the human soul." And if the nature of things at present refuses to grant us a reality adequate to our desires, reduces us to merely one of a crowd of whistling and deserted emperors, that is no reason for renouncing the desire.

M. H. Abrams has noted that the Romantic doctrine of man's "saving insatiability" neatly "reverses the cardinal neoclassic ideal of setting only accessible goals, by converting what had been man's tragic error—the inordinacy of his 'pride' that persists in setting infinite aims for finite man—into his specific glory and his triumph." It is quite true that "man's infinite hopes can never be matched by the world as it is," but this is no reason to repudiate hope. For "in the magnitude of the disappointment lies its consolation; . . . the gap between the inordinacy of his hope and the limits of possibility is the measure of man's dignity and greatness."[66] For the believer, then, the hell of unsatisfiable desire and the heaven of inaccessible fulfillment are both contained in the circumference of the same Eternal Cause, as the two lines from Milton Emerson habitually used as shorthand for the experience of interminability—"Another morn is risen on mid-noon" and "Under every deep a lower deep opens"—are both subsumed in the deliberately ambiguous line of poetry that ends "Montaigne": "If my bark sink, 't is to another sea."

Textual References

A Note on Abbreviations and Editions Cited

References to Emerson's works, sermons, and letters are indicated by abbreviated title, volume number, and page number following the quotation. Since the new Harvard editions of the *Journals* and *Collected Works* are not yet complete, it has been necessary to use the Centenary Edition of both journals and works as well.

JMN   *The Journals and Miscellaneous Notebooks of Ralph Waldo Emerson*, ed. William Gillman et al. (Cambridge, Mass.: The Belknap Press of Harvard University Press, 1960–   ).

J   *The Journals of Ralph Waldo Emerson*, ed. Edward Waldo Emerson and Waldo Emerson Forbes, 10 vols., Centenary Edition (Boston and New York: Houghton Mifflin Co., 1910–1914).

CW   *The Collected Works of Ralph Waldo Emerson*, ed. Robert Spiller, Alfred Ferguson, et al. (Cambridge, Mass.: The Belknap Press of Harvard University Press, 1971–   ).

W   *The Complete Works of Ralph Waldo Emerson*, ed. Edward Waldo Emerson, 12 vols., Centenary Edition (Boston and New York: Houghton Mifflin Co., 1903–1904).

EL   *The Early Lectures of Ralph Waldo Emerson*, ed. Stephen Whicher, Robert Spiller, et al., 3 vols. (Cambridge, Mass.: The Belknap Press of Harvard University Press, 1960–1972).

L   *The Letters of Ralph Waldo Emerson*, ed. Ralph L. Rusk, 6 vols. (New York: Columbia University Press, 1939).

CEC   *The Correspondence of Emerson and Carlyle*, ed. Joseph Slater (New York: Columbia University Press, 1964).

YES   *Young Emerson Speaks: Unpublished Discourses on Many Subjects*, ed. Arthur Cushman McGiffert, Jr. (Boston: Houghton Mifflin Co., 1938).

Preface

Chapter I/The Lapses of Uriel: Emerson's Rhetoric

11 "The tigers of wrath . . . horses of instruction," J, IX, 575.
12 "valued adviser . . . doctrines of the church," CW, II, 30.
12 "On my saying . . . against it," CW, II, 30.
12 "Whoso would be . . . if it be goodness," CW, II, 29–30.
12 "Absolve you to . . . suffrage of the world," CW, II, 30.
12 "dear old doctrines," CW, II, 30.
13 "historical Christianity," CW, I, 82.
13 "the prayers and even . . . business of the people," CW, I, 86.
13 "this life within life . . . *God within us,*" J, II, 225.
13 "beware of Antinomianism," JMN, V, 496.
13 "the loss of the old . . . will not countervail," JMN, V, 496.
13 "automaton man . . . directions & repairs," JMN, III, 210.
13 "terrible freedom," JMN, V, 46.
13 "the bold sensualist . . . gild his crimes," CW, II, 42.
13 "Men do what is called . . . pay a high board," CW, II, 31.
14 "It is plain . . . Which is the Atheist?" JMN, VII, 112.
14 "life, transition, the energizing spirit," CW, II, 181.
14 "The new statement . . . abyss of skepticism," CW, II, 181.
14 "And thus . . . the true God!" CW, II, 181.
15 "I am not careful to justify myself," CW, II, 188.
15 "One man's . . . another's folly," CW, II, 187.
15–16 "I own I am . . . extreme satisfactions," CW, II, 188.
16 "And thus . . . extreme satisfactions," JMN, VII, 521.
17 "Except Rabelais and . . . filth and corruption," W, IV, 138.
17 "That pure malignity . . . last profanation," W, IV, 138.
17 "But fare . . . moral sublime," JMN, III, 304.
18 "There is not . . . new generalization," CW, II, 183.
18 "by knowledge . . . feebler sight," W, IX, 14.
19 "Martyrs with thumbscrews . . . make me sick," JMN, VII, 71.
20 "Criticism has this defense . . . desires of the mind," JMN, V, 190.
20–21 "It is remarkable . . . the sense that we affix to it," JMN, V, 226.
21 "against the sanity and authority of the soul," CW, II, 38.

Chapter II/The Riddle of the Sphinx: *Nature*

22 "The aenigma . . . its meaning," JMN, III, 51.
22 "I conversed with him . . . crack with her," JMN, V, 153.
22 "theory of nature," CW, I, 8.
23 "language, sleep . . . beasts, sex," CW, I, 8.
23 "So you have . . . modest attempt," JMN, V, 172.
23 "innocent serenity," CW, II, 204.
23 "Well assured . . . plainest argument," CW, II, 204.
23 "Mrs. Helen Bell . . . You're another!" J, X, 420.

24 "wild delight," CW, I, 9.
24 "I have seen . . . morning wind," CW, I, 13.
24 "Not less excellent . . . mute music," CW, I, 13–14.
27 "low degree of the sublime," CW, I, 31.
28 "Crack . . . soldered or welded," L, II, 32.
28 "candidate for truth," CW, II, 202.
28 "recognize all . . . being is swung," CW, II, 202.
29 "The ruin . . . but opake," CW, I, 43.
30 "I learn . . . after an earthquake," JMN, V, 333.
30 "chiefly upon Natural Ethics," L, I, 447.
30 "melancholy, penitential, self-accusing," JMN, V, 152.
31 "So you . . . modest attempt," JMN, V, 172.
31 "It were . . . practice of Ideas in us," JMN, V, 175.
31 "helpless mourning," JMN, V, 161.

1831–1833: "Correspondence" and the Moral Law

32 "one of those . . . human improvement," JMN, II, 265.
33 "men have come . . . God were dead," CW, I, 84.
33 "An exemplary . . . immortality of the soul," L, I, 128.
33 "Presbyterianism . . . ignorance of men," L, I, 128.
33 "this, I think . . . orthodoxy," L, I, 128.
34 "all things are moral," CW, I, 25.
35 "feebleness and dust," JMN, IV, 87.
35 "cannot be . . . my defeats," JMN, IV, 87.
35 "It has . . . my guilt," JMN, IV, 87.
35 "We are . . . current in the world," JMN, III, 72–73, 77.
36 "affections of the heart," JMN, II, 50.
36 "faculties of the mind," JMN, II, 50.
36 "The affections . . . loses its sting," JMN, II, 50.
36 "a very operose way . . . people good," JMN, IV, 45.
36 "You must . . . at first?" JMN, IV, 45.
37 "since I . . . was wrought," YES, 125.
37 "Blessed is . . . are synonyms," JMN, IV, 365.
37 "Is not Solomon's . . . men are not?" JMN, IV, 313.
37–38 "a correlation . . . at that time," EL, I, 1.
38 "Almost all . . . maxims of morals," JMN, III, 255, fn. 93.
38 "Natural Ethics," L, I, 447.
38 "It occurs . . . ethical sense," JMN, IV, 254.
38 "reaction is equal to action," CW, I, 21.
38 "the smallest weight . . . compensated by time," CW, I, 21–22.
38 "to learn . . . truth in ethics," JMN, IV, 322.
39 "Every object . . . what they signify," JMN, VII, 98.
39–40 "The ancients . . . heard with a smile," JMN, V, 97–98.
40 "pile of stones . . . bare blind laws," JMN, V, 98.
40 "the occult belief . . . common every day facts," JMN, V, 212.

40 "highest minds . . . manifold meaning," W, III, 4.
41 "Nature is . . . that tongue," JMN, IV, 95.

July 13, 1833–May 9, 1936: The Jardin des Plantes
to the Death of Charles

41 "as calm . . . a bridegroom," JMN, IV, 199–200.
41 "The Universe . . . be a naturalist," JMN, IV, 199–200.
42 "Not a form so . . . *man the observer*," JMN, IV, 199.
42 "I like . . . about nature," JMN, IV, 237.
43 "Insist on seeing . . . question addressed to you," JMN, V, 183.
43 "occult relation," CW, I, 10.
43 "visible things and human thoughts," CW, I, 19.
43 "The fox and . . . rend us," CW, I, 39.
43 "How few cosmogonies . . . they touch," JMN, VII, 352.
43 "The idea . . . problem in geometry," JMN, IV, 287–288.
43–44 "We must trust the . . . things can satisfy," CW, I, 8.
44 "is only a name . . . which are unpenetrated," W, VI, 31.
45 "true theory . . . all phenomena," CW, I, 8.
45 "for herein is writ . . . own history," EL, I, 26.
45 "it may be . . . human mind," EL, I, 26.
46 "noblest theme," JMN, I, 8.
46 "Also Mr. Waldo . . . Sybilline collections," JMN, I, 43.
46 "Who is he . . . still exist," JMN, II, 189–90.
46 "we love . . . is imperishable," JMN, I, 335.
46–47 "through Nature . . . her god," JMN, V, 146–147.
47 "emancipate us," CW, I, 30.
47 "one vast . . . contemplation of the soul," CW, I, 36.
47 "In these . . . viewed in God," JMN, V, 149.
48 "progressive," CW, I, 36.

May–June 1836: "The eye is closed that was to see nature for me . . ."

48 "The eye is closed . . . for me" JMN, V, 152.
49 "I think . . . unhappy again," L, II, 7.
49 "inestimable advantage . . . friend in one," JMN, V, 151.
49 "occult hereditary sympathy," JMN, V, 151–52.
49 "society . . . total exclusion from all other," L, II, 24–25.
50 "his senses . . . those of a Greek," JMN, V, 152.
50 "spheral," JMN, XI, 401.
50 "Every ship . . . that we sail in," W, III, 46.
50 "Power is one . . . must learn," JMN, V, 174.
51 "When much . . . short time," CW, I, 28–29.
51 "the roots . . . disappearance from me," JMN, V, 416.
51 "I cannot deny . . . else is shadow," CW, II, 116.
51 "Let us treat . . . perhaps they are," W, III, 60.
52 "one man," CEC, 148.

June–August 1836: The Apocalypse of the Mind

Contraction and Dislocation: Two Fables of the Fall

63–64 "Not whilst . . . Messiah come," JMN, V, 181.
  64 "a dream . . . concerted experiments," CW, I, 39.
  64 "The very . . . fits man awake," W, X, 5.
63–65 "some traditions . . . and prophecy," CW, I, 41–42.
  65 "The foundations . . . one degradation," CW, I, 42.
  65 "the argument . . . this hope," CW, II, 159.
  66 "I acknowledge . . . infinite scope," JMN, V, 332.
  66 "This fact . . . indissoluble connection," JMN, I, 75.
  66 "all history . . . one degradation," CW, I, 42.
  66 "like Nebuchadnezzar . . . an ox," CW, I, 42.
  66 "But who . . . force of spirit?" CW, I, 42.
  66 "Man is . . . dwarf of himself," CW, I, 42.
  67 "fitting . . . corresponds," CW, I, 42.
  67 "shrunk to a drop," CW, I, 42.
  67 "Why God . . . the devil?" J, X, 303.
  68 "Nature is . . . obedient," CW, I, 44.
  68 "So fast will . . . no more seen," CW, I, 45.
  69 "Nature is loved . . . no citizen," W, III, 178.
  69 "As when . . . perfect sight," CW, I, 45.
  70 "Not in nature . . . her own," CW, II, 86.
  70 "sordor and filths," CW, I, 45.
  72 "The problem . . . with himself," CW, I, 43.
  73 "The axis of vision . . . but opake," CW, I, 43.
  75 "to learn the law . . . in ethics," JMN, IV, 322.
  76 "The world . . . within itself," JMN, V, 280.
  76 "Whenever a man . . . religions forms," JMN, V, 492.
  76 "If *I* see . . . before me," JMN, VII, 435.
  76 "Every body . . . the great laws," JMN, V, 506.
  76 "Do something . . . of your character," JMN, VII, 297.
  76 "There is a . . . be coincident," CW, II, 136.
  76 "the soul's emphasis is always right," CW, II, 84.
  76 "a selecting . . . wherever he goes," CW, II, 84.
  76 "Those facts . . . other minds," CW, II, 84.
  77 "there is . . . go again," JMN, V, 189.
  77 "As the law . . . to gain," JMN, IV, 87.
  77 "Every body . . . a million," JMN, IV, 34.
  77 "I write . . . see again," J, IX, 468.
  77 "I am God . . . by the wall," CW, II, 182.
  78 "Our faith . . . is habitual," CW, II, 159.
  78 "But suddenly . . . null the circumstances," JMN, V, 275.
  78 "The ruin . . . but opake," CW, I, 43.
  79 "has penetrated . . . single formula," CW, I, 34.
  79 "In the highest . . . are a vision," JMN, V, 467.
  79 "boy that . . . spoke truth," JMN, V, 102.
  79 "It required . . . of the world," W, IV, 117.

Chapter III/Portable Property

The Empty American Parnassus

*The Morning After the Earthquake: Emerson and
the Depression of 1837*

Tradition and the Individual Talent: The American Scholar

102 "Late in . . . for fame," JMN, II, 244.
102 "dinned to . . . Greece & Rome," JMN, II, 244.
103 "slipshod newspaper style," JMN, VII, 43.
104 "Whilst I read . . . morning and evening," CW, I, 106.
104 "But go . . . alike unattempted," CW, I, 106.
104 "direct pragmatical analysis of objects," JMN, III, 39.
104 "mauls the moon . . . main business," JMN, III, 39.
105 "a certain . . . but empty," CW, I, 100.
106 "How much . . . a thought," JMN, V, 454.
106 "Sleep lingers . . . our perception," W, III, 45.
106 "We live . . . to them," W, X, 13.
107 "glad to . . . of fear," CW, I, 288.
107 "We go . . . every hand," JMN, VII, 276.
107 "our debt to Literature," JMN, VII, 276.
107 "Now shall . . . hundred charities?" W, VIII, 187–188.
108 "A man is . . . other minds," CW, II, 84.
109 "Nature is . . . is obedient," CW, I, 44.
109 "All that you . . . powers of thought," CW, I, 204.
109 "transfer of . . . the consciousness," CW, I, 203.
110 "republish themselves . . . they occupy," CW, I, 131.
110 "To him . . . with reverence," JMN, VII, 180–181.
110 "Pereant qui . . . nostra dixerunt," JMN, VII, 194.
110–111 "Genius is . . . by over-influence," CW, I, 57.
111 "The English . . . two hundred years," CW, I, 57.
111 "One would . . . and monopolized," CW, I, 82.
111 "Our debt . . . minds quote," W, VIII, 178.
111 "There is . . . of invention," W, VIII, 179.
111 "This vast . . . involves bankruptcy," W, VIII, 189.
112 "undoubtedly there . . . of reading," CW, I, 57.
112 "We attach . . . hating another," JMN, I, 230.
113 "The subject . . . the dead," JMN, IV, 269.
113 "trust thyself," CW, II, 28.
113 "Who is the Trustee?" CW, II, 37.
114 "In every kind . . . being superfluous," W, VIII, 188–189.
114 "restorers of . . . all degrees," CW, I, 56.
114 "occupy," W, III, 240.
114 "an abdication . . . present empire," JMN, V, 178.
114 "for good . . . to the book," JMN, XI, 166.
114 "receive always . . . fatal disservice," CW, I, 57.
115 "Our poetry . . . *miow miow*," JMN, VIII, 173.
115 "the one . . . active soul," CW, I, 56.
115 "imitation is suicide," CW, II, 27.
115 "Books are for . . . idle times," CW, I, 57.

The Divinity School Address

The Universal Grudge: "The Protest" and "Circles"

"Self-Reliance"

Chapter IV/The Curse of Kehama

"Experience"

     148 "It is . . . Fall of Man," W, III, 75.
     149 "There are . . . sons and lovers," W, III, 48.
     149 "We believe . . . the felon," W, III, 48.
     149 "shun father . . . and brother," CW, II, 30.
     149 "men cease . . . with him," CW, II, 182–183.
149–150 "will it . . . a particular?" W, III, 56.
     150 "ruins the . . . of love," W, III, 77.
     150 "shown the . . . for souls," W, IV, 184.
     151 "Every ship . . . the horizon," W, III, 46.
     151 "each man . . . his imagination," CW, II, 100.
     151 "How easily . . . and years!" W, III, 67.
     151 "capital stock," JMN, V, 307.
     151 "would quickly . . . of life," W, III, 67.
     152 "Where do . . . place again," W, III, 45.
     152 "Did our . . . their dams," W, III, 45–46.
152–153 "I have . . . & seldom," JMN, II, 153.
     153 "In the pageant . . . Experience exhibits," JMN, II, 148–149.
     153 "We dreamed . . . practical effect," JMN, II, 149.
     153 "The momentary . . . in Society," JMN, II, 149.
153–154 "Alas. As . . . human expectations," JMN, II, 149.
     154 "The dreams . . . & condition," JMN, II, 153.
     154 *"periods* of . . . a dunce," JMN, II, 389.
     155 "opposite negations . . . is swung," CW, II, 202.
     155 "Lethean stream . . . of unreality," JMN, V, 20.
     155 "The astonishment . . . to converge," W, IV, 178–179.
     156 "Very little . . . a lifetime," JMN, V, 277.
     156 "It is . . . without time," CW, II, 187–188.
     156 "in the . . . join these," JMN, V, 56.
     156 "on the way back to Annihilation," JMN, V, 20.
     157 "certain brief experience," CW, I, 213.
     157 "we have . . . of none," JMN, II, 161.
     157 "Scotch Goliath," L, I, 138.
     157 "Where is . . . followed since," L, I, 138.
     158 "Internal evidence . . . they do," JMN, III, 214.
     158 "yield to Hume . . . probably false," JMN, III, 215.
     159 "life is . . . the other," W, III, 245.
     159 "The sublime . . . outcast corpse," CW, I, 34.
     159 "I know . . . of afterwards," L, II, 384–385.
     160 "Idealism seems . . . universal holiness," JMN, III, 363.
     160 "belief consists . . . denying them," W, IV, 180.
     160 "Religion does . . . of Reason," JMN, V, 123.
     160 "piety or passion . . . of change," CW, I, 34–35.

160 "The best . . . its God," CW, I, 30.
161 "The senses . . . *their channel*," JMN, III, 362.
161 "I fear . . . be written," JMN, II, 224–225.
162 "train of . . . own hue," W, III, 50.
162 "Grief too . . . us idealists," W, III, 48.
163 "swim and glitter," W, III, 45.
163 "If any . . . begun in us," W, III, 46.
164 "What a . . . on mid-noon," JMN, V, 38.
164 "the years . . . never know," W, III, 46.
164 "The individual is always mistaken," W, III, 69.
164 "All our . . . calendar day," W, III, 46.
165 "Some heavenly days . . . be born," W, III, 46.
165 "What opium . . . dodge us," W, III, 48–49.
166 "the most . . . our condition," W, III, 49.
167 "innavigable sea," W, III, 48.
167 "even the . . . sons and lovers," W, III, 48.
167 "Alas! I chiefly grieve . . . & Kehama," L, III, 9–10.
167–168 "The dearest . . . dodge us," W, III, 49.
168 "Such as . . . help you," W, VI, 239.
168 "*Ate Dea* is gentle," W, III, 48.
168 "Grief too . . . us idealists," W, III, 48.
168 "I cannot . . . to me," W, III, 48.
169 "Religion makes . . . its god," JMN, V, 124.
169 "these caducous . . . them ever," JMN, V, 363.
169 "I told . . . all things," JMN, VII, 132.
169 "could not . . . enriching me," W, III, 49.
170 "Where do we find ourselves?" W, III, 45.
170 "Let us . . . is nature?" CW, I, 7.
170 "colored and distorting lenses," W, III, 75.
170 "Men seem . . . and reference," W, III, 46.
170 "a prison . . . cannot see," W, III, 52.
170 "noble doubt," CW, I, 29.
171 "Men resist . . . of religion," W, III, 52.
171 "capital exception," W, III, 52.
171 "a fatal partialist . . . universalist," W, III, 248.
171 "the crime . . . the felon," W, III, 78–79.
171 "every man . . . greater possibility," CW, II, 182.
171 "links of . . . physical necessity," W, III, 54.
171 "But it . . . a state," W, III, 54–55.
172 "We need . . . of objects," W, III, 55.
172 "one central . . . of Naples," CW, I, 66.
172 "Like a bird . . . that one," W, III, 58.
172 "what help . . . not dialectics," W, III, 58.
172 "Life is . . . but sturdy," W, III, 59.
172 "To fill . . . on them," W, III, 59.
173 "due metes and bounds," W, III, 69.

173 "Underneath the ... or seam," W, III, 71.
173 "this august ... the West," W, III, 71–72.
173 "If I ... states of mind," W, III, 72.
173 "The consciousness ... in infinite degrees," W, III, 72.
173 "vast-flowing vigor ... no hunger," W, III, 73.
173 "we have ... vast-flowing vigor," W, III, 73.
174 "It is ... its ideas," W, III, 75–76.
174 "a door ... creator passes," W, III, 54.
174 "the chagrins ... in us," W, III, 54.
175 "Ours is ... We philosophise," EL, II, 168.
175 "innavigable sea ... converse with," W, III, 48.
175 "what more ... idealist say," CW, II, 202.
175 "Marriage ... the picture," W, III, 77.
175 "of a ... *no co-life,*" W, III, 78.
175–176 "It is ... be contemplated," W, III, 78.
176 "in its sequel ... all relations," W, III, 78.
176 "Let us ... they are," W, III, 60.
176 "stated over ... we know!" JMN, XI, 447.
176 "the Sea ... that condition," JMN, V, 329.
176 "Men generally ... himself *solus,*" JMN, IX, 236.
177 "How long ... solitary performance?" W, III, 80.
177 "sharp peaks ... of truth," W, III, 48.
177 "the native ... another's facts," W, III, 81.
177 "it takes ... for Rachel," JMN, V, 489.
177 "I am not ... nor seven years ago," W, III, 83.
177 "Let who will ... fruit sufficient," W, III, 83.
178 "I am not satisfied," L, III, 239.
178 "ugly breaks," JMN, IX, 65.
178 "He did ... demand Victory," JMN, VIII, 228.
178 "Patience and ... at the last," W, III, 85.
178 "but in ... sanity," W, III, 85.
178 "Never mind ... practical power," W, III, 85–86.

The Adequate Genesis: "The Poet"

179 "the timely ... things await," W, III, 37.
179 "Dante's praise ... are yet unsung," W, III, 37–38.
180 "the double ... sensuous fact," W, III, 4.
180 "The poet ... adequate genesis," W, VIII, 71.
180 "the essential ... thought and volition," W, III, 4.
180 "Theologians think it ... historical evidence," W, III, 4.
180 "things admit ... every part," W, III, 13.
180 "The Universe ... around it," W, III, 14.
180 "For all poetry ... miswrite the poem," W, III, 8.
180 "far off ... of the intuition," CW, II, 39.
181 "Language is fossil poetry," W, III, 34.

181 "... the quality of ... for homestead," W, III, 34.
181 "the religions ... imaginative men," W, III, 34.
181 "The history of... of language," W, III, 35.
181 "substantial & central," JMN, VIII, 386.
181 "the discovery ... we exist," W, III, 75.
181–182 "intellectual ... Central Life," JMN, VIII, 386.
182 "if the ... Centre of Life," JMN, VIII, 386.
182 "the slight ... facts *knowingly*," JMN, VIII, 386.
182 "He is ... Jews possess," W, IV, 75.
182 "a distinction ... teach thus," JMN, III, 185.
182 "Character is ... the Daimonisches," JMN, V, 318.
182–183 "a reserved force ... cannot impart," W, III, 89–90.
183 "I suppose ... voice of God," JMN, III, 107.
183 "Can you ... two roads," JMN, IV, 264.
183–184 "There is no ... not end," JMN, XIV, 284.
184 "What others ... of affairs," W, III, 90.
184 "He spoke ... Gold again," W, III, 87.
184 "great Defeat," JMN, VIII, 227.
184 "the mind ... of character," JMN, VIII, 228.
184 "The mind ... moral agents," W, III, 114.
185 "If his ... beneficent power?" W, XI, 204.
185 "animal good ... property," W, XI, 204.
185 "recent writer ... eternal man," W, III, 9.
185 "men of talent ... the music," W, III, 9.
186 "consecrated by ... parse & spell?" L, II, 331.
186 "I wish ... as he," L, II, 171.
186 "At first sight ... mono *Sania*," L, II, 173.
186 "charmed us ... us all," JMN, VII, 124.
186 "He is ... he breathes," JMN, VII, 122–123.
186 "He thinks ... showing,) Truth," JMN, VII, 122–123.
186 "He would obey, obey," JMN, VII, 122.
186 "who has ... his finger," CW, II, 40.
187 "It is a ... through this world," W, III, 26–27.
187 "Conversion from ... perceives God," JMN, III, 186.
187 "... take this fact ... the Lord," JMN, III, 290–291.
187 "He felt ... of the Spirit," JMN, VII, 123.
187–188 "Because in ... thy breast," JMN, III, 292.
189 "the sense ... their cause," CW, II, 37.
189–190 "By degrees ... magazine of power," CW, I, 23.
190 "a horse ... this other," W, IV, 121.
190 "In nature ... real being," W, IV, 121.
190 "the metamorphosis," W, III, 35.
191 "Its smoothness ... perpetual inchoation," CW, I, 124.
191 "through Nature ... striving upward," JMN, V, 146.
191 "to what ... is nature?" CW, I, 7.
191 "does not ... particular ends," CW, I, 126–127.

191 "I grow . . . new stars," CW, I, 126.
192 "excess of . . . call *ecstasy*," CW, I, 127.
192 "As the power . . . bright casualty," CW, I, 132.
192 "suggests a . . . his own," CW, II, 171.
192 "if the imagination . . . liberating gods," W, III, 30.
192 "the value . . . any form," W, VIII, 15.
192 "Before him . . . their hands," W, III, 35.
193 "the problem . . . of the soul," CW, I, 43.
193 "Power ceases . . . of repose," CW, II, 40.
194 "perceives the . . . of the symbol," W, III, 20.
194 "it is not . . . new thing," CW, II, 9–10.
194 "the books . . . quite exhausted," CW, I, 66.
194 "The Greek . . . is old," CW, II, 179–180.
194 "the experience . . . its poet," W, III, 10.
194–195 "the melodies . . . infinite time," W, III, 24.
195 "songs of the nations," W, III, 8.
195 "repairs the decays of things," W, III, 22.
195 "true and only doctor," W, III, 8.
195 "into the science of the real," W, III, 12.
195 "sharing the . . . to others," W, III, 26.
195 "at all risks," W, III, 26.
195 "the divine . . . through things," W, III, 26.
195 "splendor . . . visible world," W, IV, 216.
195 "rested in . . . themselves say?" W, IV, 217.
195 ". . . other men . . . in them," W, IV, 218–219.
196 "its poet-priest, a reconciler," W, IV, 219.
196 "is not . . . bound together," YES, 4.
196 "a man . . . selecting principle," CW, II, 84.
196 "life within . . . *within us*," J, II, 225.
197 "Thou true . . . for thee," W, III, 42.
197 "when an . . . our opulence," W, III, 33.
197 "Dream delivers . . . to illusion," W, III, 50.
197 "And this . . . invulnerable essence," W, III, 42.
198 "The Indian . . . every drop," W, III, 48.
198 "upheave and . . . his brain," EL, III, 354.

"*Montaigne*": The Middle Way

199 "sweetly torments . . . inaccessible homes," W, IV, 206.
199 "is not . . . but sturdy," W, III, 59.
199 "the mid world is best," W, III, 64.
199 "everything good . . . the highway," W, III, 62.
199 "if we . . . heaping measures," W, III, 62.
199 "delight and wonder," W, IV, 162.
199 "It seemed . . . and experience," W, IV, 336.
199 "Montaigne has . . . sit down," W, IV, 336.

200 "want of sufficient *bottom*," JMN, II, 240.
200 "Talent without . . . its value?" W, IV, 340.
200 "Come, no . . . in the bush," W, IV, 159.
200 "Every fact . . . names beside," W, IV, 149.
201 "middle ground," W, IV, 155.
201 "He finds . . . the balance," W, IV, 155.
201 "If there . . . the judgment?" W, IV, 159.
201 "There is . . . all sides," W, IV, 157.
201 "universal denying . . . and good," W, IV, 159.
201 "the considerer . . . his means," W, IV, 159–160.
202 "a golden impossibility," W, III, 66.
202 "We are . . . the sea," W, IV, 161.
202 "vigorous and original thinker," W, IV, 162.
202 "sufficiently related . . . and London," W, IV, 162.
202 "Here is . . . or stinging," W, IV, 166.
202 "Cut these words . . . and alive," W, IV, 168.
202 "positive degree," W, IV, 168.
202 "Montaigne talks . . . the road," W, IV, 169.
203 "doubts and negations," W, IV, 173.
203 "I have . . . this chapter," W, III, 69.
203 "I shall . . . of me," W, IV, 173.
203 "the exaggeration . . . and blockheads," W, IV, 171.
203 "levity of intellect," W, IV, 174.
203 "The dull . . . light mockers," W, IV, 174.
203 "the subject . . . less fame," W, IV, 174–175.
203 "What flutters . . . of faith," W, IV, 175.
203 "if the . . . have two," EL, II, 171.
204 "Our age . . . truth dry?" CW, I, 66–67.
204 "For my . . . and musical," EL, II, 171.
204 "power of . . . and beliefs," W, IV, 175.
204 "Our life . . . best citizen," W, IV, 175–176.
205 "Are the . . . a week," W, IV, 176.
205 "As far . . . the states?" W, IV, 176.
205 "These varieties . . . average tendency," CW, II, 34.
205 "main resistance . . . impulse finds," W, IV, 177.
205 "doctrine of . . . emptiest name," W, IV, 177.
205 "There are . . . easily amused," W, VI, 313.
205 "In the life . . . rosy hue," W, VI, 312.
206 "They say . . . the same?" JMN, VIII, 162.
206 "Every god . . . him alone," W, VI, 312.
206 "absence of any . . . to converge," W, IV, 178–179.
207 "I am . . . shall beat," W, VI, 234–235.
207 "There is . . . am born," JMN, VIII, 228.
208 "lie for . . . no doubts," W, IV, 180.
208 "Some minds . . . a return," W, IV, 180.
208 "like an . . . false bottom," JMN, IX, 295.

208 "Once admitted . . . with divinities," W, IV, 180–81.
208 "reflex or . . . from themselves," W, IV, 181.
208 "sensual habit . . . burns the believer," W, IV, 181.
209 "The new . . . of skepticism," CW, II, 181.
209 "Great believers . . . no account," W, IV, 181.
210 "The final . . . skepticism impossible," W, IV, 183.
210 "the world . . . with law," W, IV, 183.
210 "can behold . . . all souls," W, IV, 183.
210 "Charles Fourier . . . the destinies," W, IV, 183–184.
211 "The emperor . . . the human soul," JMN, III, 96.
211 "If my . . . another sea," W, IV, 186.

Notes

Preface

1. All quotations from Emerson's works, journals, and letters are identified in the Textual References beginning on p. 213.
2. Jer. 8:20. In his journal Emerson misquotes the verse by inverting the order of the clauses. The passage is to be found in JMN, III, 50.

Chapter I

1. Charles J. Woodbury, *Talks with Ralph Walso Emerson* (New York: Baker and Baker, 1890), p. 22.
2. Ralph L. Rusk, *The Life of Ralph Waldo Emerson* (New York: Columbia University Press, 1949), p. 77.
3. Furness's remark is quoted in James Elliot Cabot, *A Memoir of Ralph Waldo Emerson*, 2 vols. (Boston and New York: Houghton Mifflin & Co.; The Riverside Press, Cambridge, 1895) I, 44.
4. Ibid., p. 56.
5. Rusk, *Life*, p. 98.
6. The remarks of the journalist J. P. Willis are reproduced in Cabot, *Memoir*, II, 570–571.
7. George Beard, *American Nervousness, Its Causes and Consequences: a Supplement to Nervous Exhaustion* (New York: G. P. Putnam's Sons, 1881), p. 80.
8. Daniel Walker Howe, *The Unitarian Conscience: Harvard Moral Philosophy, 1805–1861* (Cambridge, Mass.: Harvard University Press, 1970), p. 197.
9. The phrase "stock properties of college rhetoric" is from Jonathan Bishop, *Emerson on the Soul* (Cambridge, Mass.: Harvard University Press, 1964), p. 11. Bishop's book has perceptive discussions of Emerson's rhetorical strategies: see especially the sections on "Rhythm," "Metaphor," and "Tone." The phrase "homespun cloth-of-gold" is from James Russell Lowell, who applies it to Emerson himself in his essay "Emerson the Lecturer," first printed in *The Nation* in 1868, reprinted in *The Literary Criticism of James Russell Lowell*, ed. Herbert F. Smith (Lincoln: University of Nebraska Press, 1969), p. 208.
10. The address was printed by Elizabeth Peabody in *Aesthetic*

Papers (1849); selections from it are printed in Perry Miller, *The Transcendentalists: An Anthology* (Cambridge, Mass.: Harvard University Press, 1950), pp. 50–53. The quoted phrase can be found on p. 51.

11. Francis Bowen, *The Christian Examiner* 21 (1837): 371.

12. Roland Barthes, *The Pleasure of the Text*, trans. Richard Miller, with a note on the text by Richard Howard (New York: Hill & Wang, 1975), p. 27.

13. W. C. Brownell, *American Prose Masters* (New York: Charles Scribner's Sons, 1909), p. 201; quoted in Laurence Stapleton, *The Elected Circle: Studies in the Art of Prose* (Princeton, N.J.: Princeton University Press, 1973), p. 185.

14. *Literary Criticism of Lowell*, p. 208.

15. Stapleton, *Elected Circle*, p. 194.

16. Stanley Cavell, "An Emerson Mood," in *The Senses of "Walden": An Expanded Edition* (San Francisco: North Point Press, 1981), p. 160.

17. *Selected Prose of Robert Frost*, ed. Hyde Cox and Edward Connery Latham (New York: Holt, Rinehart & Winston, 1966), p. 114.

18. F. O. Matthiessen, *American Renaissance: Art and Expression in the Age of Emerson and Whitman* (New York: Oxford University Press, 1941), p. 20, n. 8.

19. Constance Rourke, *American Humor* (New York: Harcourt Brace Jovanovich, 1931), p. 64.

20. Ibid.

21. Jonathan Culler, *Structuralist Poetics: Structuralism, Linguistics and the Study of Literature* (Ithaca, N.Y.: Cornell University Press, 1975), p. 154. See also the article by Frederick W. Bogel, "Irony, Inference, and Critical Uncertainty," *Yale Review* 69 (1980): 503–519.

22. Yvor Winters, "Jones Very and R. W. Emerson: Aspects of New England Mysticism," in *In Defense of Reason* (Denver: Alan Swallow, 1943), p. 268.

23. Martin Price, *To the Palace of Wisdom: Studies in Order and Energy from Dryden to Blake* (New York: Doubleday & Co., Anchor Books, 1965), p. 193.

24. "Auguries of Innocence," in *The Poetry and Prose of William Blake*, ed. David Erdman, 4th printing, with revisions (New York: Doubleday & Co., 1970), p. 483.

25. Yvor Winters, "The Significance of *The Bridge*, by Hart Crane, or What Are We to Think of Professor X?" in *In Defense of Reason*, p. 581.

26. Ibid., p. 582.

27. Ibid.

28. I Cor. 1:18–19; 3:19.

29. I Cor. 1:23.

30. Annotations to Swedenborg's *Divine Love and Divine Wisdom,* in Erdman, *Blake,* p. 594.

31. See Swedenborg's "Remarks on the Ruling Love in Men and Spirits, as the Source of Their Delights," *New Jerusalem Magazine* 5 (1831–1832): 209–217.

32. Friedrich Nietzsche, *Beyond Good and Evil: Prelude to a Philosophy of the Future,* trans. Walter Kaufman (New York: Vintage Books, 1966), pp. 35–36.

33. Bishop, *Emerson on the Soul,* p. 43.

34. John Lyndenberg, "Emerson and the Dark Tradition," *Critical Quarterly* 4 (1962): 352.

35. O. W. Firkins, *Ralph Waldo Emerson* (Boston and New York: Houghton Mifflin & Co., 1915), p. 193.

Chapter II

1. Rusk, *Life,* p. 498.

2. Burke's actual words are perhaps not quite so unambiguous: "An enemy might want to rate this early essay of Emerson's as hardly other than a Happiness Pill. But I admit: I find it so charming, I'd be willing to defend it even on that level, it is so buoyant." See his "I, Eye, Ay— Emerson's Early Essay 'Nature': Thoughts on the Machinery of Transcendence," in *Transcendentalism and Its Legacy,* ed. Myron Simon and Thornton H. Parsons (Ann Arbor: The University of Michigan Press, 1966), pp. 3–24; reprinted in *Emerson's "Nature": Origin, Growth, Meaning,* ed. Merton M. Sealts and Alfred Ferguson, 2nd. ed., revised and enlarged (Carbondale, Ill.: Southern Illinois University Press, 1979), pp. 150–163. Subsequent references are to this latter edition. The quotation in question is to be found on p. 150.

3. Stephen Whicher, *Selections from Ralph Waldo Emerson: An Organic Anthology* (Boston: Houghton Mifflin Co., Riverside Editions, 1957), p. 13.

4. Bishop, *Emerson on the Soul,* p. 6.

5. Herbert N. Schneidau, *Sacred Discontent: The Bible and Western Tradition* (Berkeley and Los Angeles: University of California Press, 1977), p. 212.

6. On "supernatural rationalism" see Conrad Wright, "Rational Religion in Eighteenth-Century America," in *The Liberal Christians: Essays on American Unitarian History* (Boston: Beacon Press, 1970), pp. 1–21.

7. *Aids to Reflection,* 1st American ed., preliminary essay and additional notes by James Marsh (Burlington, Vt.: Chauncy Goodrich, 1829), p. 155.

8. Francis Bowen, *The Christian Examiner* 21 (1837): 375–376.

9. Nietzsche's sarcastic description of the philosophers' lies about the origins of their systems in *Beyond Good and Evil*, p. 12.

10. Rusk, *Life*, p. 187.

11. Whicher, *Freedom and Fate*, p. 14.

12. Ibid., p. 14.

13. Nietzsche, *Beyond Good and Evil*, p. 18.

14. Whicher, *Freedom and Fate*, p. 21.

15. The sentence, from Swedenborg's *The Economy of the Animal Kingdom*, is quoted by Emerson in his essay on Swedenborg in *Representative Men* (W, IV, 215). On the importance of the doctrine of "correspondence" for Emerson's thought, see Sherman Paul, *Emerson's Angle of Vision: Man and Nature in American Experience* (Cambridge, Mass.: Harvard University Press, 1952).

16. The remark, originally made by Nietzsche in a note to the second volume of *Human, All-Too-Human*, is quoted by Walter Kaufman in a note to section 294 of *Beyond Good and Evil*, p. 232.

17. Walt Whitman, "Crossing Brooklyn Ferry," lines 71–75, in *Leaves of Grass: Comprehensive Reader's Edition*, ed. Harold W. Blodgett and Scully Bradley (New York: W. W. Norton & Co., 1965), p. 163.

18. Rusk, *Life*, p. 201.

19. Samuel Taylor Coleridge, *The Friend* (1818), ed. Barbara E. Rooke, 2 vols. (Princeton, N.J.: Princeton University Press, Bollingen Series LXXV, 1969), I, 476.

20. Ibid., I, 50.

21. Ibid., I, 459.

22. Ibid., I, 464.

23. Ibid., I, 479.

24. Ibid.

25. Ibid., I, 481.

26. A careful study of the relationship between journal passages used in *Nature* and the text of the book itself has converted me to Merton Sealts's opinion that the traditional account of *Nature*'s composition is probably incorrect. According to that account, Emerson originally planned a five-chapter book. After he had written the material that later became "Spirits" and "Prospects," he decided to add it to the original book. But he needed a "bridge chapter"—"Idealism"—to lead the reader from the opening chapters to the visionary conclusion.

But large chunks of "Idealism" (particularly section 5) come from journal entries from February and March of 1836, when he was working feverishly to complete the first version of the book. It seems unlikely that he would have interrupted the process of composition to meditate extensively on the subject of Idealism if he were not planning to use the material in the book. Besides, it is difficult to imagine Emerson at any time in his life choosing to end a book or essay by extolling so negative a subject as "Discipline." Discipline might be necessary as a negative moment in a dialectic leading to higher things, but it could hardly rank as an end in itself. It seems far likelier that "Idealism" was the final cause to which the subordinate "uses" of nature were originally directed. When Emerson had written the material that was later included in "Spirit" and "Prospects," he was faced with the task of soldering his earlier chapters to this new material, a task he tried to complete chiefly by adding sentences and paragraphs of new material to the earlier chapters. But a "crack" in the book continued to distress him. See Merton M. Sealts, "The Composition of *Nature*," in *Emerson's "Nature,"* pp. 175–193.

27. Rusk, *Life*, p. 230.

28. William Wordsworth, "Elegiac Stanzas, suggested by a picture of Peele Castle, in a Storm, Painted by Sir George Beaumont," lines 34–36, in *The Poetical Works of William Wordsworth*, ed. E. de Selincourt, 5 vols. (Oxford: The Clarendon Press, 1940–1949), IV, 259–260.

29. Burke, "I, Eye, Ay," in *Emerson's "Nature,"* p. 161.

30. James M. Cox, "R. W. Emerson: The Circles of the Eye," in *Emerson: Prophecy, Metamorphosis, and Influence: Selected Papers from the English Institute*, ed. David Levin (New York: Columbia University Press, 1975), pp. 71–72, 74–75. See also R. A. Yoder, *Emerson and the Orphic Poet in America* (Berkeley and Los Angeles: University of California Press, 1978), pp. 23–24.

31. Burke, "I, Eye, Ay," in *Emerson's "Nature,"* p. 16; John Milton, *Complete Poems and Major Prose*, ed. Meritt Hughes (New York: The Bobbs-Merrill Co., The Odyssey Press, 1957). Subsequent references are to this edition.

32. William Ellery Channing, "Remarks on the Character and Writings of John Milton," in *The Works of William Ellery Channing*, 6 vols. (Boston: American Unitarian Association, 1903), I, 19.

33. *Paradise Lost*, Bk. 3, lines 46–50.

34. Rusk, *Life*, p. 112.

35. Anna Freud, *The Ego and the Mechanisms of Defense*, rev. ed. (New York: International Universities Press, 1966), p. 80.

36. Letter to Mrs. Thrale, 21 Sept. 1773, in *The Letters of Samuel Johnson*, ed. R. W. Chapman, 3 vols. (Oxford: The Clarendon Press, 1952), I, 326.

37. *The Prelude: or Growth of a Poet's Mind*, ed. Ernest de Selincourt, 2nd. ed., revised by Helen Darbishire (Oxford: The Clarendon Press, 1950), 1850 version, Bk. 6, lines 613–616. Subsequent references are to this edition.

38. Burke, "I, Eye, Ay," in *Emerson's "Nature,"* p. 161.

39. "Prospectus" to *The Recluse*, lines 63–68, published as part of the "Preface" to the 1814 edition of *The Excursion; Poetical Works*, V, 5.

40. Annotations to Wordsworth's "Preface" to *The Excursion*, in Erdman, *Blake*, p. 656.

41. *The [First] Book of Urizen*, Plate 27, lines 39–42, in Erdman, *Blake*, p. 82.

42. Thomas Frosch, *The Awakening of Albion: The Renovation of the Body in the Poetry of William Blake* (Ithaca, N.Y.: Cornell University Press, 1974), p. 180.

43. *The Marriage of Heaven and Hell*, Plate 14, in Erdman, *Blake*, p. 38.

44. Yoder, *Orphic Poet*, p. 36.

45. Burke, "I, Eye, Ay," in *Emerson's "Nature,"* p. 161.

46. "Prospectus" to *The Recluse*, lines 42–55, in *Poetical Works*, V, 4. See Joel Porte, *Representative Man: Ralph Waldo Emerson in His Time* (New York: Oxford University Press, 1979), pp. 72–74.

47. Wallace Stevens, "Tea at the Palaz of Hoon," *The Collected Poems of Wallace Stevens* (New York: Alfred A. Knopf, 1954), p. 65.

48. Luke 17: 20–21.

49. Porte, *Representative Man*, pp. 78–79.

50. See "The Last Judgement," in *Memorabilia of Swedenborg*, ed. George Bush (New York: John Allen, 1846), pp. 35–36.

51. David Brewster, *The Life of Sir Isaac Newton* (London: John Murray, 1831). A copy of the New York edition (J. & J. Harper, 1831), with autograph and notes, is in Emerson's library. Walter Harding, *Emerson's Library* (Charlottesville: The University Press of Virginia, 1967), p. 40.

52. Isaac Newton, *Opticks: or a Treatise of the Reflections & Colors of Light* (1704) (London: G. Bell and Sons, 1931; rpt. New York: Dover, 1952), p. 280.

53. Ibid., p. 282.

54. Brewster, *Life of Newton*, p. 75.

55. Ibid., p. 80.

56. Sampson Reed, *Observations on the Growth of the Mind* (1826), facsimile reproduction of 1838 edition with an Introduction by Carl F. Strauch (Gainesville, Fla.: Scholars' Facsimiles & Reprints, 1970), p. 42.

57. Samuel Taylor Coleridge, *Biographia Literaria*, ed. J. Shawcross, 2 vols. (Oxford: The Clarendon Press, 1907), I, 174.

58. Coleridge, *The Friend*, I, 522.

59. Guillaume Oegger, *The True Messiah: or the Old and New Testaments, Examined According to the Principles of the Language of Nature*, trans. Elizabeth Peabody, reprinted in Kenneth Walter Cameron, *The Young Emerson's Transcendental Vision: An Exposition of his World View, with an Analysis of the Structure, Backgrounds, and Meaning of "Nature" (1836)* (Hartford, Conn.: Transcendental Books, 1971), p. 338.

60. Oegger, *True Messiah*, p. 338; Coleridge, *Aids to Reflection*, p. 241.

61. See John Irwin, "The Symbol of the Hieroglyphics in the

American Renaissance," *American Quarterly* 26 (1974): 103–126. Champollion had deciphered the Rosetta Stone in 1822, and his achievement aroused great interest in New England.

62. Coleridge, *The Friend*, I, 512–513.

63. John Milton, *Paradise Lost*, Bk. 3, lines 47–49.

64. According to Coleridge, one of the tests of a truth affirmed by the Reason is that "in its own proper form it is *inconceivable*." It can "come forth out of the molds of the Understanding only in the disguise of two contradictory conceptions." *Aids to Reflection*, p. 304, n. 59.

65. Geoffrey H. Hartman, *Wordsworth's Poetry 1787–1814* (New Haven, Conn.: Yale University Press, 1964), p. 193.

66. Stephen Whicher, *Selections from Ralph Waldo Emerson*, p. 13.

67. Northrop Frye, *Fearful Symmetry: A Study of William Blake* (Princeton, N.J.: Princeton University Press, 1947), p. 308.

68. Cox, "Circles of the Eye," in *Emerson: Prophecy*, p. 66.

69. *Jerusalem*, Ch. 4, Plate 98, lines 34–38, in Erdman, *Blake*, p. 255.

70. Frosch, *Awakening of Albion*, p. 150

71. Burke, "I, Eye, Ay," in *Emerson's "Nature,"* p. 155.

Chapter III

1. Harriet Martineau, *Society in America*, 3 vols. (London: Saunders and Otley, 1837), III, 206.

2. Alexis de Tocqueville, *Democracy in America*, trans. George Lawrence, ed. J. P. Mayer (Garden City, N.Y.: Doubleday & Co., Anchor Books, 1969), p. 471.

3. Berkeley's poem, "Verses on the Prospect of Planting Arts and Learning in America," is discussed in Joseph P. Ellis's informative article, "Culture and Capitalism in Pre-Revolutionary America," *American Quarterly* 31 (1979): 169–186. For the complete text of the poem see *The Works of George Berkeley, D.D.*, ed. Alexander Fraser, 4 vols. (Oxford: The Clarendon Press, 1901), IV, 364–365.

4. *Literary Criticism of Lowell*, p. 122.

5. John Jay Chapman, "Emerson," in *Emerson and Other Essays* (1898), reprinted in *The Selected Writings of John Jay Chapman*, ed. Jacques Barzun (New York: Funk and Wagnalls, Minerva Press, 1968), p. 153.

6. Martineau, *Society in America*, III, 63–64. Martineau referred to Boston as "the headquarters of Cant" (p. 31).

7. Ibid., I, 139–142.

8. Martineau, *Retrospect of Western Travel*, 2 vols. (New York: Charles Lohman, 1838), II, 84.

9. Tocqueville, *Democracy in America*, p. 255.

10. Martineau, *Society in America*, III, 14–15.

11. Chapman, "William Lloyd Garrison," in *Selected Writings*, pp. 40–41.

12. See Quentin Anderson, *The Imperial Self: An Essay in American Literary and Cultural History* (New York: Alfred A. Knopf, 1971); and Yvor Winters, "The Significance of *The Bridge*, by Hart Crane," in *In Defense of Reason*.

13. Bruno Bettelheim, *The Informed Heart: On Retaining the Self in a Dehumanizing Society* (New York: Avon Books, 1971), pp. 27–29.

14. Anderson, *Imperial Self*, p. 31.

15. W. H. Auden, *The Dyer's Hand and Other Essays* (London: Faber and Faber, 1963), p. 336.

16. Chapman, "Society," in *Selected Writings*, p. 245.

17. Howe, *The Unitarian Conscience*, p. 277.

18. Acts 8:22–23.

19. Maurice Gonnaud, "Emerson and the Imperial Self: A European Critique," in *Emerson: Prophecy*, p. 116.

20. Wordsworth, *Poetical Works*, I, 319.

21. "Thoreau," in *Literary Criticism of Lowell*, p. 228.

22. Coleridge, *Biographia Literaria*, II, 6.

23. Reed uses the term in *Observations on the Growth of the Mind*, p. 87. For Emerson's use of the term, see JMN, IX, 259.

24. Wordsworth, "Growth of Genius from the Influences of Natural Objects, on the Imagination in Boyhood, and Early Youth," part of Bk. 1 of *The Prelude;* printed in Coleridge, *The Friend*, I, 369. Coleridge's version differs slightly from both the 1805 and 1850 versions as given by de Selincourt, *The Prelude*, pp. 28–29.

25. Whicher, *Freedom and Fate*, p. 52.

26. John Hollander's phrase; quoted in Frank Kermode, *The Genesis of Secrecy: On the Interpretation of Narrative* (Cambridge, Mass.: Harvard University Press, 1979), p. 18.

27. *Troilus and Criseyde*, Bk. 5, lines 1789–1793, in *The Works of Geoffrey Chaucer*, ed. F. N. Robinson (Boston: Houghton Mifflin Co., 1957). Subsequent references are to this edition.

28. Wordsworth, *The Prelude*, Bk. 1, lines 545–546.

29. Firkins, *Ralph Waldo Emerson*, p. 160.

30. Conrad Wright, "Emerson, Barzillai Frost, and the Divinity School *Address*," in *Liberal Christians*, pp. 41–61.

31. "Unitarian Christianity: Discourse at the Ordination of the Reverend Jared Sparks, Baltimore 1819," in *The Works of Channing*, III, 60, 102.

32. Andrew Norton, *A Statement of Reasons for Not Believing the Doctrines of the Trinitarians, Concerning the Nature of God and the Person of Christ* (Cambridge, Mass.: Brown, Shattuck, 1838, 1859 ed.), p. 144.

33. Channing, "Unitarian Christianity," in *Works of Channing*, III, 103.

34. Whicher, *Freedom and Fate*, p. 21.

35. William Hutchison, *The Transcendentalist Ministers: Church Reform in the New England Renaissance* (New Haven, Conn.: Yale University Press, 1959), p. 37.

36. *Owl's Clover*, in *Opus Posthumous*, ed. Samuel French Morse (New York: Alfred A. Knopf, 1966), pp. 53–54.

37. Matt. 28:6.

38. J. H. van den Berg, *The Changing Nature of Man: Introduction to a Historical Psychology*, trans. H. F. Croes (New York: Dell Publishing Co., 1975), p. 201. On the miracles controversy see Hutchison, *Transcendentalist Ministers*, pp. 52–97.

39. Rusk, *Life*, pp. 265–266.

40. Norton's remark, which first appeared in *The Boston Courier*, is quoted by Perry Miller in *The Transcendentalists*, p. 168.

41. Rusk, *Life*, p. 270.

42. Porte, *Representative Man*, p. 91. See also his chapter on "The Fall of Man," pp. 161–203, where he discusses Emerson's rewritings of the Fall story in "The Protest" and "Experience."

43. Cavell, "Thinking of Emerson," in *The Senses of "Walden,"* p. 136.

44. Firkins, *Ralph Waldo Emerson*, pp. 175–176.

45. *The Marriage of Heaven and Hell*, Plate 23, in Erdman, *Blake*, p. 42.

46. Ibid., Plate 10, p. 37.

47. Eccles. 9:4.

48. Cavell, *Senses of "Walden,"* p. 137.

49. *Young Emerson Speaks: Unpublished Discourses on Many Subjects*, ed. Arthur Cushman McGiffert, Jr. (Boston: Houghton Mifflin Co., 1938), p. xxxvii.

50. Hutchison, *Transcendentalist Ministers*, p. 79. The review appeared in the November 1838 issue of *The Christian Examiner* 25 (1838): 266–268.

51. Anderson, *Imperial Self*, p. 11.

52. *The Four Zoas*, Night the Third, in Erdman, *Blake*, p. 230.

Chapter IV

1. Firkins, *Ralph Waldo Emerson*, p. 112.

2. Alfred Lord Tennyson, "Ulysses," lines 18–21, in *The Poems of Tennyson*, ed. Christopher Ricks (New York: W. W. Norton & Co., 1972), p. 563.

3. "The Holy Grail," lines 438–439, from *Idylls of the King*, in *Poems of Tennyson*, p. 1674.

4. Beard, *American Nervousness*, p. 9.

5. George M. Beard, *A Practical Treatise on Nervous Exhaustion*

(*Neurasthenia*), *Its Symptoms, Nature, Sequences, Treatment* (New York: William Wood & Co., 1880), p. 66.

6. Chapman, *Selected Writings*, p. 163.

7. Firkins, *Ralph Waldo Emerson*, p. 239.

8. Albert Abrams, *The Blues* (*Splanchic Neurasthenia*): *Causes and Cures*, 2nd. ed., enlarged (New York: E. B. Treat & Co., 1905) p. 16.

9. Whicher, *Freedom and Fate*, p. 15.

10. David Hume, "Of Miracles," in *An Enquiry Concerning Human Understanding*, in: *Essays, Moral, Political, and Literary*, ed. T. H. Green and T. H. Grose, 2 vols. (London: Longmans, Green, & Co., 1875), I, 91–92.

11. Whicher, *Freedom and Fate*, p. 16.

12. Cavell, *The Senses of Walden*, p. 125.

13. Porte, *Representative Man*, p. 181, n. 10.

14. David Hume, *A Treatise of Human Nature, Being an Attempt to Introduce the Experimental Method of Reasoning into Moral Subjects*, ed. T. H. Green and T. H. Grose, 2 vols. (London: Longmans, Green, & Co., 1898), I, 311.

15. Ibid., I, 311–312.

16. Ibid., I, 311.

17. Chaucer, *Troilus and Criseyde*, Bk. 2, line 1107.

18. W. B. Yeats, *Per Amica Silentia Lunae* (London: Macmillan & Co., 1918), p. 41.

19. Shunryu Suzuki, *Zen Mind, Beginner's Mind*, ed. Trudy Dixon, with an introduction by Richard Baker (New York: John Weatherhill, 1970), p. 35.

20. *Hydrotaphia: Urne-Burial, or, A Brief Discourse of the Sepulchral Urnes Lately Found in Norfolk* (1658), in *Sir Thomas Browne: Selected Writings*, ed. Sir Geoffrey Keynes (Chicago: University of Chicago Press, 1968), pp. 150, 152. Among the sentences Emerson copied were "There is no antidote against the *Opium* of time," and "miseries are slippery, or fall like snow upon us, which notwithstanding is no unhappy stupidity." See JMN, III, 219–220.

21. *The Poetical Works of Robert Southey*, 10 vols. (London: Longman, Orme, Brown, Green, & Longmans, 1840), VIII, 21.

22. Bishop, *Emerson on the Soul*, p. 198.

23. Ibid., p. 139.

24. Ibid., pp. 196–197.

25. Wordsworth, *The Prelude*, 1850 version, Bk. 4, lines 442–445.

26. Gonnaud, *Emerson: Prophecy*, pp. 121–122.

27. Rusk, *Life*, p. 294.

28. See Bishop, *Emerson on the Soul*, pp. 193–194; Porte, *Representative Man*, p. 182; Whicher, *Freedom and Fate*, p. 121. For additional examples, see Yoder, *Orphic Poet*, pp. 45, 48.

29. Michael Cowan, *City of the West: Emerson, America, and Urban*

Metaphor (New Haven, Conn.: Yale University Press, 1967), p. 120.
Cowan's reading of "Experience" is excellent.

·30. Hume, *Treatise of Human Nature*, p. 371.

31. Cox, *Emerson: Prophecy*, p. 80.

32. Yoder, *Orphic Poet*, p. 46.

33. Firkins, *Ralph Waldo Emerson*, p. 194.

34. Whicher points out that Emerson's later thought is "characteristically an affirmation of a *second best.*" *Freedom and Fate*, p. 126.

35. Yoder, *Orphic Poet*, p. 42.

36. Bishop, *Emerson on the Soul*, p. 23.

37. The editors of the *Journals* identify this quotation as being from
Plutarch's "A Discourse Concerning Socrates' Daemon," in *Morals*,
trans. from the Greek by Several Hands, corrected and revised by W.
W. Goodwin, 5 vols. (Boston, 1870), II, 388–389.

38. Matt. 8: 8–9.

39. Chapman, *Selected Writings*, p. 175.

40. Ibid., p. 162.

41. Whicher, *Freedom and Fate*, p. 24.

42. Winters, *In Defense of Reason*, p. 263.

43. Very's sonnet is quoted by Winters, *In Defense of Reason*, pp.
275–276.

44. W. K. Wimsatt, "Two Meanings of Symbolism," in *Hateful
Contraries: Studies in Literature and Criticism* (Kentucky: University
of Kentucky Press, 1965), p. 58.

45. Ibid., p. 60.

46. Wordsworth, *The Prelude*, 1850 version, Bk. 6, lines 624–629,
635–640.

47. Quoted in Signe Toskvig, *Emanuel Swedenborg: Scientist and
Mystic* (New Haven, Conn.: Yale University Press, 1948), p. 24.

48. On the doctrine of the Affections Clothed, see James Reed, *Swedenborg and the New Church* (Cambridge, Mass.: Riverside Press,
1880), p. 32. James Reed was Sampson Reed's son.

49. Vivian Hopkins, *Spires of Form: A Study of Emerson's Aesthetic
Theory* (Cambridge, Mass.: Harvard University Press, 1951), p. 130.

50. Frye, *Fearful Symmetry*, p. 8.

51. Hopkins, *Spires of Form*, p. 130.

52. Stevens, *Opus Posthumous*, p. 49.

53. Whitman, *Song of Myself*, section 24, line 506, in *Walt Whitman's Leaves of Grass: The First (1855) Edition*, edited, with an
Introduction, by Malcolm Cowley (New York: Viking Press, 1959),
p. 48.

54. Ibid., section 5, lines 82–83, 86–89, p. 29.

55. Whitman, "As I Ebb'd with the Ocean of Life," in Blodgett and
Bradley, *Leaves of Grass*, p. 254.

56. Wordsworth, "Resolution and Independence," 23–25, in *Poetical
Works*, II, 236.

57. Kazin, review of *Representative Man* by Joel Porte, in *The New Republic*, Feb. 24, 1979, p. 31.

58. Whicher, *Freedom and Fate*, p. 136.

59. Ibid., p. 138.

60. Yoder, *Orphic Poet*, p. 42.

61. Firkins, *Ralph Waldo Emerson*, p. 27.

62. Gonnaud, *Emerson: Prophecy*, p. 122.

63. Ibid., p. 123.

64. Richard Popkin, *The History of Scepticism from Erasmus to Descartes*, rev. ed. (New York: Harper and Row, 1968), p. 54.

65. *Apology for Raymond Sebond*, in *The Complete Essays of Montaigne*, trans. Donald Frame (Stanford, Cal.: Stanford University Press, 1965), pp. 374–375, 415.

66. M. H. Abrams, "English Romanticism: The Spirit of the Age," in *Romanticism Reconsidered: Selected Papers from the English Institute*, ed. Northrop Frye (New York: Columbia University Press, 1963), pp. 56–57.